C-339   CAREER EXAMINATION SERIES

This is your
PASSBOOK for...

Housing Inspector

Test Preparation Study Guide
Questions & Answers

NATIONAL LEARNING CORPORATION®

COPYRIGHT NOTICE

This book is SOLELY intended for, is sold ONLY to, and its use is RESTRICTED to individual, bona fide applicants or candidates who qualify by virtue of having seriously filed applications for appropriate license, certificate, professional and/or promotional advancement, higher school matriculation, scholarship, or other legitimate requirements of education and/or governmental authorities.

This book is NOT intended for use, class instruction, tutoring, training, duplication, copying, reprinting, excerption, or adaptation, etc., by:

1) Other publishers
2) Proprietors and/or Instructors of "Coaching" and/or Preparatory Courses
3) Personnel and/or Training Divisions of commercial, industrial, and governmental organizations
4) Schools, colleges, or universities and/or their departments and staffs, including teachers and other personnel
5) Testing Agencies or Bureaus
6) Study groups which seek by the purchase of a single volume to copy and/or duplicate and/or adapt this material for use by the group as a whole without having purchased individual volumes for each of the members of the group
7) Et al.

Such persons would be in violation of appropriate Federal and State statutes.

PROVISION OF LICENSING AGREEMENTS – Recognized educational, commercial, industrial, and governmental institutions and organizations, and others legitimately engaged in educational pursuits, including training, testing, and measurement activities, may address request for a licensing agreement to the copyright owners, who will determine whether, and under what conditions, including fees and charges, the materials in this book may be used them. In other words, a licensing facility exists for the legitimate use of the material in this book on other than an individual basis. However, it is asseverated and affirmed here that the material in this book CANNOT be used without the receipt of the express permission of such a licensing agreement from the Publishers. Inquiries re licensing should be addressed to the company, attention rights and permissions department.

All rights reserved, including the right of reproduction in whole or in part, in any form or by any means, electronic or mechanical, including photocopying, recording, or by any information storage and retrieval system, without permission in writing from the Publisher.

Copyright © 2025 by
National Learning Corporation

212 Michael Drive, Syosset, NY 11791
(516) 921-8888 • www.passbooks.com
E-mail: info@passbooks.com

PASSBOOK® SERIES

THE *PASSBOOK® SERIES* has been created to prepare applicants and candidates for the ultimate academic battlefield – the examination room.

At some time in our lives, each and every one of us may be required to take an examination – for validation, matriculation, admission, qualification, registration, certification, or licensure.

Based on the assumption that every applicant or candidate has met the basic formal educational standards, has taken the required number of courses, and read the necessary texts, the *PASSBOOK® SERIES* furnishes the one special preparation which may assure passing with confidence, instead of failing with insecurity. Examination questions – together with answers – are furnished as the basic vehicle for study so that the mysteries of the examination and its compounding difficulties may be eliminated or diminished by a sure method.

This book is meant to help you pass your examination provided that you qualify and are serious in your objective.

The entire field is reviewed through the huge store of content information which is succinctly presented through a provocative and challenging approach – the question-and-answer method.

A climate of success is established by furnishing the correct answers at the end of each test.

You soon learn to recognize types of questions, forms of questions, and patterns of questioning. You may even begin to anticipate expected outcomes.

You perceive that many questions are repeated or adapted so that you can gain acute insights, which may enable you to score many sure points.

You learn how to confront new questions, or types of questions, and to attack them confidently and work out the correct answers.

You note objectives and emphases, and recognize pitfalls and dangers, so that you may make positive educational adjustments.

Moreover, you are kept fully informed in relation to new concepts, methods, practices, and directions in the field.

You discover that you are actually taking the examination all the time: you are preparing for the examination by "taking" an examination, not by reading extraneous and/or supererogatory textbooks.

In short, this PASSBOOK®, used directedly, should be an important factor in helping you to pass your test.

HOUSING INSPECTOR

DUTIES AND RESPONSIBILITIES
Under general supervision, performs technical work in the inspection of dwellings and other structures for the enforcement of the multiple dwelling law, housing maintenance code, and other laws, rules, and regulations that govern occupancy, safety, and sanitary conditions of such dwellings and structures; performs related work.

EXAMPLES OF TYPICAL TASKS
Makes inspections of dwellings to insure compliance with the multiple dwelling law, housing maintenance code, and other statutes. Explains and interprets housing codes to property owners and tenants. Inspects for illegal conversion of one-or two-family homes to multiple dwellings, or for change in occupancy or use of multiple-dwellings. Inspects rooms which are used for living quarters to demine whether they are crowded beyond ordinance requirements. Checks for adequacy of light and ventilation and plumbing facilities. Checks gas appliances in dwelling units for detection and measurement of emitted carbon monoxide. Inspects yards, courts, and occupied premises for the presence of garbage, refuse, stagnant water, sewage, improper drainage, and other hazards or nuisances which might be present. Performs inspections on any structure, part thereof, or related areas based on citizens' complaints concerning lack of water, water leaks, piping noises, water hammer, etc.; insufficient or lack of heat when the outside temperature falls below specified amounts; unsanitary conditions in the public parts of buildings, yards, courts, areaways, alleyways, roofs, etc.; rodents and insect infestation and conducive conditions, and various damages such as holes in walls, floors, ceilings, broken locks on hallway doors, etc. Inspects coal-fired heating and hot water plants, chimneys, and flues for escape of coal gas or carbon monoxide, and for violations. Investigates complaints and makes emergency inspections of hazardous conditions created by explosions, fires, etc. Prepares reports of inspections, and draws floor diagrams for the official records of the department. Places violations on dwellings and prepares cases for court prosecution, appearing in court as witness. Makes such reinspections as ordered by the court. May supervise and train subordinates. May be required to operate a motor vehicle in the performance of his duties.

SCOPE OF THE WRITTEN TEST
The written test may include questions on:
1. Building mechanical systems (such as plumbing, heating, and ventilation) and other parts of dwellings, such as windows, doors, and public access areas;
2. Various building materials used in construction and completion of residences and multiple-dwellings, and related trade practices (such as carpentry, plumbing, and plastering);
3. Comprehension and interpretation of housing laws, rules, and regulations, and related agency directives;
4. Reading building plans; and
5. Other related areas.

HOW TO TAKE A TEST

I. YOU MUST PASS AN EXAMINATION

A. WHAT EVERY CANDIDATE SHOULD KNOW

Examination applicants often ask us for help in preparing for the written test. What can I study in advance? What kinds of questions will be asked? How will the test be given? How will the papers be graded?

As an applicant for a civil service examination, you may be wondering about some of these things. Our purpose here is to suggest effective methods of advance study and to describe civil service examinations.

Your chances for success on this examination can be increased if you know how to prepare. Those "pre-examination jitters" can be reduced if you know what to expect. You can even experience an adventure in good citizenship if you know why civil service exams are given.

B. WHY ARE CIVIL SERVICE EXAMINATIONS GIVEN?

Civil service examinations are important to you in two ways. As a citizen, you want public jobs filled by employees who know how to do their work. As a job seeker, you want a fair chance to compete for that job on an equal footing with other candidates. The best-known means of accomplishing this two-fold goal is the competitive examination.

Exams are widely publicized throughout the nation. They may be administered for jobs in federal, state, city, municipal, town or village governments or agencies.

Any citizen may apply, with some limitations, such as the age or residence of applicants. Your experience and education may be reviewed to see whether you meet the requirements for the particular examination. When these requirements exist, they are reasonable and applied consistently to all applicants. Thus, a competitive examination may cause you some uneasiness now, but it is your privilege and safeguard.

C. HOW ARE CIVIL SERVICE EXAMS DEVELOPED?

Examinations are carefully written by trained technicians who are specialists in the field known as "psychological measurement," in consultation with recognized authorities in the field of work that the test will cover. These experts recommend the subject matter areas or skills to be tested; only those knowledges or skills important to your success on the job are included. The most reliable books and source materials available are used as references. Together, the experts and technicians judge the difficulty level of the questions.

Test technicians know how to phrase questions so that the problem is clearly stated. Their ethics do not permit "trick" or "catch" questions. Questions may have been tried out on sample groups, or subjected to statistical analysis, to determine their usefulness.

Written tests are often used in combination with performance tests, ratings of training and experience, and oral interviews. All of these measures combine to form the best-known means of finding the right person for the right job.

II. HOW TO PASS THE WRITTEN TEST

A. NATURE OF THE EXAMINATION

To prepare intelligently for civil service examinations, you should know how they differ from school examinations you have taken. In school you were assigned certain definite pages to read or subjects to cover. The examination questions were quite detailed and usually emphasized memory. Civil service exams, on the other hand, try to discover your present ability to perform the duties of a position, plus your potentiality to learn these duties. In other words, a civil service exam attempts to predict how successful you will be. Questions cover such a broad area that they cannot be as minute and detailed as school exam questions.

In the public service similar kinds of work, or positions, are grouped together in one "class." This process is known as *position-classification*. All the positions in a class are paid according to the salary range for that class. One class title covers all of these positions, and they are all tested by the same examination.

B. FOUR BASIC STEPS

1) Study the announcement

How, then, can you know what subjects to study? Our best answer is: "Learn as much as possible about the class of positions for which you've applied." The exam will test the knowledge, skills and abilities needed to do the work.

Your most valuable source of information about the position you want is the official exam announcement. This announcement lists the training and experience qualifications. Check these standards and apply only if you come reasonably close to meeting them.

The brief description of the position in the examination announcement offers some clues to the subjects which will be tested. Think about the job itself. Review the duties in your mind. Can you perform them, or are there some in which you are rusty? Fill in the blank spots in your preparation.

Many jurisdictions preview the written test in the exam announcement by including a section called "Knowledge and Abilities Required," "Scope of the Examination," or some similar heading. Here you will find out specifically what fields will be tested.

2) Review your own background

Once you learn in general what the position is all about, and what you need to know to do the work, ask yourself which subjects you already know fairly well and which need improvement. You may wonder whether to concentrate on improving your strong areas or on building some background in your fields of weakness. When the announcement has specified "some knowledge" or "considerable knowledge," or has used adjectives like "beginning principles of..." or "advanced ... methods," you can get a clue as to the number and difficulty of questions to be asked in any given field. More questions, and hence broader coverage, would be included for those subjects which are more important in the work. Now weigh your strengths and weaknesses against the job requirements and prepare accordingly.

3) Determine the level of the position

Another way to tell how intensively you should prepare is to understand the level of the job for which you are applying. Is it the entering level? In other words, is this the position in which beginners in a field of work are hired? Or is it an intermediate or advanced level? Sometimes this is indicated by such words as "Junior" or "Senior" in the class title. Other jurisdictions use Roman numerals to designate the level – Clerk I, Clerk II, for example. The word "Supervisor" sometimes appears in the title. If the level is not indicated by the title, check the description of duties. Will you be working under very close supervision, or will you have responsibility for independent decisions in this work?

4) Choose appropriate study materials

Now that you know the subjects to be examined and the relative amount of each subject to be covered, you can choose suitable study materials. For beginning level jobs, or even advanced ones, if you have a pronounced weakness in some aspect of your training, read a modern, standard textbook in that field. Be sure it is up to date and has general coverage. Such books are normally available at your library, and the librarian will be glad to help you locate one. For entry-level positions, questions of appropriate difficulty are chosen – neither highly advanced questions, nor those too simple. Such questions require careful thought but not advanced training.

If the position for which you are applying is technical or advanced, you will read more advanced, specialized material. If you are already familiar with the basic principles of your field, elementary textbooks would waste your time. Concentrate on advanced textbooks and technical periodicals. Think through the concepts and review difficult problems in your field.

These are all general sources. You can get more ideas on your own initiative, following these leads. For example, training manuals and publications of the government agency which employs workers in your field can be useful, particularly for technical and professional positions. A letter or visit to the government department involved may result in more specific study suggestions, and certainly will provide you with a more definite idea of the exact nature of the position you are seeking.

III. KINDS OF TESTS

Tests are used for purposes other than measuring knowledge and ability to perform specified duties. For some positions, it is equally important to test ability to make adjustments to new situations or to profit from training. In others, basic mental abilities not dependent on information are essential. Questions which test these things may not appear as pertinent to the duties of the position as those which test for knowledge and information. Yet they are often highly important parts of a fair examination. For very general questions, it is almost impossible to help you direct your study efforts. What we can do is to point out some of the more common of these general abilities needed in public service positions and describe some typical questions.

1) General information

Broad, general information has been found useful for predicting job success in some kinds of work. This is tested in a variety of ways, from vocabulary lists to questions about current events. Basic background in some field of work, such as sociology or economics, may be sampled in a group of questions. Often these are principles which have become familiar to most persons through exposure rather than through formal training. It is difficult to advise you how to study for these questions; being alert to the world around you is our best suggestion.

2) Verbal ability

An example of an ability needed in many positions is verbal or language ability. Verbal ability is, in brief, the ability to use and understand words. Vocabulary and grammar tests are typical measures of this ability. Reading comprehension or paragraph interpretation questions are common in many kinds of civil service tests. You are given a paragraph of written material and asked to find its central meaning.

3) Numerical ability

Number skills can be tested by the familiar arithmetic problem, by checking paired lists of numbers to see which are alike and which are different, or by interpreting charts and graphs. In the latter test, a graph may be printed in the test booklet which you are asked to use as the basis for answering questions.

4) Observation

A popular test for law-enforcement positions is the observation test. A picture is shown to you for several minutes, then taken away. Questions about the picture test your ability to observe both details and larger elements.

5) Following directions

In many positions in the public service, the employee must be able to carry out written instructions dependably and accurately. You may be given a chart with several columns, each column listing a variety of information. The questions require you to carry out directions involving the information given in the chart.

6) Skills and aptitudes

Performance tests effectively measure some manual skills and aptitudes. When the skill is one in which you are trained, such as typing or shorthand, you can practice. These tests are often very much like those given in business school or high school courses. For many of the other skills and aptitudes, however, no short-time preparation can be made. Skills and abilities natural to you or that you have developed throughout your lifetime are being tested.

Many of the general questions just described provide all the data needed to answer the questions and ask you to use your reasoning ability to find the answers. Your best preparation for these tests, as well as for tests of facts and ideas, is to be at your physical and mental best. You, no doubt, have your own methods of getting into an exam-taking mood and keeping "in shape." The next section lists some ideas on this subject.

IV. KINDS OF QUESTIONS

Only rarely is the "essay" question, which you answer in narrative form, used in civil service tests. Civil service tests are usually of the short-answer type. Full instructions for answering these questions will be given to you at the examination. But in case this is your first experience with short-answer questions and separate answer sheets, here is what you need to know:

1) Multiple-choice Questions

Most popular of the short-answer questions is the "multiple choice" or "best answer" question. It can be used, for example, to test for factual knowledge, ability to solve problems or judgment in meeting situations found at work.

A multiple-choice question is normally one of three types—
- It can begin with an incomplete statement followed by several possible endings. You are to find the one ending which *best* completes the statement, although some of the others may not be entirely wrong.
- It can also be a complete statement in the form of a question which is answered by choosing one of the statements listed.

- It can be in the form of a problem – again you select the best answer.

Here is an example of a multiple-choice question with a discussion which should give you some clues as to the method for choosing the right answer:

When an employee has a complaint about his assignment, the action which will *best* help him overcome his difficulty is to
- A. discuss his difficulty with his coworkers
- B. take the problem to the head of the organization
- C. take the problem to the person who gave him the assignment
- D. say nothing to anyone about his complaint

In answering this question, you should study each of the choices to find which is best. Consider choice "A" – Certainly an employee may discuss his complaint with fellow employees, but no change or improvement can result, and the complaint remains unresolved. Choice "B" is a poor choice since the head of the organization probably does not know what assignment you have been given, and taking your problem to him is known as "going over the head" of the supervisor. The supervisor, or person who made the assignment, is the person who can clarify it or correct any injustice. Choice "C" is, therefore, correct. To say nothing, as in choice "D," is unwise. Supervisors have and interest in knowing the problems employees are facing, and the employee is seeking a solution to his problem.

2) True/False Questions

The "true/false" or "right/wrong" form of question is sometimes used. Here a complete statement is given. Your job is to decide whether the statement is right or wrong.

SAMPLE: A roaming cell-phone call to a nearby city costs less than a non-roaming call to a distant city.

This statement is wrong, or false, since roaming calls are more expensive.

This is not a complete list of all possible question forms, although most of the others are variations of these common types. You will always get complete directions for answering questions. Be sure you understand *how* to mark your answers – ask questions until you do.

V. RECORDING YOUR ANSWERS

Computer terminals are used more and more today for many different kinds of exams.

For an examination with very few applicants, you may be told to record your answers in the test booklet itself. Separate answer sheets are much more common. If this separate answer sheet is to be scored by machine – and this is often the case – it is highly important that you mark your answers correctly in order to get credit.

An electronic scoring machine is often used in civil service offices because of the speed with which papers can be scored. Machine-scored answer sheets must be marked with a pencil, which will be given to you. This pencil has a high graphite content which responds to the electronic scoring machine. As a matter of fact, stray dots may register as answers, so do not let your pencil rest on the answer sheet while you are pondering the correct answer. Also, if your pencil lead breaks or is otherwise defective, ask for another.

Since the answer sheet will be dropped in a slot in the scoring machine, be careful not to bend the corners or get the paper crumpled.

The answer sheet normally has five vertical columns of numbers, with 30 numbers to a column. These numbers correspond to the question numbers in your test booklet. After each number, going across the page are four or five pairs of dotted lines. These short dotted lines have small letters or numbers above them. The first two pairs may also have a "T" or "F" above the letters. This indicates that the first two pairs only are to be used if the questions are of the true-false type. If the questions are multiple choice, disregard the "T" and "F" and pay attention only to the small letters or numbers.

Answer your questions in the manner of the sample that follows:

32. The largest city in the United States is
    A. Washington, D.C.
    B. New York City
    C. Chicago
    D. Detroit
    E. San Francisco

1) Choose the answer you think is best. (New York City is the largest, so "B" is correct.)
2) Find the row of dotted lines numbered the same as the question you are answering. (Find row number 32)
3) Find the pair of dotted lines corresponding to the answer. (Find the pair of lines under the mark "B.")
4) Make a solid black mark between the dotted lines.

VI. BEFORE THE TEST

Common sense will help you find procedures to follow to get ready for an examination. Too many of us, however, overlook these sensible measures. Indeed, nervousness and fatigue have been found to be the most serious reasons why applicants fail to do their best on civil service tests. Here is a list of reminders:

- Begin your preparation early – Don't wait until the last minute to go scurrying around for books and materials or to find out what the position is all about.
- Prepare continuously – An hour a night for a week is better than an all-night cram session. This has been definitely established. What is more, a night a week for a month will return better dividends than crowding your study into a shorter period of time.
- Locate the place of the exam – You have been sent a notice telling you when and where to report for the examination. If the location is in a different town or otherwise unfamiliar to you, it would be well to inquire the best route and learn something about the building.
- Relax the night before the test – Allow your mind to rest. Do not study at all that night. Plan some mild recreation or diversion; then go to bed early and get a good night's sleep.
- Get up early enough to make a leisurely trip to the place for the test – This way unforeseen events, traffic snarls, unfamiliar buildings, etc. will not upset you.
- Dress comfortably – A written test is not a fashion show. You will be known by number and not by name, so wear something comfortable.

- Leave excess paraphernalia at home – Shopping bags and odd bundles will get in your way. You need bring only the items mentioned in the official notice you received; usually everything you need is provided. Do not bring reference books to the exam. They will only confuse those last minutes and be taken away from you when in the test room.
- Arrive somewhat ahead of time – If because of transportation schedules you must get there very early, bring a newspaper or magazine to take your mind off yourself while waiting.
- Locate the examination room – When you have found the proper room, you will be directed to the seat or part of the room where you will sit. Sometimes you are given a sheet of instructions to read while you are waiting. Do not fill out any forms until you are told to do so; just read them and be prepared.
- Relax and prepare to listen to the instructions
- If you have any physical problem that may keep you from doing your best, be sure to tell the test administrator. If you are sick or in poor health, you really cannot do your best on the exam. You can come back and take the test some other time.

VII. AT THE TEST

The day of the test is here and you have the test booklet in your hand. The temptation to get going is very strong. Caution! There is more to success than knowing the right answers. You must know how to identify your papers and understand variations in the type of short-answer question used in this particular examination. Follow these suggestions for maximum results from your efforts:

1) Cooperate with the monitor

The test administrator has a duty to create a situation in which you can be as much at ease as possible. He will give instructions, tell you when to begin, check to see that you are marking your answer sheet correctly, and so on. He is not there to guard you, although he will see that your competitors do not take unfair advantage. He wants to help you do your best.

2) Listen to all instructions

Don't jump the gun! Wait until you understand all directions. In most civil service tests you get more time than you need to answer the questions. So don't be in a hurry. Read each word of instructions until you clearly understand the meaning. Study the examples, listen to all announcements and follow directions. Ask questions if you do not understand what to do.

3) Identify your papers

Civil service exams are usually identified by number only. You will be assigned a number; you must not put your name on your test papers. Be sure to copy your number correctly. Since more than one exam may be given, copy your exact examination title.

4) Plan your time

Unless you are told that a test is a "speed" or "rate of work" test, speed itself is usually not important. Time enough to answer all the questions will be provided, but this does not mean that you have all day. An overall time limit has been set. Divide the total time (in minutes) by the number of questions to determine the approximate time you have for each question.

5) Do not linger over difficult questions

If you come across a difficult question, mark it with a paper clip (useful to have along) and come back to it when you have been through the booklet. One caution if you do this – be sure to skip a number on your answer sheet as well. Check often to be sure that you have not lost your place and that you are marking in the row numbered the same as the question you are answering.

6) Read the questions

Be sure you know what the question asks! Many capable people are unsuccessful because they failed to *read* the questions correctly.

7) Answer all questions

Unless you have been instructed that a penalty will be deducted for incorrect answers, it is better to guess than to omit a question.

8) Speed tests

It is often better NOT to guess on speed tests. It has been found that on timed tests people are tempted to spend the last few seconds before time is called in marking answers at random – without even reading them – in the hope of picking up a few extra points. To discourage this practice, the instructions may warn you that your score will be "corrected" for guessing. That is, a penalty will be applied. The incorrect answers will be deducted from the correct ones, or some other penalty formula will be used.

9) Review your answers

If you finish before time is called, go back to the questions you guessed or omitted to give them further thought. Review other answers if you have time.

10) Return your test materials

If you are ready to leave before others have finished or time is called, take ALL your materials to the monitor and leave quietly. Never take any test material with you. The monitor can discover whose papers are not complete, and taking a test booklet may be grounds for disqualification.

VIII. EXAMINATION TECHNIQUES

1) Read the general instructions carefully. These are usually printed on the first page of the exam booklet. As a rule, these instructions refer to the timing of the examination; the fact that you should not start work until the signal and must stop work at a signal, etc. If there are any *special* instructions, such as a choice of questions to be answered, make sure that you note this instruction carefully.

2) When you are ready to start work on the examination, that is as soon as the signal has been given, read the instructions to each question booklet, underline any key words or phrases, such as *least, best, outline, describe* and the like. In this way you will tend to answer as requested rather than discover on reviewing your paper that you *listed without describing*, that you selected the *worst* choice rather than the *best* choice, etc.

3) If the examination is of the objective or multiple-choice type – that is, each question will also give a series of possible answers: A, B, C or D, and you are called upon to select the best answer and write the letter next to that answer on your answer paper – it is advisable to start answering each question in turn. There may be anywhere from 50 to 100 such questions in the three or four hours allotted and you can see how much time would be taken if you read through all the questions before beginning to answer any. Furthermore, if you come across a question or group of questions which you know would be difficult to answer, it would undoubtedly affect your handling of all the other questions.

4) If the examination is of the essay type and contains but a few questions, it is a moot point as to whether you should read all the questions before starting to answer any one. Of course, if you are given a choice – say five out of seven and the like – then it is essential to read all the questions so you can eliminate the two that are most difficult. If, however, you are asked to answer all the questions, there may be danger in trying to answer the easiest one first because you may find that you will spend too much time on it. The best technique is to answer the first question, then proceed to the second, etc.

5) Time your answers. Before the exam begins, write down the time it started, then add the time allowed for the examination and write down the time it must be completed, then divide the time available somewhat as follows:
    - If 3-1/2 hours are allowed, that would be 210 minutes. If you have 80 objective-type questions, that would be an average of 2-1/2 minutes per question. Allow yourself no more than 2 minutes per question, or a total of 160 minutes, which will permit about 50 minutes to review.
    - If for the time allotment of 210 minutes there are 7 essay questions to answer, that would average about 30 minutes a question. Give yourself only 25 minutes per question so that you have about 35 minutes to review.

6) The most important instruction is to *read each question* and make sure you know what is wanted. The second most important instruction is to *time yourself properly* so that you answer every question. The third most important instruction is to *answer every question*. Guess if you have to but include something for each question. Remember that you will receive no credit for a blank and will probably receive some credit if you write something in answer to an essay question. If you guess a letter – say "B" for a multiple-choice question – you may have guessed right. If you leave a blank as an answer to a multiple-choice question, the examiners may respect your feelings but it will not add a point to your score. Some exams may penalize you for wrong answers, so in such cases *only*, you may not want to guess unless you have some basis for your answer.

7) Suggestions
    a. Objective-type questions
        1. Examine the question booklet for proper sequence of pages and questions
        2. Read all instructions carefully
        3. Skip any question which seems too difficult; return to it after all other questions have been answered
        4. Apportion your time properly; do not spend too much time on any single question or group of questions

5. Note and underline key words – *all, most, fewest, least, best, worst, same, opposite*, etc.
6. Pay particular attention to negatives
7. Note unusual option, e.g., unduly long, short, complex, different or similar in content to the body of the question
8. Observe the use of "hedging" words – *probably, may, most likely*, etc.
9. Make sure that your answer is put next to the same number as the question
10. Do not second-guess unless you have good reason to believe the second answer is definitely more correct
11. Cross out original answer if you decide another answer is more accurate; do not erase until you are ready to hand your paper in
12. Answer all questions; guess unless instructed otherwise
13. Leave time for review

  b. Essay questions
    1. Read each question carefully
    2. Determine exactly what is wanted. Underline key words or phrases.
    3. Decide on outline or paragraph answer
    4. Include many different points and elements unless asked to develop any one or two points or elements
    5. Show impartiality by giving pros and cons unless directed to select one side only
    6. Make and write down any assumptions you find necessary to answer the questions
    7. Watch your English, grammar, punctuation and choice of words
    8. Time your answers; don't crowd material

8) Answering the essay question

Most essay questions can be answered by framing the specific response around several key words or ideas. Here are a few such key words or ideas:

M's: manpower, materials, methods, money, management
P's: purpose, program, policy, plan, procedure, practice, problems, pitfalls, personnel, public relations

  a. Six basic steps in handling problems:
    1. Preliminary plan and background development
    2. Collect information, data and facts
    3. Analyze and interpret information, data and facts
    4. Analyze and develop solutions as well as make recommendations
    5. Prepare report and sell recommendations
    6. Install recommendations and follow up effectiveness

  b. Pitfalls to avoid
    1. *Taking things for granted* – A statement of the situation does not necessarily imply that each of the elements is necessarily true; for example, a complaint may be invalid and biased so that all that can be taken for granted is that a complaint has been registered

2. *Considering only one side of a situation* – Wherever possible, indicate several alternatives and then point out the reasons you selected the best one
3. *Failing to indicate follow up* – Whenever your answer indicates action on your part, make certain that you will take proper follow-up action to see how successful your recommendations, procedures or actions turn out to be
4. *Taking too long in answering any single question* – Remember to time your answers properly

IX. AFTER THE TEST

Scoring procedures differ in detail among civil service jurisdictions although the general principles are the same. Whether the papers are hand-scored or graded by machine we have described, they are nearly always graded by number. That is, the person who marks the paper knows only the number – never the name – of the applicant. Not until all the papers have been graded will they be matched with names. If other tests, such as training and experience or oral interview ratings have been given, scores will be combined. Different parts of the examination usually have different weights. For example, the written test might count 60 percent of the final grade, and a rating of training and experience 40 percent. In many jurisdictions, veterans will have a certain number of points added to their grades.

After the final grade has been determined, the names are placed in grade order and an eligible list is established. There are various methods for resolving ties between those who get the same final grade – probably the most common is to place first the name of the person whose application was received first. Job offers are made from the eligible list in the order the names appear on it. You will be notified of your grade and your rank as soon as all these computations have been made. This will be done as rapidly as possible.

People who are found to meet the requirements in the announcement are called "eligibles." Their names are put on a list of eligible candidates. An eligible's chances of getting a job depend on how high he stands on this list and how fast agencies are filling jobs from the list.

When a job is to be filled from a list of eligibles, the agency asks for the names of people on the list of eligibles for that job. When the civil service commission receives this request, it sends to the agency the names of the three people highest on this list. Or, if the job to be filled has specialized requirements, the office sends the agency the names of the top three persons who meet these requirements from the general list.

The appointing officer makes a choice from among the three people whose names were sent to him. If the selected person accepts the appointment, the names of the others are put back on the list to be considered for future openings.

That is the rule in hiring from all kinds of eligible lists, whether they are for typist, carpenter, chemist, or something else. For every vacancy, the appointing officer has his choice of any one of the top three eligibles on the list. This explains why the person whose name is on top of the list sometimes does not get an appointment when some of the persons lower on the list do. If the appointing officer chooses the second or third eligible, the No. 1 eligible does not get a job at once, but stays on the list until he is appointed or the list is terminated.

X. HOW TO PASS THE INTERVIEW TEST

The examination for which you applied requires an oral interview test. You have already taken the written test and you are now being called for the interview test – the final part of the formal examination.

You may think that it is not possible to prepare for an interview test and that there are no procedures to follow during an interview. Our purpose is to point out some things you can do in advance that will help you and some good rules to follow and pitfalls to avoid while you are being interviewed.

What is an interview supposed to test?

The written examination is designed to test the technical knowledge and competence of the candidate; the oral is designed to evaluate intangible qualities, not readily measured otherwise, and to establish a list showing the relative fitness of each candidate – as measured against his competitors – for the position sought. Scoring is not on the basis of "right" and "wrong," but on a sliding scale of values ranging from "not passable" to "outstanding." As a matter of fact, it is possible to achieve a relatively low score without a single "incorrect" answer because of evident weakness in the qualities being measured.

Occasionally, an examination may consist entirely of an oral test – either an individual or a group oral. In such cases, information is sought concerning the technical knowledges and abilities of the candidate, since there has been no written examination for this purpose. More commonly, however, an oral test is used to supplement a written examination.

Who conducts interviews?

The composition of oral boards varies among different jurisdictions. In nearly all, a representative of the personnel department serves as chairman. One of the members of the board may be a representative of the department in which the candidate would work. In some cases, "outside experts" are used, and, frequently, a businessman or some other representative of the general public is asked to serve. Labor and management or other special groups may be represented. The aim is to secure the services of experts in the appropriate field.

However the board is composed, it is a good idea (and not at all improper or unethical) to ascertain in advance of the interview who the members are and what groups they represent. When you are introduced to them, you will have some idea of their backgrounds and interests, and at least you will not stutter and stammer over their names.

What should be done before the interview?

While knowledge about the board members is useful and takes some of the surprise element out of the interview, there is other preparation which is more substantive. It *is* possible to prepare for an oral interview – in several ways:

1) **Keep a copy of your application and review it carefully before the interview**

This may be the only document before the oral board, and the starting point of the interview. Know what education and experience you have listed there, and the sequence and dates of all of it. Sometimes the board will ask you to review the highlights of your experience for them; you should not have to hem and haw doing it.

2) **Study the class specification and the examination announcement**

Usually, the oral board has one or both of these to guide them. The qualities, characteristics or knowledges required by the position sought are stated in these documents. They offer valuable clues as to the nature of the oral interview. For example, if the job involves supervisory responsibilities, the announcement will usually indicate that knowledge of modern supervisory methods and the qualifications of the candidate as a supervisor will be tested. If so, you can expect such questions, frequently in the form of a hypothetical situation which you are expected to solve. NEVER go into an oral without knowledge of the duties and responsibilities of the job you seek.

3) Think through each qualification required

Try to visualize the kind of questions you would ask if you were a board member. How well could you answer them? Try especially to appraise your own knowledge and background in each area, *measured against the job sought*, and identify any areas in which you are weak. Be critical and realistic – do not flatter yourself.

4) Do some general reading in areas in which you feel you may be weak

For example, if the job involves supervision and your past experience has NOT, some general reading in supervisory methods and practices, particularly in the field of human relations, might be useful. Do NOT study agency procedures or detailed manuals. The oral board will be testing your understanding and capacity, not your memory.

5) Get a good night's sleep and watch your general health and mental attitude

You will want a clear head at the interview. Take care of a cold or any other minor ailment, and of course, no hangovers.

What should be done on the day of the interview?

Now comes the day of the interview itself. Give yourself plenty of time to get there. Plan to arrive somewhat ahead of the scheduled time, particularly if your appointment is in the fore part of the day. If a previous candidate fails to appear, the board might be ready for you a bit early. By early afternoon an oral board is almost invariably behind schedule if there are many candidates, and you may have to wait. Take along a book or magazine to read, or your application to review, but leave any extraneous material in the waiting room when you go in for your interview. In any event, relax and compose yourself.

The matter of dress is important. The board is forming impressions about you – from your experience, your manners, your attitude, and your appearance. Give your personal appearance careful attention. Dress your best, but not your flashiest. Choose conservative, appropriate clothing, and be sure it is immaculate. This is a business interview, and your appearance should indicate that you regard it as such. Besides, being well groomed and properly dressed will help boost your confidence.

Sooner or later, someone will call your name and escort you into the interview room. *This is it.* From here on you are on your own. It is too late for any more preparation. But remember, you asked for this opportunity to prove your fitness, and you are here because your request was granted.

What happens when you go in?

The usual sequence of events will be as follows: The clerk (who is often the board stenographer) will introduce you to the chairman of the oral board, who will introduce you to the other members of the board. Acknowledge the introductions before you sit down. Do not be surprised if you find a microphone facing you or a stenotypist sitting by. Oral interviews are usually recorded in the event of an appeal or other review.

Usually the chairman of the board will open the interview by reviewing the highlights of your education and work experience from your application – primarily for the benefit of the other members of the board, as well as to get the material into the record. Do not interrupt or comment unless there is an error or significant misinterpretation; if that is the case, do not hesitate. But do not quibble about insignificant matters. Also, he will usually ask you some question about your education, experience or your present job – partly to get you to start talking and to establish the interviewing "rapport." He may start the actual questioning, or turn it over to one of the other members. Frequently, each member undertakes the questioning on a particular area, one in which he is perhaps most competent, so you can expect each member to participate in the examination. Because time is limited, you may also expect some rather abrupt switches in the direction the questioning takes, so do not be upset by it. Normally, a board member will not pursue a single line of questioning unless he discovers a particular strength or weakness.

After each member has participated, the chairman will usually ask whether any member has any further questions, then will ask you if you have anything you wish to add. Unless you are expecting this question, it may floor you. Worse, it may start you off on an extended, extemporaneous speech. The board is not usually seeking more information. The question is principally to offer you a last opportunity to present further qualifications or to indicate that you have nothing to add. So, if you feel that a significant qualification or characteristic has been overlooked, it is proper to point it out in a sentence or so. Do not compliment the board on the thoroughness of their examination – they have been sketchy, and you know it. If you wish, merely say, "No thank you, I have nothing further to add." This is a point where you can "talk yourself out" of a good impression or fail to present an important bit of information. Remember, *you close the interview yourself*.

The chairman will then say, "That is all, Mr. _____, thank you." Do not be startled; the interview is over, and quicker than you think. Thank him, gather your belongings and take your leave. Save your sigh of relief for the other side of the door.

How to put your best foot forward
Throughout this entire process, you may feel that the board individually and collectively is trying to pierce your defenses, seek out your hidden weaknesses and embarrass and confuse you. Actually, this is not true. They are obliged to make an appraisal of your qualifications for the job you are seeking, and they want to see you in your best light. Remember, they must interview all candidates and a non-cooperative candidate may become a failure in spite of their best efforts to bring out his qualifications. Here are 15 suggestions that will help you:

1) Be natural – Keep your attitude confident, not cocky
If you are not confident that you can do the job, do not expect the board to be. Do not apologize for your weaknesses, try to bring out your strong points. The board is interested in a positive, not negative, presentation. Cockiness will antagonize any board member and make him wonder if you are covering up a weakness by a false show of strength.

2) Get comfortable, but don't lounge or sprawl
Sit erectly but not stiffly. A careless posture may lead the board to conclude that you are careless in other things, or at least that you are not impressed by the importance of the occasion. Either conclusion is natural, even if incorrect. Do not fuss with your clothing, a pencil or an ashtray. Your hands may occasionally be useful to emphasize a point; do not let them become a point of distraction.

3) Do not wisecrack or make small talk
This is a serious situation, and your attitude should show that you consider it as such. Further, the time of the board is limited – they do not want to waste it, and neither should you.

4) Do not exaggerate your experience or abilities

In the first place, from information in the application or other interviews and sources, the board may know more about you than you think. Secondly, you probably will not get away with it. An experienced board is rather adept at spotting such a situation, so do not take the chance.

5) If you know a board member, do not make a point of it, yet do not hide it

Certainly you are not fooling him, and probably not the other members of the board. Do not try to take advantage of your acquaintanceship – it will probably do you little good.

6) Do not dominate the interview

Let the board do that. They will give you the clues – do not assume that you have to do all the talking. Realize that the board has a number of questions to ask you, and do not try to take up all the interview time by showing off your extensive knowledge of the answer to the first one.

7) Be attentive

You only have 20 minutes or so, and you should keep your attention at its sharpest throughout. When a member is addressing a problem or question to you, give him your undivided attention. Address your reply principally to him, but do not exclude the other board members.

8) Do not interrupt

A board member may be stating a problem for you to analyze. He will ask you a question when the time comes. Let him state the problem, and wait for the question.

9) Make sure you understand the question

Do not try to answer until you are sure what the question is. If it is not clear, restate it in your own words or ask the board member to clarify it for you. However, do not haggle about minor elements.

10) Reply promptly but not hastily

A common entry on oral board rating sheets is "candidate responded readily," or "candidate hesitated in replies." Respond as promptly and quickly as you can, but do not jump to a hasty, ill-considered answer.

11) Do not be peremptory in your answers

A brief answer is proper – but do not fire your answer back. That is a losing game from your point of view. The board member can probably ask questions much faster than you can answer them.

12) Do not try to create the answer you think the board member wants

He is interested in what kind of mind you have and how it works – not in playing games. Furthermore, he can usually spot this practice and will actually grade you down on it.

13) Do not switch sides in your reply merely to agree with a board member

Frequently, a member will take a contrary position merely to draw you out and to see if you are willing and able to defend your point of view. Do not start a debate, yet do not surrender a good position. If a position is worth taking, it is worth defending.

14) Do not be afraid to admit an error in judgment if you are shown to be wrong

The board knows that you are forced to reply without any opportunity for careful consideration. Your answer may be demonstrably wrong. If so, admit it and get on with the interview.

15) Do not dwell at length on your present job

The opening question may relate to your present assignment. Answer the question but do not go into an extended discussion. You are being examined for a *new* job, not your present one. As a matter of fact, try to phrase ALL your answers in terms of the job for which you are being examined.

Basis of Rating

Probably you will forget most of these "do's" and "don'ts" when you walk into the oral interview room. Even remembering them all will not ensure you a passing grade. Perhaps you did not have the qualifications in the first place. But remembering them will help you to put your best foot forward, without treading on the toes of the board members.

Rumor and popular opinion to the contrary notwithstanding, an oral board wants you to make the best appearance possible. They know you are under pressure – but they also want to see how you respond to it as a guide to what your reaction would be under the pressures of the job you seek. They will be influenced by the degree of poise you display, the personal traits you show and the manner in which you respond.

ABOUT THIS BOOK

This book contains tests divided into Examination Sections. Go through each test, answering every question in the margin. We have also attached a sample answer sheet at the back of the book that can be removed and used. At the end of each test look at the answer key and check your answers. On the ones you got wrong, look at the right answer choice and learn. Do not fill in the answers first. Do not memorize the questions and answers, but understand the answer and principles involved. On your test, the questions will likely be different from the samples. Questions are changed and new ones added. If you understand these past questions you should have success with any changes that arise. Tests may consist of several types of questions. We have additional books on each subject should more study be advisable or necessary for you. Finally, the more you study, the better prepared you will be. This book is intended to be the last thing you study before you walk into the examination room. Prior study of relevant texts is also recommended. NLC publishes some of these in our Fundamental Series. Knowledge and good sense are important factors in passing your exam. Good luck also helps. So now study this Passbook, absorb the material contained within and take that knowledge into the examination. Then do your best to pass that exam.

EXAMINATION SECTION

EXAMINATION SECTION
TEST 1

DIRECTIONS: Each question or incomplete statement is followed by several suggested answers or completions. Select the one that BEST answers the question or completes the statement. *PRINT THE LETTER OF THE CORRECT ANSWER IN THE SPACE AT THE RIGHT.*

1. Assume you are a housing inspector assigned to make an inspection of an apartment house.
   The MOST desirable procedure to follow is:

   A. Before beginning this inspection, you should make an appointment with the owner so that he may have a representative present when you arrive
   B. You should make your inspection without revealing your identity
   C. You should reveal your identity only if challenged
   D. Upon arrival at the premises, you should identify yourself to the owner or his representative before proceeding with your inspection

   1._____

2. Suppose that you were preparing a report on your investigation of a tenant complaint.
   Of the following, the item that you should consider LEAST necessary for inclusion in your report is the

   A. height of the building
   B. address of the building
   C. specific violations discovered
   D. name of the complaining tenant

   2._____

3. During an inspection of a tenant's apartment, you are asked for information about enforcement of orders to correct violations.
   Of the following, the MOST proper reply to the tenant is to

   A. advise the tenant to write a letter to Department headquarters so that his inquiry can be treated as an official matter
   B. refuse to tell the tenant anything since this is a matter between the owner and the Department
   C. explain briefly the usual procedure in connection with the processing of complaints in your Department
   D. advise the tenant to withhold rent payment until the violations found in her apartment are removed

   3._____

Questions 4-7.

DIRECTIONS: Questions 4 through 7 are to be answered on the basis of the following situation.

Assume you are an Inspector of Housing. While investigating a complaint about broken plaster, the tenant who made the complaint tells you that the building is vermin- and rat-infested. Your inspection shows the plaster to be in very unsatisfactory condition, but you see no evidence of vermin or rats. The tenant tells you that vermin and rats appear only in the evening. The apartment is kept in a very slovenly manner.

1

4. Of the following statements, the MOST important one to include in your report in addition to your findings regarding the plaster is:

    A. The apartment is slovenly kept
    B. The apartment is not vermin- and rat-infested
    C. the tenant said the apartment was infested
    D. there was no evidence of vermin- or rat-infestation as the tenant had claimed

5. In making your investigation, you should be

    A. very short with the tenant
    B. very loquacious so that you encourage the tenant to tell you about other violations
    C. very polite and agree with everything the tenant says
    D. pleasant but discourage undue conversation

6. With regard to the slovenly way in which the apartment is kept, you should

    A. make no mention of it to the tenant
    B. point out to the tenant that he does not deserve to have the plaster fixed
    C. be diplomatic by pointing out that it will be easier to keep the apartment clean when the plaster is fixed
    D. tell the tenant that dirt breeds vermin and it would be a good idea for him to start cleaning up

7. Assume that the Department requires reports to be made on a blank card.
    Of the following, the BEST statement to enter on your card concerning your findings is:

    A. Complaint exaggerated but there is a violation
    B. Inspected Apt. 2B at 700 West 400th Street and found wall plaster badly cracked with several breaks showing lath in all rooms
    C. Inspected Apt. 2B at 700 West 400th Street. Violations exist.
    D. Inspected Apt. 2B at 700 West 400th Street. Found plaster badly cracked and broken in some rooms.

8. Of the following equipment, the item that is LEAST likely to be required by an Inspector of Housing on a routine inspection is a

    A. 6' rule   B. 25' tape
    C. flashlight   D. notebook

9. According to the Multiple Dwelling Law, in all new-law-tenements there shall be access to every living room and bedroom and to at least one bathroom without passing through any bedroom.
    Of the following, the MOST important reason for this requirement is that it

    A. provides better ventilation of apartments
    B. assures privacy to occupants
    C. reduces fire and health hazards
    D. improves the arrangement of rooms of apartments

10. While investigating a complaint of a condition not dangerous or detrimental to life or health, an inspector is asked by the complainant, a tenant, if this condition constitutes a violation.
    Of the following, the MOST acceptable answer is:

    A. It is none of your business
    B. Yes. We will take him into court immediately.
    C. Yes. We will notify him of the violation immediately and the condition will be corrected in a few days or we will prosecute.
    D. Yes. The landlord will be notified and allowed a reasonable period in which to correct the condition.

    10.____

11. While making an inspection in the apartment of a tenant, you are informed by him that the janitor makes minor repairs only when he is tipped.
    Of the following, the MOST appropriate action you should take upon receipt of this information is to

    A. discuss the matter of tipping with the owner of the building
    B. advise the janitor that required repairs must be made regardless of the receipt of a gratuity
    C. tell the tenant to discuss the matter with the owner of the building
    D. ask for more information as to the existence of neglected defects in the building

    11.____

12. Your supervisor asks you to make a re-inspection of a building which you know was recently inspected by a fellow inspector. You are told that this assignment is confidential and is not to be discussed with anyone.
    Of the following, the MOST desirable action to take is to

    A. advise your superior that you do not want to check up on the work of another inspector
    B. discuss the assignment with the other inspector before going out on the inspection
    C. accept the assignment and follow the instructions of your supervisor without comment
    D. insist that you be permitted to see the report of the other inspector before accepting the assignment

    12.____

Question 13.

DIRECTIONS: Question 13 is to be answered on the basis of the following statement.

When the lot of such a dwelling abuts upon two or more streets, and the difference in level between the highest and the lowest points of the curbs adjoining the lot is more than ten feet, a room below the highest curb point may be used for living purposes provided it opens upon a street or upon a lawful court or yard which connects directly with a street or, if the floor of such a room is not more than twelve feet below the highest curb point, upon an interior court with a least dimension of not less than thirty feet if such court is situated on a lot line.

13. According to the above statement, it is CORRECT to say that   13.____
    A. the room described as acceptable for living purposes must in all instances open on a court or yard connecting directly with a street
    B. if the floor of the room is less than twelve feet below the highest curb point, it may not be used for living purposes
    C. no room in such a dwelling may be used for living purposes if the difference in curb points is less than ten feet
    D. a room whose floor is more than twelve feet below
    E. the highest curb point may be used for living purposes if it opens upon a street

Questions 14-15.

DIRECTIONS: Questions 14 and 15 are to be answered on the basis of the following statement.

Whatever is dangerous to human life or detrimental to health, and whatever dwelling is overcrowded with occupants or is not provided with adequate ingress or egress or is not sufficiently supported, ventilated, sewered, drained, cleaned, or lighted in reference to its intended or actual use, and whatever renders the air or human food or drink unwholesome are nuisances. All such nuisances are unlawful.

14. According to the above paragraph,   14.____
    A. dwellings with more occupants than one per room are dangerous and are nuisances
    B. dwellings may be considered overcrowded when there is inadequate ingress or egress
    C. if a dwelling is untenanted, it cannot be considered a nuisance under this paragraph
    D. a dwelling may be considered a nuisance if the number of exits from the building is insufficient

15. The word *ingress,* as used in the above paragraph, means MOST NEARLY   15.____
    A. entrance   B. water supply
    C. recess   D. water closet

16. Existing cubicles complying with other provisions of this section may be maintained.   16.____
    In this sentence, the word *cubicles* means MOST NEARLY
    A. exceptions   B. aisles or halls
    C. party walls   D. enclosed sections

17. An officer or employee of the Department shall be free from liability for acts done by him in good faith in the performance of his official duties.   17.____
    In this sentence, the word *liability* means MOST NEARLY
    A. responsibility   B. personal damages
    C. compliance   D. necessary insurance

18. Encumbrances of any kind are forbidden on fire escapes. The word *encumbrances*, as used in this sentence, means MOST NEARLY

    A. braces
    B. shackles
    C. attachments
    D. obstructions

19. If more than one dormer faces a street, their aggregate frontage at any level shall not exceed the frontage length herein permitted at such level.
    The word *aggregate,* as used in this sentence, means MOST NEARLY

    A. total
    B. individual
    C. excess
    D. permitted

20. The location and design of all buildings and structures on the plot shall be consistent with the predominantly residential character of the district.
    The word *predominantly*, as used in this sentence, means MOST NEARLY

    A. prepared
    B. approximate
    C. prevailing
    D. predetermined

Questions 21-24.

DIRECTIONS: In answering Questions 21 through 24, choose the term in Column II MOST closely identified with the item in Column I. Each term may be used more than once or not at all.

COLUMN I

21. Scratch coat
22. Flashing
23. Parapet
24. Newel

COLUMN II

A. Roofing
B. Stair building
C. Plastering
D. Plumbing
E. Painting

25. Of the following, the term which is LEAST related to the others is

    A. ground
    B. lath
    C. plaster
    D. ledger board

26. The upright finished board in the side of a door opening is called a

    A. batten   B. saddle   C. jamb   D. stile

27. Which one of the following terms is LEAST related to the others?

    A. Stop   B. Jamb   C. Buck   D. Siding

28. Which one of the following terms is LEAST related to the others?

    A. Pipe   B. Riser   C. Tread   D. Nosing

29. Of the following terms, the one which is LEAST related to the others is

    A. baseboard   B. base mold
    C. casing   D. base plate

30. A ribband or ribbon is a horizontal strip of wood notched into the studs. It is used ONLY in _____-frame construction.

    A. balloon   B. braced   C. platform   D. Western

31. The bracing between wood floor beams is called

    A. internal bracing   B. bridging
    C. reinforcing   D. cross-bracing

32. The MAXIMUM allowable spacing for the bracing described in Question 31 above, according to the City Building Code, is

    A. 6'   B. 8'   C. 10'   D. 12'

33. In wooden floor construction, the bracing described in Question 31 above is used PRIMARILY to

    A. prevent the joists from turning over before the flooring is placed
    B. transfer load from the joist directly under a load on the floor to adjacent joists
    C. keep a uniform spacing of the joists
    D. eliminate the need for header and trimmer beams at floor openings

34. In floor construction, the bracing described in Question 31 above should

    A. be nailed at the top and the lower ends left loose until the sub-flooring is nailed in position
    B. be nailed at both ends before the sub-flooring is placed in position
    C. not be nailed at all until after the sub-flooring is nailed in position
    D. not be nailed until after the sub-flooring is nailed and the finished flooring placed

35. The timbers that support the rough flooring are called

    A. lintels   B. sills   C. beams   D. studs

36. Wood for the wearing surface of a floor should PREFERABLY be

    A. flat-sawed   B. quarter-sawed
    C. cross-cut   D. rip-sawed

37. Wainscoting is

    A. the moulding around a room for hanging pictures
    B. the moulding around a room to protect the plaster from the backs of chairs
    C. panel work covering part or all of a wall
    D. the tile or cement flooring in a kitchen around the stove or range

38. The small bars separating the panes of glass in a panelled window are

    A. rails   B. muntins   C. moldings   D. mullions

39. An extra window, hung over a window of a building, to help keep out wind and cold is a(n) _____ window. 39._____

   A. storm
   B. casement
   C. oriel
   D. double-hung

Questions 40-44.

DIRECTIONS: In Questions 40 through 44, for each figure in Column I, representing a cross-section of a piece of lumber, select the letter preceding the term in Column II which is MOST closely associated with figure. NOTE: These figures are not to scale.

COLUMN I / COLUMN II

A. Flooring
B. Siding
C. Baseboard
D. Window steel
E. Threshold
F. Shingle

40. _____
41. _____
42. _____
43. _____
44. _____

45. A dry well 45._____

   A. provides drainage without the use of a sewer
   B. is a reservoir for storage of drainage water until such time as the flooded sewer is able to carry this water
   C. is an auxiliary cesspool
   D. provides an approved storage space for rubbish

46. A wall of a building which supports any load other than its own weight is called a _____ wall. 46.___

    A. curtain B. retaining C. parapet D. bearing

47. Soffits are USUALLY located in 47.___

    A. the roofing B. bathrooms
    C. stairways D. the flooring

48. Piles are used in building construction 48.___

    A. to provide waterproof construction
    B. to eliminate the need for a cellar
    C. when the building is located on sloping ground
    D. to help support the foundation

49. Employees of the department are not permitted to engage in any activity connected with construction, alteration, or equipment of buildings PRIMARILY because 49.___

    A. they are required to work fulltime for the city
    B. their employment with the city might give them unfair advantage over others in the same activity who were not employed by the city
    C. such activity might influence their enforcement of the law
    D. they would tend to specialize in a phase of their work in the department which concerned their outside activity, to the detriment of other phases

50. Of the following, the MOST acceptable reason for the enforcement of the Building Code and Multiple Dwelling Law is: 50.___

    A. Since all builders are governed by a single code of practice, no builder will have any advantage over any other builder
    B. Minimum standards of safety and comfort are assured for the occupants of buildings
    C. It stimulates the growth of undeveloped sections of the city
    D. It prevents the decline of real estate values

KEY (CORRECT ANSWERS)

1. D	11. C	21. C	31. B	41. D
2. A	12. C	22. A	32. B	42. E
3. C	13. D	23. A	33. B	43. A
4. D	14. D	24. B	34. A	44. B
5. D	15. A	25. D	35. C	45. A
6. A	16. D	26. C	36. B	46. D
7. B	17. B	27. D	37. C	47. C
8. B	18. D	28. A	38. B	48. D
9. B	19. A	29. D	39. A	49. C
10. D	20. C	30. A	40. C	50. B

TEST 2

DIRECTIONS: Each question or incomplete statement is followed by several suggested answers or completions. Select the one that BEST answers the question or completes the statement. *PRINT THE LETTER OF THE CORRECT ANSWER IN THE SPACE AT THE RIGHT.*

1. In determining the dimensions of a rectangular court, a surveyor measured the width as 12'0"; but instead of measuring the depth, measured the length of a diagonal as 20'0". The depth of the court, in feet, is

    A. 18   B. 16   C. 14   D. 12

    1._____

2. Assuming that 6 sq. ft. are allowed per person, the capacity of an assembly hall that is 45 feet wide at the front, 60 feet wide at the rear (front and rear walls parallel), and 75 feet long is MOST NEARLY

    A. 600   B. 650   C. 700   D. 750

    2._____

3. The volume of a rectangular room is 1063 3/4 cu. ft. It is 10'0" and 9'3" wide. Its length is MOST NEARLY

    A. 11'0"   B. 11'3"   C. 11'6"   D. 11'9"

    3._____

4. Seven hundred twenty (720) reports are to be checked. Inspector X can do this job alone in 6 days. Inspector Y, less experienced, can do the job in 10 days. To expedite the work, both inspectors are assigned to share the work in such manner that they will both require the same time for completion.
The number of reports that Y will check is MOST NEARLY

    A. 270   B. 288   C. 312   D. 330

    4._____

5. In a C district, a building may occupy 60% of the area of a lot.
If a lot measures 30' x 100', the maximum permissible length of a rectangular building 25 feet wide is MOST NEARLY

    A. 66'   B. 68'   C. 70'   D. 72'

    5._____

6. A room measures 9' x 12'. The light fixture is located in the center of the ceiling. The distance from a corner of the room to the center of the light fixture, measured along the ceiling, is MOST NEARLY

    A. 6'6"   B. 7'0"   C. 7'6"   D. 8'0"

    6._____

7. In a class one district, no building shall be erected to a height in excess of 7/8 times the width of the street; but for each one foot that the building or a portion of it sets back from the street line, 1 1/2 feet shall be added to the height limit of such building or such portion thereof.
According to the above statement, the maximum height of a building in a class one district on a street 100 feet wide where the building is set back 4 feet from the street line is MOST NEARLY

    A. 93'   B. 87'   C. 112'   D. 76'

    7._____

8. An old law tenement is one that was constructed before

 A. April 18, 1929 B. April 15, 1887
 C. April 18, 1912 D. April 12, 1901

9. Of the following, the type of building which is NOT covered by the provisions of the Multiple Dwelling Law is a

 A. converted dwelling B. two-family dwelling
 C. hotel D. clubhouse

10. According to the City Administrative Code, the power to regulate and limit the height and bulk of buildings and to regulate and determine the areas of yards, courts, and other open spaces is delegated to the

 A. Department of Housing and Buildings
 B. City Planning Commission
 C. Board of Standards and Appeals
 D. City Council

11. The regulations of the department with respect to lodging houses do NOT cover

 A. cleanliness of sheets and pillowcases
 B. amount of space per bed
 C. hours of use of beds by lodgers
 D. fire-retarding of cooking spaces used by lodgers

12. The Multiple Dwelling Law requires the landlord of a tenement to

 A. provide a resident janitor for the building if it is occupied by six or more families
 B. have previous coats of wallpaper removed before new wallpaper can be applied
 C. paint walls of halls and stairs every three years or less
 D. keep bulkhead doors and scuttles locked with a key lock at all times

13. The MINIMUM sized light, in watts, required in halls and stairs of multiple dwellings, according to the Multiple Dwelling Law, is

 A. 15 B. 30 C. 40 D. 60

14. Of the following, the type of building which may NOT be erected in a residence district is

 A. railroad passenger station
 B. hospital
 C. bank building
 D. philanthropic institution

15. A fireproof building

 A. is fire-retarded
 B. must be fire-stopped
 C. must be constructed entirely of incombustible material
 D. is a fire-protected structure

16. Of the following items relating to fire escapes, the one that is NOT permitted, according to the Multiple Dwelling Law, is

    A. balconies
    B. gooseneck ladders
    C. vertical ladder fire escapes
    D. drop ladder

17. A certificate of occupancy is issued by the

    A. Commissioner of Housing and Buildings
    B. Deputy Commissioner of Housing
    C. Deputy Commissioner of Buildings
    D. Borough Superintendent

18. The structure above the roof of a building enclosing a stairway is described by the building code as a(n)

    A. scuttle   B. extension
    C. penthouse   D. bulkhead

19. When a structure containing a party wall is demolished, protection for the party wall is specified by the Building Code.
    Of the following items relating to such protection, the one that is NOT specified by the Code is

    A. the owner of the building being demolished must pay for protecting the party wall
    B. the anchors at the beam ends in the standing wall shall be bent over
    C. the party wall shall be shored up and made secure
    D. all open beam holes shall be bricked in

20. According to the Multiple Dwelling Law, the MINIMUM area of a bedroom in newly constructed Class A multiple dwellings is_____ sq. ft.

    A. 132   B. 116   C. 100   D. 80

21. The height of a room, for the purpose of determining compliance with requirements of the Multiple Dwelling Law, shall be measured from the

    A. top of the floor beams to the bottom of the ceiling beams
    B. center of the floor beams to the center of the ceiling beams
    C. finished floor to the finished ceiling
    D. rough flooring to the finished ceiling

22. The outside temperature below which heat must be supplied to tenants of centrally heated buildings during the day is

    A. 32° F   B. 60° F   C. 55° F   D. 45° F

23. A wiped joint is MOST likely to be found in_____ piping.

    A. vitrified clay sewer   B. cast iron sewer
    C. steel water   D. lead

24. A caulked joint is MOST likely to be found in 24.____

  A. vitrified clay sewer piping
  B. bell and spiget metal piping
  C. brass water piping
  D. a connection between a brass pipe and a lead pipe

25. Of the following materials, the one that the city building code does NOT permit for use in underground piping is _____ pipe. 25.____

  A. wrought iron   B. cast iron
  C. lead   D. brass

26. The drainage system of a building is that part of the plumbing system which receives, conveys, and removes 26.____

  A. the discharge of any fixture except water closets
  B. storm water only
  C. liquid and water carried wastes and storm water
  D. the discharge of water closets only

27. The purpose of a trap in a plumbing system is to 27.____

  A. provide a means of cleaning out a clogged drain
  B. prevent back syphonage
  C. provide a means of venting the plumbing system
  D. prevent the passage of air or gas through a pipe or fixture

28. Of the following piping, the one that can NOT be termed a stack is _____ piping. 28.____

  A. soil   B. house drain
  C. vent   D. waste

29. The roughing-in of plumbing constitutes 29.____

  A. delivery of plumbing supplies to the site of a building
  B. the installation of the piping
  C. the installation of the plumbing fixtures
  D. the testing of the plumbing

30. Hydrated lime is 30.____

  A. lime mixed in mortar   B. quick lime
  C. pre-slaked lime   D. waterproof lime

31. A concrete mix is tested for slump to indicate its 31.____

  A. freshness   B. water content
  C. plasticity   D. strength

32. Rock wool is used in buildings MAINLY to 32.____

  A. increase the fire resistive qualities of the walls
  B. act as an insulator of heat in walls
  C. form a barrier against vermin or rodent travel in walls
  D. reduce moisture or condensation on wall surfaces

33. Hair is added to plaster in order to 33.____

   A. delay the time of set
   B. make it more workable
   C. bond the finish coat to the brown coat
   D. increase its strength

34. A terrazzo-finish floor consists of 34.____

   A. cement, sand, and gravel ground to a smooth finish
   B. cement, sand, and marble chips
   C. tile squares set in fresh mortar
   D. asphaltic tiles set in asphaltic cement

35. A 1:2:4 concrete contains one sack of cement(,) 35.____

   A. two cubic feet of sand, and four cubic feet of gravel
   B. two gallons of water, and four cubic feet of aggregate
   C. two wheelbarrows of sand, and four wheelbarrows of gravel
   D. to four cubic feet of aggregate

Questions 86-90.

DIRECTIONS: In answering Questions 86 through 90, choose the term in Column II MOST closely identified with the item in Column I. Each term may be used more than once or not at all.

COLUMN I		COLUMN II	
36. Wane		A. Carpentry	36.____
		B. Plumbing	
37. Parging		C. Masonry	37.____
		D. Riveting	
38. Smoke test		E. Welding	38.____
		F. Plastering	
39. Mortise		G. Roofing	39.____
40. Struck joint			40.____

41. In brick work, a bat is 41.____

   A. never used in laying up a brick wall
   B. sometimes used so that it appears to be a header
   C. a bonding unit
   D. a stretcher

42. When painting, nail holes and cracks should be 42.____

   A. filled with putty before starting
   B. filled with putty after the priming coat is applied
   C. filled with paint by careful working
   D. ignored

43. The white deposit on a new brick wall is due to

    A. efflorescence
    B. slaking
    C. sedimentation
    D. condensation

44. Wire glass is used MAINLY where

    A. light is required but it is desired to obscure the view
    B. fire-retarding qualities are required
    C. strength is required without the extra cost of heavy plate glass
    D. a diffused light is required

45. Glazier's points are used to

    A. hold glass in wooden window sash
    B. scratch glass so that it can be broken to size
    C. force putty into narrow spaces between glass and sash
    D. remove broken glass from a pane

46. When pipes are to be hung from the ceilings of a concrete building, it is GOOD practice to provide in the construction

    A. inserts
    B. nailing strips
    C. lag screws
    D. clamps

47. A good flashing

    A. is as narrow as possible
    B. usually requires periodic painting
    C. never requires counter-flashing
    D. may be copper or zinc

48. The PRIMARY reason for using headers in brickwork is to

    A. obtain a particular architectural effect
    B. make a stronger wall
    C. have all bricklayers follow the same pattern
    D. permit easier pointing

49. The process of filling the joints of masonry with mortar and pressing the mortar into the joints is called

    A. grouting
    B. buttering
    C. pointing
    D. caulking

50. Dwellings may be located on a sanitary landfill. Such landfill that is young in age may present certain hazards. Of the following, the one that is NOT such a hazard is

    A. spontaneous combustion
    B. explosion of combustible gases
    C. contamination of water supply
    D. excavating for utilities may result in the release of bad odors

KEY (CORRECT ANSWERS)

1. B	11. D	21. C	31. C	41. B
2. B	12. B	22. C	32. B	42. B
3. C	13. A	23. D	33. D	43. A
4. A	14. C	24. B	34. B	44. B
5. D	15. D	25. A	35. A	45. A
6. C	16. C	26. C	36. A	46. A
7. A	17. D	27. D	37. C	47. D
8. D	18. D	28. B	38. B	48. B
9. B	19. C	29. B	39. A	49. C
10. B	20. D	30. C	40. C	50. C

EXAMINATION SECTION
TEST 1

DIRECTIONS: Each question or incomplete statement is followed by several suggested answers or completions. Select the one that BEST answers the question or completes the statement. *PRINT THE LETTER OF THE CORRECT ANSWER IN THE SPACE AT THE RIGHT.*

1. The basis of differentiating between a *Class A* and a *Class B* multiple dwelling is   1.____

    A. the date when the building was erected
    B. the size of the building
    C. whether residents are permanent or transient
    D. the number of families living in the building

2. The basis of differentiating between a *cellar* and a *basement* is   2.____

    A. whether or not there are windows
    B. the relationship of its height to curb level
    C. the ventilation available
    D. the number of exists provided

3. The MINIMUM horizontal dimension permitted for a living room in an apartment house erected after 1929 is   3.____

    A. 8'0"   B. 8'6"   C. 9'0"   D. 9'6"

4. It is proposed to build a garage for two cars for use by the tenants in a three-family dwelling. The garage will be on the same lot as the dwelling.
Of the following, the statement that MOST completely gives the type or types of construction that would be permitted for the garage is _____ with concrete roof.   4.____

    A. frame or block walls with flat wood roof or block walls with wood peak roof, or block walls
    B. block walls with flat wood roof or block walls with wood peak roof or block walls
    C. block walls with wood peak roof or block walls
    D. block walls

5. A restaurant is permitted in a hotel of non-fireproof construction providing that   5.____

    A. there are automatic sprinkler heads in the kitchen
    B. there are two means of egress from the kitchen
    C. the kitchen has windows opening to a required yard
    D. the walls of the kitchen have one hour fire rating

6. The one of the following that is considered a *living room* is a   6.____

    A. bathroom   B. foyer
    C. public room   D. kitchen

7. In certain types of occupancies, gas-fueled space heaters may be used instead of a central heating system. One of the requirements that MUST be met in order that space heaters be permitted in an apartment is that the   7.____

17

A. building be of fireproof construction
B. apartment must consist of two or more living rooms
C. building is not a tenement
D. apartment has two means of egress

8. Where a parapet wall is required, the MINIMUM height permitted is 8.___

   A. 3'0"   B. 3'6"   C. 4'0"   D. 4'6"

9. Ceilings over boilers in converted dwellings MUST be fire-retarded with 9.___

   A. two layers of 3/8" sheet rock
   B. wire lath and 3/4" cement mortar
   C. 3/8" rock lath and 1/2" gypsum mortar
   D. 3/8" sheet rock with #26 U.S. gage stamped metal

10. A fire alarm signal is required in all multiple dwellings which have the following type of occupancy: 10.___

    A. tenement   B. hotel
    C. converted dwelling D. single room

11. The multiple dwelling law requires that every living room be ventilated by windows having an area of at least 10% of the floor surface of the room. Assume that a certain living room is 10'6" long by 9'6" wide. 11.___
    Of the following, the MINIMUM window size that would be acceptable is

    A. 3'2" x 3'6"   B. 3'4" x 3'6"
    C. 3'4" x 3'8"   D. 3'6" x 3'8"

12. The multiple dwelling law specifies the minimum area and height of living rooms. 12.___
    The PRINCIPAL reason for this is to

    A. insure adequate light and air
    B. make inspections easier
    C. reduce possibility of serious fires
    D. control the number of occupants

13. The one of the following that is considered a multiple dwelling when located in a building separate from other buildings is a 13.___

    A. jail   B. monastery
    C. nurses' residence D. asylum

14. When any part of a building is to be fire-retarded, that part of the building MUST be protected by materials having a fire rating of at least _____ hour(s). 14.___

    A. 1   B. 2   C. 3   D. 4

15. A *fire damper* is necessary to 15.___

    A. adjust the draft in a chimney
    B. wet down combustible material in case of fire
    C. prevent the passage of heat and smoke through an air duct
    D. control the flame in an incinerator

Questions 16-18.

DIRECTIONS: Questions 16 through 18 must be answered in accordance with the following paragraph.

When constructed within a multiple dwelling, such storage space shall be equipped with a sprinkler system and also with a system of mechanical ventilation in no way connected with any other ventilating system. Such storage space shall have no opening into any other part of the dwelling except through a fireproof vestibule. Any such vestibule shall have a minimum superficial floor area of fifty square feet and its maximum area shall not exceed seventy-five square feet. It shall be enclosed with incombustible partitions having a fire-resistive rating of three hours. The floor and ceiling of such vestibule shall also be of incombustible material having a fire-resistive rating of at least three hours. There shall be two doors to provide access from the dwelling to the car storage space. Each such door shall have a fire-resistive rating of one and one-half hours and shall be provided with a device to prevent the opening of one door until the other door is entirely closed.

16. According to the above paragraph, the one of the following that is REQUIRED in order for cars to be permitted to be stored in a multiple dwelling is a(n)

    A. fireproof vestibule
    B. elevator from the garage
    C. approved heating system
    D. sprinkler system

17. According to the above paragraph, the one of the following materials that would NOT be acceptable for the walls of a vestibule connecting a garage to the dwelling portion of a building is

    A. 3" solid gypsum blocks
    B. 4" brick
    C. 4" hollow gypsum blocks, plastered both sides
    D. 6" solid cinder concrete blocks

18. According to the above paragraph, the one of the following that would be ACCEPTABLE for the width and length of a vestibule connecting a garage that is within a multiple dwelling to the dwelling portion of the building is

    A. 3'8" x 13'0"   B. 4'6" x 18'6"
    C. 4'9" x 14'6"   D. 4'3" x 19'3"

Questions 19-20.

DIRECTIONS: Questions 19 and 20 must be answered in accordance with the following paragraph.

It shall be unlawful to place, use, or to maintain in a condition intended, arranged or designed for use, any gas-fired cooking appliance, laundry stove, heating stove, range or water heater or combination of such appliances in any room or space used for living or sleeping in any new or existing multiple dwelling unless such room or space has a window opening to the outer air or such gas appliance is vented to the outer air. All automatically operated gas appliances shall be equipped with a device which shall shut off automatically the gas supply to the main burners when the pilot light in such appliance is extinguished. A gas range or the cooking portion of a gas appliance incorporating a room heater shall not be deemed an automatically operated gas appliance. However, burners in gas ovens and broilers which can be turned on and off or ignited by non-manual means shall be equipped with a device which shall shut off automatically the gas supply to those burners when the operation of such non-manual means fails.

19. According to the above paragraph, an automatic shut-off device is NOT required on a gas

    A. hot water heater
    B. laundry drier
    C. space heater
    D. range

20. According to the above paragraph, a gas-fired water heater is permitted

    A. only in kitchens
    B. only in bathrooms
    C. only in living rooms
    D. in any type of room

21. A tenant tells an inspector that the spring on the entrance door to his apartment is broken and the door remains open.
    Of the following, the BEST action for the inspector to take, after verifying the facts, is to

    A. tell the tenant to get the janitor to fix it
    B. tell the janitor to get it fixed
    C. tell the landlord to hire someone to fix it
    D. report it as a violation and tell the janitor to get it fixed

22. An owner of a two-family house tells you, an inspector, that he wants to convert his house to a three-family dwelling. He asks you for your advice as to the requirements that must be met for this change.
    You should

    A. inspect the building so that you can give him all the necessary information
    B. refer him to your supervisor for fuller advice
    C. tell him to consult a competent architect
    D. tell him you can't give him the information unless he gives you the plans of the building to check

23. An inspector receiving a complaint from a tenant should consider it as

    A. most likely the result of a quarrel with the landlord
    B. usually an exaggerated statement of the facts
    C. a matter which should be investigated
    D. something to be checked after all other work has been completed

24. In a dispute about a matter covered by the multiple dwelling law, an inspector should carefully AVOID

    A. taking the attitude that the landlord is always wrong
    B. sounding out both the landlord and the tenant when both sides disagree
    C. investigating the basis of the disagreement
    D. getting involved in the matter until both the landlord and the tenant agree on the facts

25. If an inspector does not clearly understand one of the provisions of the multiple dwelling law, he should

   A. interpret it as best he can
   B. get his superior to explain it to him
   C. avoid having to enforce this provision
   D. consider this provision unimportant

26. If a tenant continues to ask an inspector a great many questions, the inspector should

   A. tell the tenant not to ask so many questions because the inspector has too many other things to do
   B. pretend he does not hear the tenant unless the tenant persists
   C. tell the tenant that all questions should be referred to the main office
   D. answer the questions as briefly as he can without creating the impression he is trying to *brush off* the tenant

27. If an inspector is dissatisfied with his assignment, he should

   A. demand that he be re-assigned to another task
   B. slow down his work so that his superior knows he is dissatisfied
   C. continue doing his work as well as he can but request a reassignment at the earliest opportunity
   D. make sure his fellow inspectors know his feelings

28. The MAIN reason why an inspector should know the value of his work is that

   A. he will have more of an incentive to do a better job
   B. he can better explain his job to the public
   C. it will be easier for him to get a promotion
   D. he will be able to ignore minor inspections

29. A landlord has made an unjustified complaint about an inspector to the inspector's superiors.
   In future contacts with this landlord, the inspector should be

   A. cool and distant to avoid more trouble
   B. smiling and friendly to ease matters
   C. courteous and fair in enforcing the law
   D. strict so that the landlord knows he must comply with his orders

30. Assume that an inspector believes that one of the provisions of the multiple dwelling law is unfair.
   The inspector should

   A. refuse to enforce this provision because it is unfair
   B. enforce this provision because it does not matter whether the law is fair or not
   C. refuse to enforce this provision because it is impossible to make the public comply with this provision
   D. enforce the provision because it is the law

31. In wood frame construction, mortise and tenon joints may be illegal. The basis for determining whether or not such a joint is legal is

   A. type of wood
   B. size of members
   C. load carried by the members
   D. age of wood

32. Of the following terms, the one LEAST related to the others is

   A. scuttle   B. buttress   C. bulkhead   D. parapet

33. Of the following terms, the one LEAST related to the others is

   A. egress   B. fire tower
   C. fire wall   D. fire escape

34. A deformed bar would MOST likely be used in

   A. masonry work
   B. steel construction
   C. wood construction
   D. reinforced concrete construction

35. A party wall is a(n)

   A. wall serving two structures
   B. interior wall
   C. retaining wall
   D. wall without openings

36. Of the following types of walls, the one LEAST related to the others is

   A. faced   B. spandrel   C. apron   D. panel

37. A bar bending table would MOST likely be used in the following type of construction:

   A. steel   B. reinforced concrete
   C. wood   D. masonry

38. Of the following terms, the one which is LEAST related to the others is

   A. down-spout   B. ground seat
   C. gutter   D. leader

39. Of the following terms, the one which is LEAST related to the others is

   A. ball-peen   B. doublecut flat
   C. file card   D. rat tail

40. Of the following, the one which is LEAST related to the others is

   A. chase   B. footing   C. pier   D. pile

Questions 41-45.

DIRECTIONS: Questions 41 through 45 are to be answered in accordance with the floor plan of one floor of a converted dwelling shown on the last page of this test.

41. The depth of the linen closet, indicated by the letter S, is

　A. 1'4"　　B. 1'5"　　C. 1'6"　　D. 1'7"

42. The door that should have a fire rating is indicated by the letter

　A. G　　B. H　　C. J　　D. K

43. The walls of the building are of

　A. frame construction　　B. solid brick
　C. brick and block　　D. solid block

44. Of the following types of steel sections, the one that MOST closely resembles, in appearance, the steel beams used to support the floor joists is

　A. ⊔　　B. ST　　C. L　　D. WF

45. The grade of lumber indicated for joists FORMERLY was called #

　A. 1 common　　B. 1 select　　C. 2 common　　D. 2 select

8 (#1)

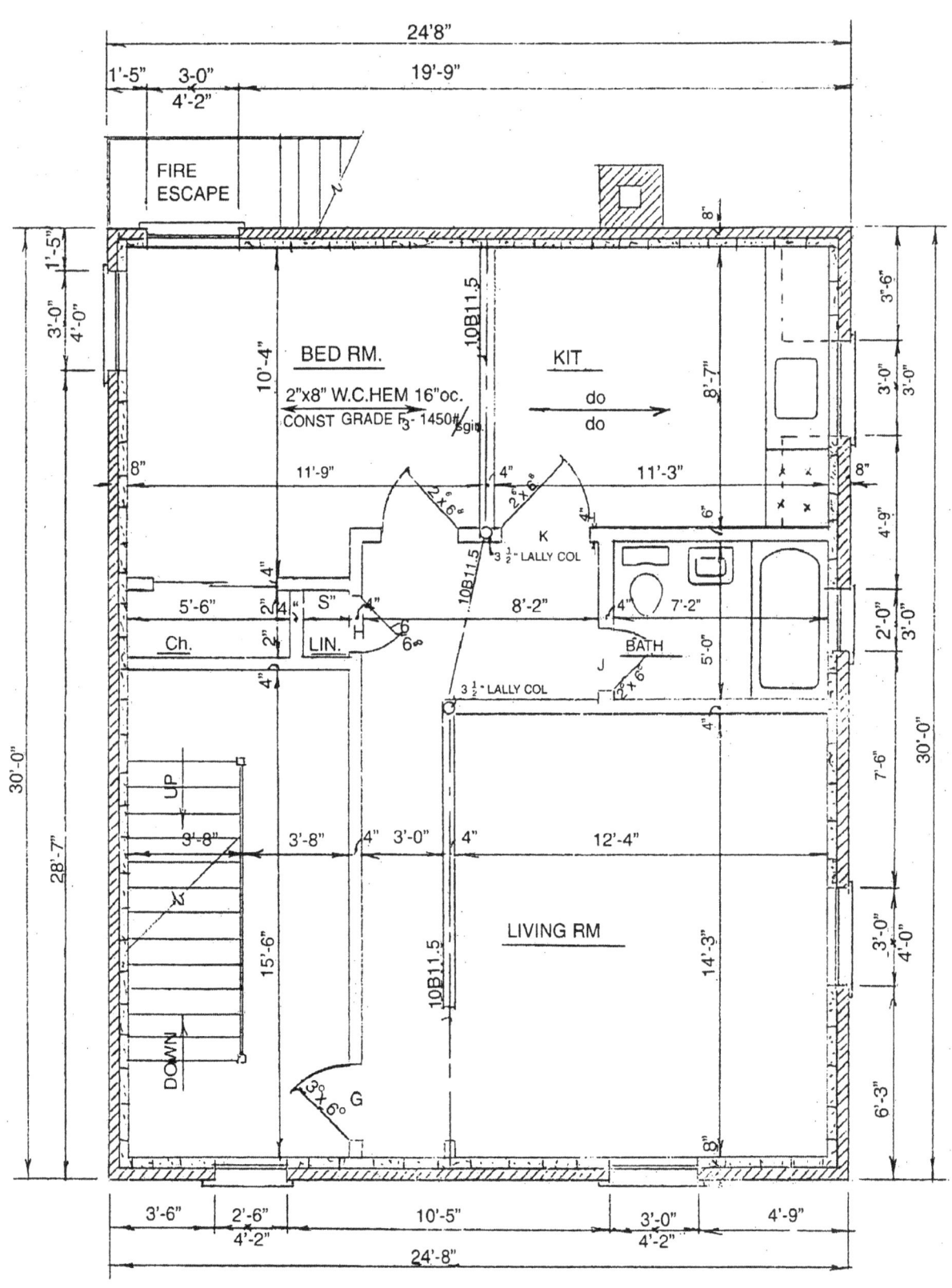

FLOOR PLAN

KEY (CORRECT ANSWERS)

1. C	11. A	21. D	31. B	41. C
2. B	12. A	22. C	32. B	42. A
3. A	13. C	23. C	33. C	43. C
4. D	14. A	24. A	34. D	44. D
5. A	15. C	25. B	35. A	45. A
6. D	16. D	26. D	36. A	
7. B	17. B	27. C	37. B	
8. B	18. C	28. A	38. B	
9. B	19. D	29. C	39. A	
10. D	20. D	30. D	40. A	

EXAMINATION SECTION
TEST 1

DIRECTIONS: Each question or incomplete statement is followed by several suggested answers or completions. Select the one that BEST answers the question or completes the statement. *PRINT THE LETTER OF THE CORRECT ANSWER IN THE SPACE AT THE RIGHT.*

1. A kitchenette is defined as a cooking space having a floor area of LESS than _____ square feet.
    A. 57 B. 58 C. 59 D. 60

2. The one of the following that is classed as a converted dwelling is a(n)
    A. apartment house erected prior to 1929, now used as a hotel
    B. lodging house erected prior to 1913, now used as a multiple dwelling
    C. one-family house erected prior to 1929, now used as a multiple dwelling
    D. rooming house erected prior to 1913, now used as a hotel

3. A *fire-retarded* partition must have a fire-resistive rating of AT LEAST _____ hour(s).
    A. 1 B. 2 C. 3 D. 4

4. The multiple dwelling law states that the total window area of a room must be at least one-tenth of the floor surface area of the room.
   The one of the following types of rooms that is exempted from this provision is a
    A. bedroom   B. kitchen
    C. recreation room D. bathroom

5. In a non-fireproof multiple dwelling, the HIGHEST story in which a factory may be operated is the
    A. 1st B. 2nd C. 3rd D. 4th

6. In a multiple dwelling under construction, the MINIMUM required width of an entrance hall, from the entrance to the first stair, is
    A. 3'4" B. 3'8" C. 4'0" D. 4'4"

7. Access to a required fire escape, used as a legal second means of egress from an apartment, may be from a
    A. public hall B. kitchen
    C. bathroom   D. closet

8. The basis for differentiating between a *tenement* and any other *Class A multiple dwelling* is
    A. the year in which it was built
    B. the number of families now residing therein
    C. whether residents are permanent or transient
    D. classification of construction

2 (#1)

9. In a 6-story multiple dwelling under construction, wood floor joists would NOT be used for   9.___

   A. apartments
   B. recreation rooms
   C. toilets
   D. public halls

10. If plans were to be filed now for a change of occupancy, the type of occupancy for which   10.___
    a fire escape is NOT acceptable as a second means of egress is

    A. club house
    B. single room
    C. tenement
    D. garden type maisonette

11. The multiple dwelling law requires self-closing doors between apartments and halls in all   11.___
    Class A multiple dwellings.
    The PRINCIPAL reason for this is to

    A. insure privacy of the tenants
    B. protect other tenants from excessive noise
    C. reduce heat loss
    D. prevent the spread of fire

12. The multiple dwelling law prohibits the erection of a building the height of which is in   12.___
    excess of one and one-half times the width of the widest street on which it faces.
    The MAIN reason for this prohibition is to

    A. insure that tenants will not have to travel too far to the street in case of fire
    B. provide adequate light and air
    C. prevent excessive loadings on the footings
    D. provide adequate water pressure on the top floor

13. The multiple dwelling law requires that the walls of all interior courts shall be built with a   13.___
    light-colored brick. The PRINCIPAL reason for this is that

    A. light-colored brick is easier to clean
    B. more light will be reflected into the apartments
    C. light-colored brick is usually stronger
    D. rain will not penetrate light-colored brick readily

14. The multiple dwelling law requires that every fire escape constructed of material subject   14.___
    to rusting shall be painted with two or more coats of paint of contrasting colors.
    The reason that each coat is required to be of a different color is that

    A. the different pigments in the two coats will better protect the steel from rust
    B. when two colors are used, the sun will not bleach the top color as rapidly as when only one color is used
    C. the contrasting colors make inspection easier
    D. a better bond is obtained between paint of different color

15. The multiple dwelling law requires that every fire escape at the top story of a building   15.___
    shall be provided with a stairway or ladder to the roof, except where the roof is a peak
    roof with a pitch in excess of twenty degrees. The reason that access to the roof from the
    fire escape is NOT required where the pitch of the roof is in excess of twenty degrees is
    that

    A. it would be difficult to walk on a roof with such a slope
    B. a steep roof would tend to catch fire quicker, so people should not be on the roof

C. sparks from a fire would tend to roll down the roof toward any person climbing up the ladder
D. it is almost impossible to anchor a ladder to a steep roof

16. The multiple dwelling law states that for stairs, each tread shall be not less than nine and one-half inches wide; each riser shall not exceed seven and three-quarters inches in height; and the product of the number of inches in the width of the tread and the number of inches in the height of the riser shall be at least seventy and at most seventy-five. The one of the following sets of dimensions that is acceptable for the stairs of a multiple dwelling is tread _____, riser _____.

    A. 9 3/4"; 7 1/8"
    B. 9 1/4"; 8"
    C. 10 1/4"; 7 1/8"
    D. 10 1/2"; 7 1/2"

16.____

17. The multiple dwelling law prohibits construction of a frame multiple dwelling. The PRINCIPAL reason for this is that

    A. frame buildings are more susceptible to vermin infection
    B. the heavier loads occurring in multiple dwellings can not be supported in frame buildings
    C. frame buildings, used as multiple dwellings, tend to become slums
    D. fire in a frame building is more dangerous than in other types of buildings

17.____

18. The multiple dwelling law states that no radio or other wires shall be attached to any vent line extending above the roof.
The PRINCIPAL reason for this prohibition is that

    A. vent lines are relatively weak structures
    B. wires increase the danger of electric shock due to lightning
    C. low wires are a safety hazard
    D. ventilation will be blocked

18.____

19. In a non-fireproof building, the multiple dwelling law requires that certain partitions shall be fire-stopped. This means that

    A. fireproof doors must be used
    B. the partitions must be constructed of incombustible material
    C. the covering of the studs must be of incombustible material
    D. the spaces between the top of a partition and the ceiling and floors above must be filled with incombustible material

19.____

20. The building code states that the floor of a multiple dwelling shall be designed for a live load of 40 pounds per square foot.
Live load means weight of

    A. floor joists, beams, and girders
    B. tenants only
    C. tenants and their furniture
    D. floor joists, beams, girders, tenants, and furniture

20.____

21. An anonymous complaint is made to the Department of Buildings. This complaint should be

    A. ignored because it is not signed
    B. investigated because it may be valid
    C. filed to see if further complaints of a like nature are made
    D. ignored because only troublemakers make anonymous complaints

22. In order to make certain emergency repairs to an occupied multiple dwelling, a fire escape must be removed. The owner asks you, an inspector, for permission to do this. You should

    A. grant the request, since the only way to make the repair is to remove the fire escape
    B. tell the owner to find another method of making the repair since a fire escape may not be removed
    C. refer the owner to your superiors, since you do not have the authority to grant the request
    D. grant the request only if fire extinguishers are provided to prevent danger of fire

23. The cellar ceiling of a converted multiple dwelling is to be fire-retarded by applying two layers of 1/2" plaster boards to the existing ceiling. The owner tells you that the existing lath is too weak to support the weight of the additional plaster boards. You should

    A. insist that the plaster boards shall be applied on the existing ceiling
    B. tell the owner that the plaster boards will not be necessary since their application would be dangerous
    C. permit installation of only one layer of plaster boards in order to reduce the load on the lath
    D. require that the lath be strengthened first and then that the two layers of plaster boards be applied

24. A tenant has made a complaint that water leaking from a pipe in the apartment above has damaged the ceiling of the tenant's apartment. While the premises are being inspected, the tenant mentions other complaints to you. You should

    A. tell the tenant you are there to inspect the original complaint only
    B. listen courteously to the tenant, but discourage further complaints
    C. check each of the complaints to determine their validity
    D. place a violation on the landlord for all the complaints

25. The public halls of a multiple dwelling were painted two months ago. A tenant has filed a complaint stating that the walls are now peeling and are in a dirty, deteriorated condition. When investigating this complaint, you find that it is justified. You should

    A. test the paint to find out why it peeled so rapidly
    B. notify the landlord to repaint the walls properly
    C. tell the tenant that since the walls were painted within three years, nothing further can be done
    D. refer the complaint to the legal department so that court action may be taken

26. A multiple dwelling is being erected with one wall on a lot line. On the adjoining lot is a two-family house. The owner of this house complaints that the new building is cutting off light and ventilation from the two-family house.
You should

   A. tell the small home owner that nothing can be done since the law permits such construction
   B. tell the small home owner that nothing can be done since two-family houses are not within your jurisdiction
   C. stop construction of the multiple dwelling since it is illegal to block ventilation of another house
   D. tell the small home owner to sue the city for the decrease in the value of his property

27. The approved plans for a converted multiple dwelling call for fireproofing the stair enclosure with metal lath and cement plaster. The contractor would like to substitute two layers of 1/2 inch plaster board since this has the same fire-resistive rating as the lath and plaster.
The inspector should

   A. permit this, since the fire ratings are the same
   B. deny this, since the structural strengths may not be the same
   C. permit this only if an amended plan showing the substitution is approved
   D. permit this only if the structural strengths and the fire-resistive ratings are the same

28. During a routine inspection of a multiple dwelling, an inspector discovers that a fire door has been blocked open.
The FIRST action of the inspector should be to

   A. order the owner or his representative to remove the blocking immediately
   B. notify the owner in writing that a violation of the law exists on the premises
   C. warn the tenants that a fire hazard exists
   D. remove the blocking himself

29. When writing a report of an investigation of a tenant's complaint, the item that you should consider LEAST important for inclusion in the report is the

   A. name of tenant   B. apartment number
   C. age of building   D. location of building

30. A tenant asks you about the procedures the Department of Buildings uses in processing a violation complaint.
You should

   A. refer the tenant to your superiors since they are the only ones permitted to give official information
   B. tell the tenant that such information is none of his business
   C. give the tenant the information in as concise a manner as possible
   D. explain completely and in detail all the ramifications of departmental procedure

31. In investigating the adequacy of the exits of a multiple dwelling, the LEAST important item to check is the

    A. location of exits
    B. width of stairs
    C. size of stair platforms
    D. number of treads and risers

32. In a 8-story fireproof multiple dwelling of skeleton steel construction, the one of the following members that would be LEAST likely to have a fire-resistive enclosure is a

    A. beam B. column C. joist D. lintel

33. The one of the following that is LEAST related to the others is

    A. pile B. footing C. caisson D. pilaster

34. A pit at the low point of a cellar floor is known as a(n)

    A. sump
    B. well
    C. accumulator
    D. drain

35. The structure above the roof of a building that encloses a stairway is called a

    A. bulkhead
    B. penthouse
    C. mezzanine
    D. stairwell

36. To prevent flying sparks, incinerator chimneys in multiple dwellings are frequently covered with

    A. cement copings
    B. draft hoods
    C. goosenecks
    D. wire mesh

37. A valve used to prevent boiler explosions due to excessive pressure is a _____ valve.

    A. check B. gate C. relief D. fuller

38. The one of the following that is acceptable according to the building code for a 3-hour fire partition is 6"

    A. solid brick
    B. solid stone concrete blocks
    C. solid cinder concrete blocks
    D. plain concrete

39. A fire tower is a

    A. means of egress from a building
    B. water tank on the roof of a building
    C. piece of Fire Department equipment
    D. draft space through which fire will spread

Questions 40-45.

DIRECTIONS: Questions 40 through 45, inclusive, refer to the sketch of an apartment building shown on the last page. All questions are to be answered on the basis of this sketch.

40. The dimension of the bedroom indicated by the letter Y is

   A. 9'1 5/16"
   B. 9'1 13/16"
   C. 9'2 3/16"
   D. 9'2 11/16"

41. Following is an abstract of the multiple dwelling law:
   1. Every living room (including bedrooms) shall contain at least 80 square feet of floor space.
   2. Every living room shall be at least eight feet in least horizontal dimension except that any number of bedrooms up to one-half the total number in any apartment containing three or more bedrooms may have a least horizontal dimension of seven feet or more.

   In order to increase the width of the hall, it is necessary to decrease the width of the bedroom indicated by the letter Y.
   The one of the following that is the smallest acceptable width of this room is

   A. 7'0"   B. 7'6"   C. 8'0"   D. 8'6"

42. The columns shown are

   A. wood posts
   B. concrete filled pipes
   C. I beams
   D. built up channels

43. The letter indicating the partition that is MOST likely to be a bearing partition is

   A. M
   B. W
   C. X
   D. There are no bearing partitions

44. The exit door

   A. does not swing in the direction of egress
   B. is too large
   C. will block the stairs
   D. is not fireproof

45. The one of the following general notes that is MOST likely to appear in connection with this plan is:

   A. Masonry walls shall be braced horizontally at maximum intervals of twenty times the wall thickness
   B. Buttresses shall be bonded into the wall by masonry in the same manner as employed in the construction of the wall
   C. Masonry walls shall be anchored at maximum intervals of four feet, to each tier of joists bearing on such walls, by metal anchors
   D. Openings in the masonry wall shall be spanned by a lintel or arch of incombustible materia

8 (#1)

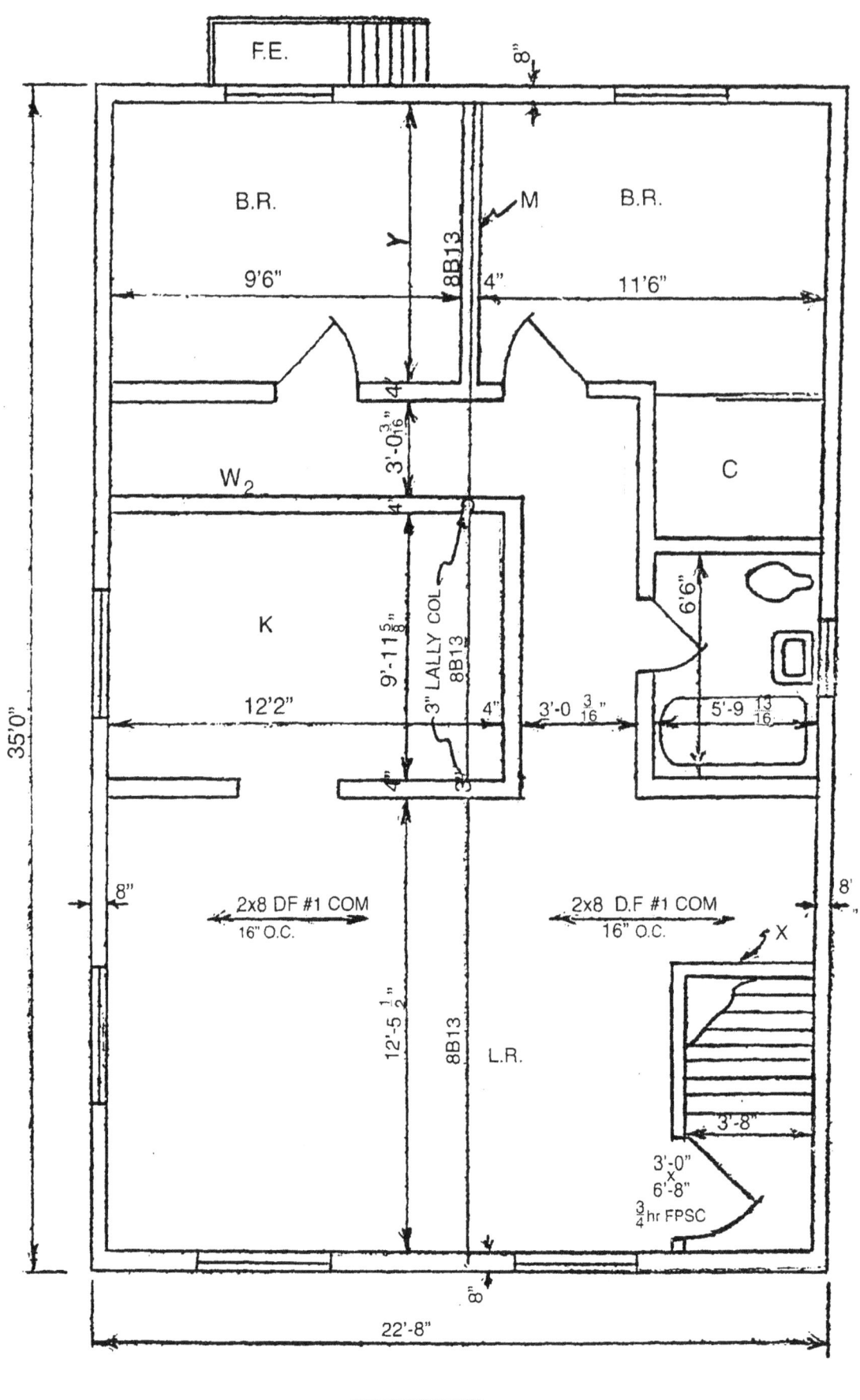

34

KEY (CORRECT ANSWERS)

1. C	11. D	21. B	31. D	41. D
2. C	12. B	22. C	32. D	42. B
3. A	13. B	23. D	33. D	43. D
4. D	14. C	24. C	34. A	44. C
5. B	15. A	25. B	35. A	45. C
6. C	16. C	26. A	36. D	
7. B	17. D	27. C	37. C	
8. A	18. A	28. A	38. C	
9. D	19. D	29. C	39. A	
10. B	20. C	30. C	40. D	

EXAMINATION SECTION
TEST 1

DIRECTIONS: Each question or incomplete statement is followed by several suggested answers or completions. Select the one that BEST answers the question or completes the statement. *PRINT THE LETTER OF THE CORRECT ANSWER IN THE SPACE AT THE RIGHT.*

Questions 1-5.

DIRECTIONS: Questions 1 through 5 are to be answered on the basis of the following statement. Use ONLY the information contained in this statement in answering these questions.

    No multiple dwelling shall be erected to a height in excess of one and one-half times the width of the widest street on which it faces, except that above the level of such height, for each one foot that the front wall of such dwelling sets back from the street line, three feet shall be added to the height limit of such dwelling, but such dwelling shall not exceed in maximum height three feet plus one and three-quarter times the width of the widest street on which it faces.
    Any such dwelling facing a street more than one hundred feet in width shall be subject to the same height limitations as though such dwelling faced a street one hundred feet in width.

1. The MAXIMUM height of a multiple dwelling set back five feet from the street line and facing a 60 foot wide street is _____ feet.

   A. 60   B. 90   C. 105   D. 165

   1.____

2. The MAXIMUM height of a multiple dwelling set back six feet from the street line and facing a 120 foot wide street is _____ feet.

   A. 198   B. 168   C. 120   D. 105

   2.____

3. The MAXIMUM height of a multiple dwelling is

   A. 100 ft.   B. 150 ft.   C. 178 ft.   D. unlimited

   3.____

4. The MAXIMUM height of a multiple dwelling set back 10 feet from the street line and facing a 110 foot wide street is _____ feet.

   A. 178   B. 180   C. 195   D. 205

   4.____

5. The MAXIMUM height of a multiple dwelling set back eight feet from the street line and facing a 90 foot wide street is _____ feet.

   A. 135   B. 147   C. 178   D. 159

   5.____

Questions 6-10.

DIRECTIONS: Questions 6 through 10 are to be answered on the basis of the following statement. Use ONLY the information contained in this statement in answering these questions.

The number of persons accommodated on any story in a lodging house shall not be greater than the sum of the following components.
    a. 22 persons for each full multiple of 22 inches in the smallest clear width for each means of egress approved by the department, other than fire escapes.
    b. 20 persons for each lawful fire escape accessible from such story.

6. The MAXIMUM number of persons that may be accommodated on a story in a lodging house depends on the

    A. number of lawful fire escapes *only*
    B. number of approved means of egress *only*
    C. smallest clear width in each approved means of egress *only*
    D. number of lawful fire escapes and sum total of smallest clear widths in each approved means of egress

6.____

7. The MAXIMUM number of persons that may be accommodated on a story of a lodging house having one lawful fire escape and a sum total of 44 inches in the smallest clear widths of the two approved means of egress is

    A. 20   B. 22   C. 42   D. 64

7.____

8. The MAXIMUM number of persons that may be accommodated on a story of a lodging house having two lawful fire escapes and a sum total of 60 inches in the smallest clear width of the approved means of egress is

    A. 64   B. 84   C. 100   D. 106

8.____

9. The MAXIMUM number of persons that may be accommodated on a story of a lodging house having one lawful fire escape and a sum total of 33 inches in the smallest clear width of the approved means of egress is

    A. 42   B. 53   C. 64   D. 73

9.____

10. The MAXIMUM number of persons that may be accommodated on a story of a lodging house having two lawful fire escapes and two approved means of egress, with 40 inches and 44 inches in the smallest clear widths, respectively, is

    A. 84   B. 104   C. 106   D. 108

10.____

11. An employee of the Department of Housing and Buildings may take outside employment in private industry as a(n)

    A. architect   B. mason
    C. plumber   D. none of the above

11.____

12. The one of the following that is NOT a multiple dwelling is a

    A. college dormitory
    B. dwelling occupied by three families
    C. hospital
    D. lodging house

12.____

13. The one of the following that is a Class A multiple dwelling is a

    A. commercial building containing a janitor's apartment
    B. furnished room house

13.____

C. hotel
D. tenement

14. A dwelling occupied by one family with five transient roomers is a _____ dwelling.   14.____

    A. Class A multiple   B. Class B multiple
    C. single family private   D. two-family private

15. The one of the following that is deemed a living room by the multiple dwelling law is a   15.____

    A. bathroom
    B. bedroom
    C. dinette, 45 sq. ft. in area
    D. kitchenette, 45 sq. ft. in area

16. The MAXIMUM number of stories to which a new multiple dwelling may be erected without having a passenger elevator is   16.____

    A. 4   B. 5   C. 6   D. 7

17. In a new multiple dwelling, which of the following rooms are required to have windows?   17.____

    A. Bathroom
    B. Kitchen
    C. Water-closet compartment
    D. All of the above

18. New multiple dwellings three stories or more in height must have hot water supplied during   18.____

    A. the hours between 6 A.M. and Midnight *only*
    B. the hours between 8 A.M. and 8 P.M. *only*
    C. the hours between 6 A.M. and Noon and 6 P.M. and Midnight *only*
    D. all hours

19. A winding stair in a new multiple dwelling is   19.____

    A. not permitted under any circumstances
    B. permitted under all circumstances
    C. permitted only when the building is more than 6 stories high
    D. permitted only when the building is less than 6 stories high

20. All elevator shaft walls in new multiple dwellings MUST be   20.____

    A. at least 4 inches thick   B. fireproof
    C. hollow   D. made of gypsum plaster

21. The one of the following statements about new multiple dwellings that is NOT true is: 21.____

    A. Boiler rooms in multiple dwellings four stories or more in height must have fireproof doors
    B. Every open roof area must have a guard rail or parapet wall at least 3'6" high
    C. A new multiple dwelling may be placed on the same lot with a frame building
    D. A new multiple dwelling may be used for parking of passenger motor vehicles

22. A tenement within the meaning of the multiple dwelling law is a building erected BEFORE

    A. April 18, 1929
    B. April 6, 1948
    C. April 12, 1949
    D. March 25, 1952

23. Every entrance hall in a multiple dwelling must be provided with a light of AT LEAST _____ watts.

    A. 5
    B. 10
    C. 15
    D. 40

24. From the entrance to the first stair, every entrance hall in a new multiple dwelling must be, in clear width, AT LEAST

    A. 3'8"
    B. 4'
    C. 6'
    D. 8'

25. A basement in a new multiple dwelling exceeding seven stories in height MUST have AT LEAST one-half of its height _____ curb level and is _____ as a story.

    A. above; counted
    B. above; not counted
    C. below; counted
    D. below; not counted

26. The lower ends of mitred cross bridging should be nailed to the beams

    A. at the same time that the top ends are nailed
    B. before the rough flooring is placed
    C. after the plastering is complete
    D. after the flooring is placed

27. The maximum distance between lines of bridging should NOT exceed

    A. 10'0"
    B. 8'0"
    C. 6'6"
    D. 4'6"

28. The building code states that it shall be unlawful to corbel walls less than twelve inches thick, except for fire-stopping.
    From this, it may be concluded that

    A. walls 12 inches or more in thickness shall not be corbelled
    B. if a wall is less than 12 inches thick, it is permissible to corbel provided some of the corbelling is used for fire-stopping
    C. fire-stopping shall not be considered to be corbelling
    D. corbelling and fire-stopping are the same

29. The building code states that curtain walls of solid masonry shall be at least eight inches thick for the uppermost thirteen feet and at least twelve inches thick for the next fifty-two feet or fraction thereof below and shall be increased four inches in thickness for each succeeding sixty feet or fraction thereof below.
    This means that the thickness of a solid masonry curtain wall 126 feet high should be AT LEAST

    A. 20 inches throughout its height
    B. 20 inches at the base
    C. 16 inches throughout its height
    D. 16 inches at the base

30. The term *curb cut* refers to 30.____

    A. openings in a curb
    B. tire cuts made while parking
    C. surveying marks chiseled in a curb
    D. rental for sidewalk stands

31. A bearing wall is a wall which 31.____

    A. carries its own weight *only*
    B. carries load other than its own weight
    C. bears on structural supports at each story
    D. is more than 12 feet high

32. A column is an _____ member. 32.____

    A. upright compression   B. inclined compression
    C. upright tension   D. inclined tension

33. A lintel could be broadly classified as a 33.____

    A. beam   B. column   C. footing   D. strut

34. A flat slab is MOST commonly used in _____ construction. 34.____

    A. sidewalk   B. roadway   C. conduit   D. building

35. Of the following, the member which would MOST likely be supported on a footing is the 35.____

    A. beam   B. girder   C. column   D. joist

36. A parapet wall would MOST likely support 36.____

    A. a coping   B. roof joists
    C. floor joists   D. partitions

37. Jack arches are used 37.____

    A. in ornamental iron work
    B. in fancy stairways
    C. when lintels are omitted
    D. in foundations

38. If green lumber is used for joists, shrinkage will have its MOST serious effect in _____ of joists. 38.____

    A. length   B. width   C. depth   D. weight

39. The phrase *concealed draft openings* is MOST likely to be used in connection with 39.____

    A. fireplaces   B. flues
    C. fire-stopping   D. automatic dampers

40. Of the following terms, the one which is LEAST related to the others is the 40.____

    A. jamb   B. strike plate
    C. latch bolt   D. pulley stile

Questions 41-45.

DIRECTIONS: Questions 41 through 45 are to be answered in accordance with the following sketch.

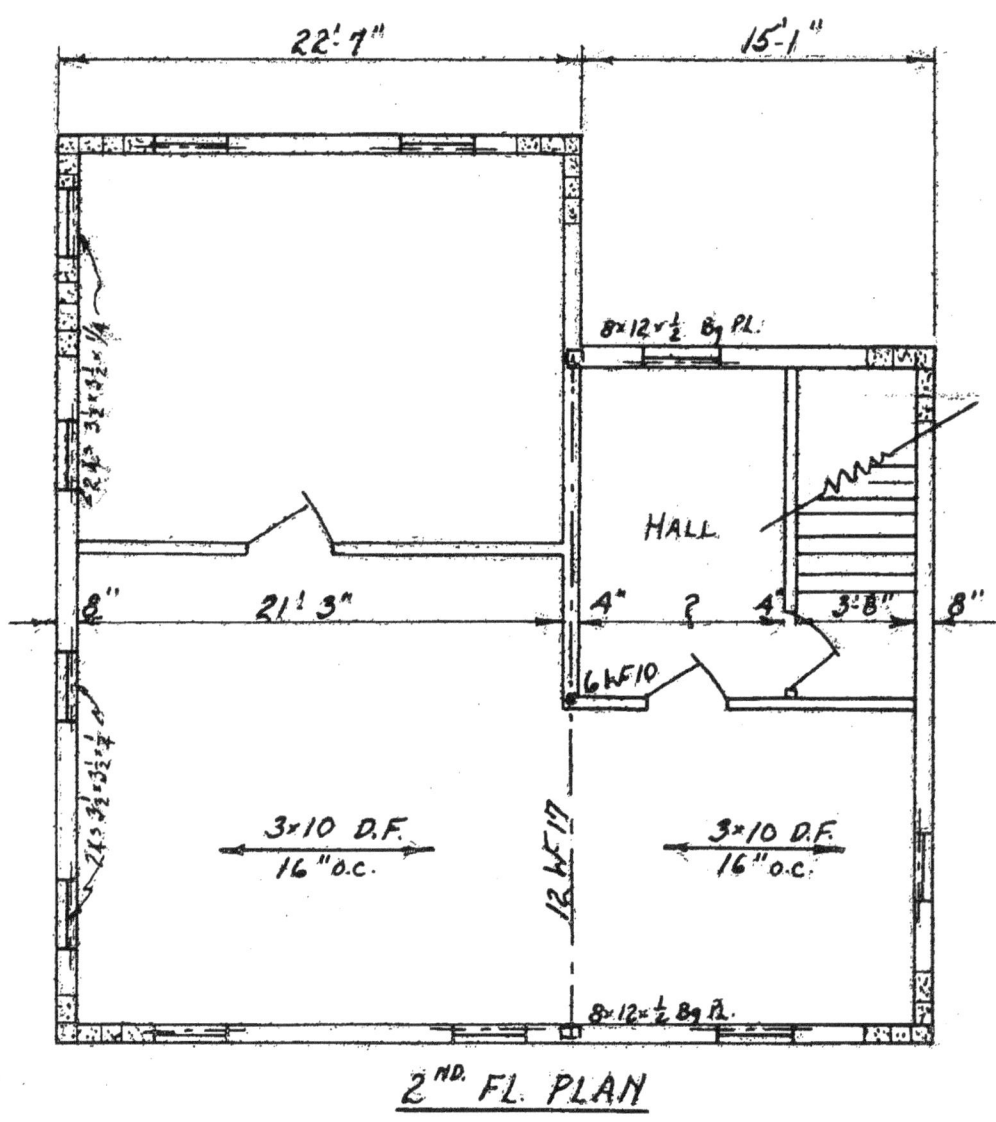

2ND. FL. PLAN

41. The one of the following statements that is CORRECT is: The building

   A. is of fireproof construction
   B. has masonry walls, with wood joists
   C. is of wood frame construction
   D. has timber posts and girders

42. The one of the following statements that is CORRECT is:

   A. The stairway from the ground floor continues through the roof
   B. There are two means of egress from the second floor of this building
   C. The door on the second floor stair landing opens in the direction of egress
   D. The entire stair is shown on this plan

43. The width of the hall is 43.____

    A. 10'3"   B. 10'5"   C. 10'7"   D. 10'9"

44. The lintels shown are 44.____

    A. angles
    B. a channel and an angle
    C. an I-beam
    D. precast concrete

45. The one of the following statements that is CORRECT is: The steel beam is 45.____

    A. supported by columns at the center and at the ends
    B. entirely supported by the walls
    C. supported on columns at the ends only
    D. supported at the center by a column and at the ends by the walls

KEY (CORRECT ANSWERS)

1. C	11. D	21. C	31. B	41. B
2. B	12. C	22. A	32. A	42. C
3. C	13. D	23. C	33. A	43. D
4. A	14. B	24. B	34. D	44. A
5. D	15. B	25. A	35. C	45. D
6. D	16. C	26. D	36. A	
7. D	17. D	27. B	37. C	
8. B	18. A	28. C	38. C	
9. A	19. A	29. B	39. C	
10. C	20. B	30. A	40. D	

EXAMINATION SECTION

DIRECTIONS: Each question or incomplete statement is followed by several suggested answers or completions. Select the one that BEST answers the question or or completes the statement. *PRINT THE LETTER OF THE CORRECT ANSWER IN THE SPACE AT THE RIGHT.*

1. A lintel is MOST CLOSELY associated with a
    A. wall opening
    B. floor opening
    C. roof opening
    D. fire escape

    1.____

2. An apron is MOST CLOSELY associated with a
    A. door
    B. window
    C. yard
    D. bulkhead

    2.____

3. In remodeling a multiple dwelling, brickwork has been removed from an interior steel column and replaced with 3/4" plaster. The MOST SERIOUS consequence of this alteration relates to
    A. strength
    B. corrosion
    C. fire
    D. accidental damage

    3.____

4. In multiple dwellings, hand-rails must be provided on each side of a stairway if the stairway exceeds CERTAIN
    A. height
    B. width
    C. steepness
    D. tread-riser ratio

    4.____

5. A rectangular court is 16'0" wide by 20'0" long. The length of a diagonal is, in feet, most nearly,
    A. 25.2
    B. 25.4
    C. 25.6
    D. 25.8

    5.____

6. If concrete weighs 4000 pounds per cubic yard, the weight of a slab of concrete 2'6" by 6'9" by 3'2" is, in pounds, most nearly,

    A. 7920
    B. 7830
    C. 7740
    D. 7650

    6.____

7. In the case of new construction, a certificate of occupancy is required for
    A. class A multiple dwellings
    B. class A and class B multiple dwellings
    C. all dwellings
    D. all buildings

    7.____

8. A sewer which carries BOTH sewage and storm water is known as a ____ sewer.
    A. sanitary
    B. combined
    C. separate
    D. storm

    8.____

9. A fire-restrictive rating of an assembly indicates that the assembly
    A. is incombustible
    B. is non-flammable
    C. can withstand a fire of given duration without serious failure
    D. prevents the passage of heat

    9.____

10. Major classifications of districts established by the Zoning Resolution do NOT Include _____ districts.
    A. Use   B. Height   C. Residence   D. Area

11. The distinction between a Business District and a Business-1 District relates to
    A. types of businesses
    B. size of businesses
    C. types of business signs
    D. area allowed for manufacturing

12. The *MAXIMUM* hight to which a multiple dwelling fronting on a 100-foot street may be erected in a class one and on-half district is
    A. 178 ft.   B. 175 ft.   C. 150 ft.   D. 125 ft.

13. As a senior supervisor of Housing, you are directed to interview several men whom the department is considering for provisional employment as a supervisor of Housing. During the course of your interview with one of these men, you learn that he has good building construction experience, owns his home outright in the City for the past four years, and even owns the patent rights on certain items now being used in building construction work. With respect to this man, you should recommend that he
    A. be employed for a trial period of 30 days
    B. be employed for a provisional period of 90 days
    C. should not be employed unless further questioning shows that he complies with the Residence Law
    D. should not be employed unless he divests himself of certain properties

14. Multiple dwellings of non-fireproof construction may NOT exceed
    A. 75 feet in height
    B. 6 stories in height unless provided with elevators
    C. 5 stories in height
    D. 60 feet in height

15. Construction in a non-fireproof multiple dwelling more than three stories high must be fireproof in all of the following locations EXCEPT
    A. first floor
    B. stairs
    C. elevator shaft below first floor
    D. roof

16. Flue or chimney connections for every apartment are *MOST LIKELY* to be required in
    A. tenements
    B. class A multiple dwellings
    C. class B multiple dwellings
    D. buildings used for single-room occupancy

17. In a 6-story multiple dwelling, the required access to the yard form a street may NOT be provided by a
    A. court
    B. fire proof passage
    C. fire-retarded passage
    D. direct passage 3'6" clear width by 7'0" high

18. The required area a function of the of windows in a living room is
    A. floor area
    B. room volume
    C. wall area
    D. number of occupants

19. A living room in a class A multiple dwelling is 8'0" wide by 9'6" long by 8'6" high. This room fails to meet requirements of the Multiple Dwelling Law with respect to
    A. height
    B. volume
    C. area
    D. least horizontal dimension

20. A tenant complains to an inspector that the interior lock on his dumbwaiter door is faulty and that the door is continually coming open. The inspector should, after verifying the facts,
    A. tell the tenant to notify the landlord
    B. notify the janitor and report a violation to the Department
    C. tell the tenant to fix it himself
    D. tell the janitor to fix this lock

21. Fire escapes constructed of material subject to rusting should be painted
    A. every year
    B. every two years
    C. whenever they become rusty
    D. twice a year

22. A building fronts on an unpaved street without curbs or sidewalk. The legal height of the building
    A. can not be established
    B. is established by the architect
    C. may be established from the equivalent curb level
    D. is established by the owner

23. The story heights of a class B multiple dwelling are as follows: cellar, 12 ft.; first floor, 20 ft.; second floor, 15 ft.; third through sixth floors, 12 ft. The story height of the building is
    A. 6   B. 7   C. 8   D. 9

24. The distinction between "cellar" and "basement" is concerned with
    A. relative position with respect to curb elevation
    B. use
    C. height
    D. area

25. The distinction between fire-tower and fire-stair is based upon
    A. position with respect to building walls
    B. degree of fire-proofing
    C. height
    D. use of self-closing fireproof doors

26. Yards may NOT be omitted under any circumstances when a multiple dwelling occupies
    A. two or more entire blocks
    B. an interior lot
    C. an interior lot running through from street to street
    D. an entire block

27. A multiple dwelling is one which is occupied by at least
    A. 2 families   B. 3 families   C. 4 families   D. 5 familles

28. The distinction between class A and class B multiple dwellings relates to
    A. size   B. quality   C. fireproofing   D. residence

29. A portion of a multiple dwelling which is considered to be an apartment contains
    A. more than one room
    B. a kitchen
    C. a bathroom
    D. a water-closet compartment

30. Living rooms include
    A. water-closet compartments
    B. bathrooms
    C. kitchens
    D. foyers

31. Of the following, the one which is NOT considered to be an alteration is
    A. replacing wainscoting with plaster
    B. moving a building from one lot to another
    C. replacing bearing wall to make one large room from two small ones
    D. increasing the height of a building without increasing the number of stories

32. A trimmer arch is used in connection with a
    A. fireplace   B. window   C. closet door   D. stairway

33. A sidewalk shed
    A. is never permitted
    B. is used when demolishing buildings
    C. is allowed in front of public buildings
    D. must have an open roof

Questions 34-39.
Questions 34 through 39 refer to the two columns below. Each item in Column 1 is associated with an item in Column 2. Place the letter of the item in Column 2 after the number of the item in Column 1 with which it is most closely associated. Items in Column 2 may be used more than once or not at all.

Column 1

34. Scratch coat
35. Flashing
36. Louvre
37. Bond
38. Soil stack
39. Shoring

Column 2

A. Welding
B. Bricklaying
C. Plumbing
D. Plastering
E. Roofing
F. Flooring
G. Excavating
H. Ventilatin

34._____
35._____
36._____
37._____
38._____
39._____

40. Of the following terms, the one which LEAST relates to the other is
    A. soffit   B. newel   C. nosing   D. trimmer

41. Of the following terms, the one which LEAST relates to the others is
    A. muntin   B. stop-bead   C. jamb   D. sill

42. Fire-stopping is synonymous with
    A. fireproofing
    B. fire-retarding
    C. fire-treated
    D. none of the foregoing

43. A two-story building 32'0" by 60'0" is erected on a lot 75'0" by 110'0". The floor area ratio is, most nearly,
    A. 0.46   B. 0.42   C. 0.38   D. 0.34

44. A portion of a multiple dwelling, other than an apartment or suite of rooms, separated as a unit from the rest of the building by fireproof construction, is known as a
    A. section   B. unit   C. separate   D. wing

45. Records maintained by the Department for each building in the City should include all of the following EXCEPT
    A. number of persons living in each apartment
    B. diagram of building
    C. date of erection
    D. deaths occurring in building each year

46. Hospitals are required to make a weekly report to the Department of cases of sickness received in such hospital. This report does NOT state
    A. patient's name
    B. patient's address
    C. patient's sickness
    D. whether patient is an adult or child

47. The Police Department is required to make a weekly report to the Department of arrests. The report does NOT contain
    A. name
    B. address
    C. offense
    D. disposition of case

48. Of the following City Departments, the one which must be furnished information by the Department is
    A. Hospitals
    B. Welfare
    C. Public Works
    D. Tax

49. In a new multiple dwelling, gas meters may be located in
    A. boiler rooms
    B. stair halls
    C. public halls above the cellar
    D. none of the foregoing

50. A required sink may be placed in a
    A. bathroom containing a water-closet
    B. water-closet compartment
    C. public hall
    D. none of the foregoing

(KEY (CORRECT ANSWERS)

1. A	11. C	21. C	31. A	41. C
2. B	12. A	22. C	32. A	42. D
3. C	13. D	23. C	33. B	43. A
4. B	14. A	24. A	34. D	44. A
5. C	15. D	25. A	35. E	45. A
6. A	16. A	26. B	36. H	46. A
7. D	17. C	27. B	37. B	47. D
8. B	18. A	28. D	38. C	48. D
9. C	19. C	29. C	39. G	49. D
10. C	20. B	30. C	40. D	50. D

EXAMINATION SECTION
TEST 1

DIRECTIONS: Each question or incomplete statement is followed by several suggested answers or completions. Select the one that BEST answers the question or completes the statement. *PRINT THE LETTER OF THE CORRECT ANSWER IN THE SPACE AT THE RIGHT.*

1. Assume that a two story building measures 21'6" x 53'7". It is in a district that calls for an open space ratio of .80. The required open space on this lot must be *most nearly* square feet.

    A. 922 B. 1152 C. 1843 D. 2880

2. Assume that the elevation at the back of a lot is 127.36 ft. and the elevation at the front of the same lot is 125.49 ft.
    The difference in elevation between front and back of the lot is *most nearly*

    A. 1'10 1/8" B. 1'10 1/4" C. 1'10 3/8" D. 1'10 1/2"

3. The sketch below represents the lowest story of a new building. In order for this story to be considered a basement, the elevation of the first floor must be AT LEAST

    A. 131.09 B. 131.14 C. 131.19 D. 131.24

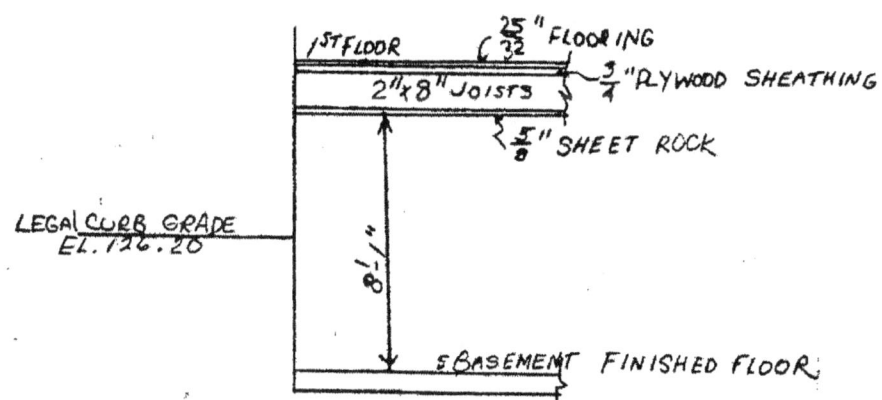

4. The MOST important requirement of a good report is that it should be

    A. properly addressed B. clear and concise
    C. verbose   D. spelled correctly

5. Of the following, in determining whether a violation should be referred for court action, the MOST important item that should be considered is

    A. the amount of available time you have to process the case
    B. the availability of the inspector
    C. whether or not the owner has indicated a desire to cooperate with the department
    D. whether or not the case is important enough to warrant court action

6. In the Zoning Resolution, the size of required side yards would be found in the chapters on

   A. Use Groups   B. Bulk Regulations
   C. Area Districts   D. District Boundaries

7. According to the Zoning Resolution, the one of the following that is NOT considered part of the floor area of a building is a(n)

   A. basement
   B. stairwell at floor level
   C. penthouse
   D. attached garage on 1st floor

8. The one of the following that is permitted by the Zoning Resolution as a home occupation is

   A. veterinary medicine   B. real estate broker
   C. teaching of music   D. public relations agency

9. For the purpose of determining the number of rooms in a dwelling unit, the Zoning Resolution adds an arbitrary number to the number of *living rooms*.
   Where there are six or less living rooms, this arbitrary number is

   A. 1/2   B. 1   C. 1 1/2   D. 2

10. Assuming the following signs are all 10 square feet in area, the one that is NOT subject to the provisions of the Zoning Resolution is one indicating

    A. a freight entrance to a building
    B. a fund drive for a civic organization
    C. vacancies in an apartment building
    D. a parking area at the rear of a structure

11. On a plan, the symbol ⎯⎯ represents

    A. earth   B. wood
    C. metal lath   D. marble

12. On a plan, the symbol represents

    A. cinder
    B. brick
    C. plywood
    D. rock lath and plaster

13. On a plan, the symbol represents

    A. glass   B. asphalt shingles
    C. concrete   D. porcelain enamel

14. A corbel is a form of

    A. cricket
    B. crown molding
    C. cantilever
    D. curtain wall

15. In balloon type framing, the second floor joists rest on a

    A. sole plate
    B. ribband
    C. header
    D. sill

16. Condensation of moisture in inadequately ventilated attics or roof spaces is usually GREATEST in

    A. summer   B. autumn   C. winter   D. spring

17. Of the following combinations of tread and riser, the one that would be acceptable for required stairs in either a new office building or a multiple dwelling is

    A. 9 1/4", 7 1/2"
    B. 9 1/2", 7 1/4"
    C. 9 1/2", 7 3/4"
    D. 10", 8"

18. A meeting rail is a common part of a

    A. door frame
    B. window sash
    C. stairwell
    D. bulkhead

19. If doors in an old building do not close, it is MOST probably an indication that the

    A. frames have shrunk
    B. building has settled
    C. hinges were not set properly
    D. wood used for the doors are of inferior grade

20. Cracks in concrete are not necessarily caused by settlement of a structure. Sometimes they are caused by

    A. shrinkage
    B. curing
    C. hydration
    D. over-troweling

KEY (CORRECT ANSWERS)

1.	C	11.	A
2.	D	12.	B
3.	A	13.	A
4.	B	14.	C
5.	C	15.	B
6.	B	16.	C
7.	D	17.	C
8.	C	18.	B
9.	C	19.	B
10.	B	20.	A

TEST 2

DIRECTIONS: Each question or incomplete statement is followed by several suggested answers or completions. Select the one that BEST answers the question or completes the statement. *PRINT THE LETTER OF THE CORRECT ANSWER IN THE SPACE AT THE RIGHT.*

1. Required exit doors from a room must open in the direction of egress when the room is occupied by more than _____ persons.   1.____

   A. 15 B. 25 C. 35 D. 50

2. A window in a masonry wall on a lot line   2.____

   A. is not permitted
   B. must have a fire resistive rating of 3/4 hour
   C. must have a fire resistive rating of 1 hour
   D. must have a fire resistive rating of 1 1/2 hours

3. Air entrained concrete is required in all cases for   3.____

   A. garage floors   B. footings
   C. grade beams   D. columns

4. A parapet wall or railing would be required on new non-residential structures where the height of the structure is greater than (give lowest height specified by law) _____ feet.   4.____

   A. 15 B. 19 C. 22 D. 25

5. Of the following statements, the one that is CORRECT is that wood joists may   5.____

   A. not be supported on a fire wall
   B. be supported on a fire wall only if fireproofed wall is used
   C. be supported on a fire wall only if they are separated from each other by at least 4 inches of solid masonry
   D. be supported on a fire wall only if they are separated from each other by at least 12 inches of solid masonry

6. A foundation wall below grade may be of hollow block only if the building   6.____

   A. is a residence
   B. is no more than one story high
   C. is of frame construction
   D. has no cellar or basement

7. The Building Code specifies that lintels are required to be fire-proofed when the opening is more than _____ feet.   7.____

   A. 3 B. 4 C. 5 D. 6

8. In a 12-inch brick wall, the MAXIMUM permitted depth of a chase is   8.____

   A. none B. 4" C. 6" D. 8"

9. Wood joists should clear flues and chimneys by at least   9.____

   A. 1" B. 2" C. 3" D. 4"

55

10. Fire retarding or enclosure in shafts of all vent ducts are required when they   10.____

    A. go through more than one floor
    B. are used for intake as well as exhaust
    C. are more than 144 square inches in area
    D. are in rooms subdivided with wood partitions

11. Assume a builder is unable to complete the pour for a continuous concrete floor slab. The   11.____
    slab is supported by beams and girders.
    The construction joint should be made at a point

    A. over a beam
    B. one quarter of the span length from the beam
    C. one third of the span length from the beam
    D. midway between beams

12. Under required stairs in a Class 3 building,   12.____

    A. it is unlawful to locate a closet
    B. a closet is permitted provided that the stringers are fire retarded
    C. a closet is permitted provided that the closet is completely lined with incombustible material
    D. a closet is permitted provided that fireproof wood is used to frame out the closet

13. In New York City, the exit provisions of the State Labor Law apply   13.____

    A. only to factories
    B. to factories and warehouses
    C. to factories, warehouses, and restaurants
    D. to all types of uses

14. A Class 3 building, two stories high, may have required stairs enclosed with stud parti-   14.____
    tions fire retarded with gypsum boards unless the building is used for a

    A. factory   B. storage warehouse
    C. bowling alley   D. department store

15. The one of the following rooms in a *place of assembly* that is required to be sprinklered is 15.____
    a

    A. performer's dressing room
    B. kitchen
    C. service pantry
    D. waiting room

16. Of the following, the FIRST operation in the demolition of a building is the   16.____

    A. shoring of the adjoining buildings
    B. erection of railings around stairwells
    C. removal of windows
    D. venting of the roof

17. As used in the Building Code, *consistency* of concrete refers to   17.____

    A. composition   B. water-cement ratio
    C. relative plasticity   D. proportion of aggregates

18. One condition that is required for a building to be considered a *Special Occupancy Structure* is that the building is used for

    A. a theater
    B. a church
    C. a restaurant
    D. motor vehicle repairs

19. A wire glass vision panel on a door opening into a fire tower is

    A. not permitted
    B. permitted if the panel has a fire rating of 3/4 hour
    C. permitted if the panel has a fire rating of 3/4 hour and is less than 100 square inches in area
    D. permitted if the panel has a fire rating of 3/4 hour, is less than 100 square inches in area, and is glazed with two thicknesses of wire glass with an air space between

20. One of the requirements that must be met before untreated wood can be used as a subdividing partition in a Class 1 building is that the partition

    A. be no more than 8 feet high
    B. enclose an area less than 200 square feet in size
    C. enclose office space only
    D. be made of a single thickness of wood

KEY (CORRECT ANSWERS)

1.	D	11.	D
2.	B	12.	C
3.	A	13.	A
4.	C	14.	C
5.	C	15.	A
6.	D	16.	C
7.	B	17.	C
8.	B	18.	A
9.	D	19.	A
10.	A	20.	D

TEST 3

DIRECTIONS: Each question or incomplete statement is followed by several suggested answers or completions. Select the one that BEST answers the question or completes the statement. *PRINT THE LETTER OF THE CORRECT ANSWER IN THE SPACE AT THE RIGHT.*

1. There are two criteria required for determining whether a multiple dwelling shall be classified as a *converted dwelling*.
The FIRST is the number of families originally occupying the dwelling, and the second is the

   A. conjunctive uses
   B. date of erection of the building
   C. classification, whether Class A or B
   D. number of families now occupying the dwelling

2. According to the Multiple Dwelling Law, a *dinette* is NOT considered a living room if its area is _____ sq. ft. or less.

   A. 50   B. 55   C. 59   D. 64

3. Where a building faces only one street, the curb level used for measuring the height of the building is the

   A. lowest curb level in front of the building
   B. highest curb level in front of the building
   C. level of the curb at the center of the front of the building
   D. average of the levels of the lowest and highest curb level in front of the building

4. According to the Multiple Dwelling Code, one of the living rooms in each apartment of a newly created multiple dwelling shall have a MINIMUM floor area of _____ square feet.

   A. 59   B. 110   C. 150   D. 175

5. It is proposed to alter an old law tenement so as to increase the number of apartments. Of the following, the one that MOST completely gives the requirements to be met before the alteration can be approved is: Each new apartment must be provided a

   A. water closet
   B. water closet and a wash basin
   C. water closet, a wash basin, and a bath or shower
   D. water closet, a wash basin, a bath or shower, and centrally supplied heat

6. Gas fueled space heaters may be permitted in lieu of centrally supplied heat.
One of the following conditions required before the use of space heaters can be permitted is that

   A. each apartment has no more than two living rooms
   B. the building is a Class A multiple dwelling
   C. all apartments are used for single room occupancy
   D. D, the gas line supplying the heater be connected directly to the main so that the tenant cannot control the flow of gas

7. An incinerator is required in all multiple

   A. dwellings
   B. dwellings four or more stories in height
   C. dwellings four or more stories in height and occupied by more than twelve families
   D. dwellings four or more stories in height occupied by more than twelve families and erected after October 1, 1951

8. Tests of required sprinkler systems in a single room occupancy building must be made

   A. monthly
   B. quarterly
   C. semi-annually
   D. annually

9. An additional apartment may be created on the first floor of a Class A frame converted dwelling provided that no more than two families will occupy this floor and

   A. the entrance hall is sprinklered
   B. the building is brick veneered
   C. there is no basement occupancy
   D. all stairs are enclosed in one hour fire partitions

10. The MAIN feature differentiating a *five tower* from a *fire stair* is the

    A. fire rating of the enclosure walls
    B. use to which the fire tower is put
    C. method of entering the fire tower from the building
    D. height of the fire tower

11. A new elevator shaft is to be built into a non-fireproof multiple dwelling.
    Of the following materials, the one that has the lowest fire resistance that would be acceptable for the enclosure walls of this shaft is

    A. 3" solid gypsum block
    B. 2" x 4" studs with 5/8" fire code 60 each side
    C. steel studs, wire mesh and 3/4" P.C. plaster
    D. 4" hollow concrete blocks, plastered both sides

12. Of the following statements, the one that is MOST complete and accurate is that a frame extension 70 sq. ft. in area added to a frame multiple dwelling is

    A. not permitted
    B. permitted only if the walls of the extension are brick filled
    C. permitted only if the walls of the extension are brick filled and the extension is to be used solely for bathrooms
    D. permitted only if the walls of the extension are brick filled, the extension is to be used solely for bathrooms and the walls are at least 3 ft. from the side lot lines

13. Assume it is proposed to extend a business use in a non-fireproof multiple dwelling by erecting an extension at the rear of the building.
    The roof the extension is required to be fireproof

    A. in all cases
    B. when the business use requires a combustible occupancy permit
    C. when there are fire escapes above the extension
    D. if the business use is a factory

14. In a Class A dwelling, two water closets may   14.____

   A. be placed in one compartment only in old law tenements
   B. be placed in one compartment in either old law or new law tenements
   C. be placed in one compartment in all types of apartment houses
   D. not be placed in one compartment

15. According to the Multiple Dwelling Law, a janitor is NOT required when the maximum   15.____
    number of families occupying the dwelling is

   A. 6   B. 9   C. 12   D. 15

16. The first floor above the lowest cellar in a non-fireproof multiple dwelling does NOT have   16.____
    to be fireproof if

   A. the cellar is used only for incombustible storage
   B. there are two means of egress from the cellar
   C. the building is no more than three stories in height
   D. the dwelling is occupied by no more than nine families

17. In a converted multiple dwelling, ventilation of a room on the top story may be obtained   17.____
    by

   A. a skylight
   B. a duct with a wind blown hood
   C. a duct with an electrically operated fan
   D. by a window only and no other method is acceptable

18. It is proposed to build a closet under the stairs leading to the second floor in a non-fire-   18.____
    proof *new law* tenement. This is

   A. not permitted
   B. permitted only if the entire closet is built of non-combustible materials
   C. permitted only if the closet is used for non-combustible storage
   D. permitted if the closet is built of fire-retarded partitions and the soffit of the stairs is also fire-retarded

19. For multiple dwellings erected after April 18, 1929, a ladder from a fire escape to a roof is   19.____
    NOT required when

   A. the building is three stories or less in height
   B. the roof is built of incombustible material
   C. the fire escape is on the front of the building
   D. there is no safe access from the roof to another building

20. It is proposed to convert a Class B multiple dwelling used for summer resort occupancy   20.____
    to year-round Class B use. This conversion is

   A. illegal
   B. legal provided the exits comply with the requirements for Class B use
   C. legal provided the exits and toilet facilities comply with the requirements for Class B use
   D. legal provided the exits, toilet facilities, and ventilation requirements comply with the requirements for Class B use

KEY (CORRECT ANSWERS)

1.	B	11.	A
2.	B	12.	A
3.	C	13.	C
4.	C	14.	A
5.	D	15.	C
6.	B	16.	C
7.	D	17.	A
8.	D	18.	A
9.	B	19.	C
10.	C	20.	A

READING COMPREHENSION
UNDERSTANDING AND INTERPRETING WRITTEN MATERIAL
EXAMINATION SECTION
TEST 1

DIRECTIONS: Each question or incomplete statement is followed by several suggested answers or completions. Select the one that BEST answers the question or completes the statement. *PRINT THE LETTER OF THE CORRECT ANSWER IN THE SPACE AT THE RIGHT.*

Questions 1-3.

DIRECTIONS: Questions 1 through 3 are to be answered SOLELY on the basis of the following paragraph.

The aging housing inventory presents a broad spectrum of conditions, from good upkeep to unbelievable deterioration. Buildings, even relatively good buildings, are likely to have numerous minor violations rather than the gross and evident sanitary violations of an earlier age. Except for the serious violations in a relatively small number of slum buildings, the task is to deal with masses of minor violations that, though insignificant in themselves, amount in the aggregate to major deprivations of health and comfort to tenants. Caused by wear and tear, by the abrasions of time, and aggravated by neglect, these conditions do not readily yield to the dramatic *vacate and restore* measures of earlier times. Moreover, the lines between *good* and *bad* housing have become blurred in many parts of our cities; we find a range of *shades of gray* blending into each other. Different kinds of code enforcement efforts may be required to deal with different degrees of deterioration.

1. The above passage suggests that code enforcement efforts may have to be

    A. developed to cope with varying levels of housing dilapidation
    B. aimed primarily at the serious violations in slum buildings
    C. modeled on the *vacate and restore* measures of earlier times
    D. modified to reduce unrealistic penalties for petty violations

2. According to the above passage, during former times some buildings had sanitary violations which were

    A. irreparable and minor
    B. blurred and gray
    C. flagrant and obvious
    D. insignificant and numerous

3. According to the above passage, the aging housing stock presents a

    A. great number of rent-controlled buildings
    B. serious problem of tenant-caused deterioration
    C. significant increase in buildings without intentional violations
    D. wide range of physical conditions

Questions 4-5.

DIRECTIONS: Questions 4 and 5 are to be answered SOLELY on the basis of the following passage.

In general, housing code provisions relating to the safe and sanitary maintenance of dwelling units prescribe the maintenance required for foundations, walls, ceilings, floors, windows, doors, stairways, and also the facilities and equipment required in other sections. The more recent codes have, in addition, extensive provisions designed to ensure that the unit be maintained in a rat-free and rat-proof condition. Also, as an example of new approaches in code provisions, one proposed Federal model housing code prohibits the landlord from terminating vital services and utilities except during temporary emergencies or when actual repairs or maintenance are in process. This provision may be used to prevent a landlord from turning off utility services as a technique of self-help eviction or as a weapon against rent strikes.

4. According to the above passage, the more recent housing codes have extensive provisions designed to 4.____

   A. maintain a reasonably fire-proof living unit
   B. prohibit tenants from participating in rent strikes
   C. maintain the unit free from rats
   D. prohibit tenants from using lead-based paints

5. According to the above passage, one housing code would permit landlords to terminate vital services during 5.____

   A. a rent strike
   B. an actual eviction
   C. a temporary emergency
   D. the planning of repairs and maintenance

Questions 6-8.

DIRECTIONS: Questions 6 through 8 are to be answered SOLELY on the basis of the following passage.

City governments have long had building codes which set minimum standards for building and for human occupancy. The code (or series of codes) makes provisions for standards of lighting and ventilation, sanitation, fire prevention, and protection. As a result of demands from manufacturers, builders, real estate people, tenement owners, and building-trades unions, these codes often have established minimum standards well below those that the contemporary society would accept as a rock-bottom minimum. Codes often become outdated so that meager standards in one era become seriously inadequate a few decades later as society"s concept of a minimum standard of living changes. Out-of-date codes, when still in use, have sometimes prevented the introduction of new devices and modern building techniques. Thus, it is extremely important that building codes keep pace with changes in the accepted concept of a minimum standard of living.

6. According to the above passage, all of the following considerations in building planning would probably be covered in a building code EXCEPT

   A. closet space as a percentage of total floor area
   B. size and number of windows required for rooms of differing sizes
   C. placement of fire escapes in each line of apartments
   D. type of garbage disposal units to be installed

7. According to the above passage, if an ideal building code were to be created, how would the established minimum standards in it compare to the ones that are presently set by city governments?
   They would

   A. be lower than they are at present
   B. be higher than they are at present
   C. be comparable to the present minimum standards
   D. vary according to the economic group that sets them

8. On the basis of the above passage, what is the reason for difficulties in introducing new building techniques?

   A. Builders prefer techniques which represent the rock-bottom minimum desired by society.
   B. Certain manufacturers have obtained patents on various building methods to the exclusion of new techniques.
   C. The government does not want to invest money in techniques that will soon be outdated.
   D. New techniques are not provided for in building codes which are not up-to-date.

Questions 9-11.

DIRECTIONS: Questions 9 through 11 are to be answered SOLELY on the basis of the following paragraph.

When constructed within a multiple dwelling, such storage space shall be equipped with a sprinkler system and also with a system of mechanical ventilation in no way connected with any other ventilating system. Such storage space shall have no opening into any other part of the dwelling except through a fireproof vestibule. Any such vestibule shall have a minimum superficial floor area of fifty square feet, and its maximum area shall not exceed seventy-five square feet. It shall be enclosed with incombustible partitions having a fire-resistive rating of three hours. The floor and ceiling of such vestibule shall also be of incombustible material having a fire-resistive rating of at least three hours. There shall be two doors to provide access from the dwelling, to the car storage space. Each such door shall have a fire-resistive rating of one and one-half hours and shall be provided with a device to prevent the opening of one door until the other door is entirely closed.

9. According to the above paragraph, the one of the following that is REQUIRED in order for cars to be permitted to be stored in a multiple dwelling is a(n)

   A. fireproof vestibule
   B. elevator from the garage
   C. approved heating system
   D. sprinkler system

10. According to the above paragraph, the one of the following materials that would NOT be acceptable for the walls of a vestibule connecting a garage to the dwelling portion of a building is

    A. 3" solid gypsum blocks
    B. 4" brick
    C. 4" hollow gypsum blocks, plastered both sides
    D. 6" solid cinder concrete blocks

10.____

11. According to the above paragraph, the one of the following that would be ACCEPTABLE for the width and length of a vestibule connecting a garage that is within a multiple dwelling to the dwelling portion of the building is

    A. 3'8" x 13'0"   B. 4'6" x 18'6"
    C. 4'9" x 14'6"   D. 4'3" x 19'3"

11.____

Questions 12-13.

DIRECTIONS: Questions 12 and 13 are to be answered SOLELY on the basis of the following paragraph.

It shall be unlawful to place, use, or maintain in a condition intended, arranged, or designed for use, any gas-fired cooking appliance, laundry stove, heating stove, range or water heater or combination of such appliances in any room or space used for living or sleeping in any new or existing multiple dwelling unless such room or space has a window opening to the outer air or such gas appliance is vented to the outer air. All automatically operated gas appliances shall be equipped with a device which shall shut off automatically the gas supply to the main burners when the pilot light in such appliance is extinguished. A gas range or the cooking portion of a gas appliance incorporating a room heater shall not be deemed an automatically operated gas appliance. However, burners in gas ovens and broilers which can be turned on and off or ignited by non-manual means shall be equipped with a device which shall shut off automatically the gas supply to those burners when the operation of such non-manual means fails.

12. According to the above paragraph, an automatic shut-off device is NOT required on a gas

    A. hot water heater   B. laundry dryer
    C. space heater   D. range

12.____

13. According to the above paragraph, a gas-fired water heater is permitted

    A. only in kitchens   B. only in bathrooms
    C. only in living rooms D. in any type of room

13.____

Questions 14-18.

DIRECTIONS: Questions 14 through 18 are to be answered SOLELY on the basis of the information contained in the statement below.

No multiple dwelling shall be erected to a height in excess of one and one-half times the width of the widest street on which it faces, except that above the level of such height, for each one foot that the front wall of such dwelling sets back from the street line, three feet shall be added to the height limit of such dwelling, but such dwelling shall not exceed in maximum height three feet plus one and three-quarter times the width of the widest street on which it faces.

Any such dwelling facing a street more than one hundred feet in width shall be subject to the same height limitations as though such dwelling faced a street one hundred feet in width.

14. The MAXIMUM height of a multiple dwelling set back five feet from the street line and facing a 60 foot wide street is ___ feet.   14._____

    A. 60   B. 90   C. 105   D. 165

15. The MAXIMUM height of a multiple dwelling set back six feet from the street line and facing a 120 foot wide street is _____ feet.   15._____

    A. 198   B. 168   C. 120   D. 105

16. The MAXIMUM height of a multiple dwelling is   16._____

    A. 100 ft.   B. 150 ft.   C. 178 ft.   D. unlimited

17. The MAXIMUM height of a multiple dwelling set back 10 feet from the street line and facing a 110 foot wide street is ___ feet.   17._____

    A. 178   B. 180   C. 195   D. 205

18. The MAXIMUM height of a multiple dwelling set back eight feet from the street line and facing a 90 foot wide street is ___ feet.   18._____

    A. 135   B. 147   C. 178   D. 159

Questions 19-23.

DIRECTIONS: Questions 19 through 23 are to be answered SOLELY on the basis of the following statement.

The number of persons accommodated on any story in a lodging house shall not be greater than the sum of the following components,

    a. 22 persons for each full multiple of 22 inches in the smallest clear width for each means of egress approved by the department, other than fire escapes
    b. 20 persons for each lawful fire escape accessible from such story.

19. The MAXIMUM number of persons that may be accommodated on a story in a lodging house depends on the   19._____

    A. number of lawful fire escapes *only*
    B. number of approved means of egress *only*
    C. smallest clear width in each approved means of egress *only*
    D. number of lawful fire escapes and sum total of smallest clear widths in each approved means of egress

20. The MAXIMUM number of persons that may be accommodated on a story of a lodging house having one lawful fire escape and a sum total of 44 inches in the smallest clear widths of the two approved means of egress is   20._____

    A. 20   B. 22   C. 42   D. 64

21. The MAXIMUM number of persons that may be accommodated on a story of a lodging house having two lawful fire escapes and a sum total of 60 inches in the smallest clear width of the approved means of egress is

    A. 64   B. 84   C. 100   D. 106

22. The MAXIMUM number of persons that may be accommodated on a story of a lodging house having one lawful fire escape and a sum total of 33 inches in the smallest clear width of the approved means of egress is

    A. 42   B. 53   C. 64   D. 73

23. The MAXIMUM number of persons that may be accommodated on a story of a lodging house having two lawful fire escapes and two approved means of egress, with 40 inches and 44 inches in the smallest clear widths, respectively, is

    A. 84   B. 104   C. 106   D. 108

Questions 24-25.

DIRECTIONS: Questions 24 and 25 are to be answered SOLELY on the basis of the following paragraph.

Though the recent trend toward apartment construction may appear to be the Region's response to large-lot zoning and centralized industry, it really is not. It is mainly a function of the age of the population. Most of the apartments are occupied by one- and two-person families young people out of school but without a family of their own and older people whose children have grown. Both groups have been increasing in number; and, in this Region, they characteristically live in apartments. It is this increased demand for apartments and the simultaneous decrease in demand for one-family houses that dramatically raised the percentage of building permits issued for multi-family housing units from 36 percent in 1977 to 67 percent in 1981. The fact that three-fourths of the apartments were built in the Core between 1977 and 1981 at the same time as the Core was losing population underscores the failure of the apartment boom to slow the outward spread of the population.

24. According to the above paragraph, one of the reasons for the increase in the number of building permits issued for multi-family construction in the City Metropolitan Region is

    A. that workers in industry want to live close to their jobs
    B. an increase in the number of elderly people living in the Region
    C. the inability of many families to afford the large lots necessary to build private homes
    D. the new zoning ordinance made it easier to build apartments

25. According to the above paragraph, the apartment construction boom

    A. increased the population density in the Core
    B. spurred a population shift to the suburbs
    C. did not halt the outward flow of the population from the Core
    D. was most significant in the outer areas of the Region

KEY (CORRECT ANSWERS)

1. A
2. C
3. D
4. C
5. C

6. A
7. B
8. D
9. D
10. B

11. C
12. D
13. D
14. C
15. B

16. C
17. A
18. D
19. D
20. D

21. B
22. A
23. C
24. B
25. C

TEST 2

DIRECTIONS: Each question or incomplete statement is followed by several suggested answers or completions. Select the one that BEST answers the question or completes the statement. *PRINT THE LETTER OF THE CORRECT ANSWER IN THE SPACE AT THE RIGHT.*

Questions 1-4.

DIRECTIONS: Questions 1 through 4 are to be answered SOLELY on the basis of the following paragraph.

Although the suburbs have provided housing and employment for millions of additional families since 1950, many suburban communities have maintained controls over the kinds of families who can live in them. Suburban attitudes have been formed by reaction against a perception of crowded, harassed city life and threatening alien city people. As population, taxable income, and jobs have left the cities for the suburbs, the *urban crisis* of substandard housing, declining levels of education and public services, and decreasing employment opportunities has been created. The crisis, however, is not urban at all, but national, and in part a result of the suburban policy that discourages outward movement by the urban poor.

1. According to the above paragraph, the quality of urban life

   A. is determined by public opinion in the cities
   B. has worsened in recent years
   C. is similar to rural life
   D. can be changed by political means

2. According to the above paragraph, suburban communities have

   A. tried to show that the urban crisis is really a national crisis
   B. avoided taking a position on the urban crisis
   C. been involved in causing the urban crisis
   D. been the innocent victims of the urban crisis

3. According to the above paragraph, the poor have

   A. become increasingly sophisticated in their attempts to move to the suburbs
   B. generally been excluded from the suburbs
   C. lost incentive for betterment of their living conditions
   D. sought improvement of the central cities

4. As used in the above paragraph, the word perception means MOST NEARLY

   A. development   B. impression
   C. opposition   D. uncertainty

Questions 5-8.

DIRECTIONS: Questions 5 through 8 are to be answered SOLELY on the basis of the following paragraph.

The concentration of publicly assisted housing in central cities -- because the suburbs do not want them and effectively bar them -- is usually rationalized by a solicitous regard for keeping intact the city neighborhoods cherished by low-income groups. If one accepted this as valid, the devotion of minorities to blighted city neighborhoods in preference to suburban employment and housing would be an historic first. Certainly no such devotion was visible among the millions who have deserted their city neighborhoods in the last 25 years even if it meant an arduous daily trip from the suburbs to their jobs in the cities.

5. The writer implies that MOST poor people 5.____

   A. prefer isolation
   B. fear change
   C. are angry
   D. seek betterment

6. The general tone of the paragraph is BEST characterized as 6.____

   A. uncertain
   B. skeptical
   C. evasive
   D. indifferent

7. As used in the above paragraph, the word rationalize means MOST NEARLY 7.____

   A. dispute
   B. justify
   C. deny
   D. locate

8. According to the above paragraph, publicly assisted housing is concentrated in the central cities PRIMARILY because 8.____

   A. city dwellers are unable to find satisfactory housing
   B. deterioration of older housing has increased in recent years
   C. suburbanites have opposed the movement of the poor to the suburbs
   D. employment opportunities have decreased in the suburbs

Questions 9-11.

DIRECTIONS: Questions 9 through 11 are to be answered SOLELY on the basis of the following paragraph.

In recent years, new and important emphasis has been placed upon the maximum use of conservation and rehabilitation techniques in carrying out programs of urban renewal and revitalization. In urban renewal projects where existing structures are hopelessly deteriorated or land uses are incompatible with the community's overall plans, the entire area may be acquired, cleared, and sold for redevelopment. However, where existing structures are basically sound but have deteriorated to the point where they are a blighting influence on the neighborhood, they may be salvaged through a program of rehabilitation and reconditioning.

9. According to the above paragraph, the one of the following which is MOST likely to cause area-wide razing of the buildings in urban renewal programs is 9.____

   A. a program of rehabilitation and reconditioning
   B. concerted insistence by landlords and tenants that certain buildings be bulldozed
   C. an inability of community groups to agree on priorities for staged clearance
   D. land use contrary to the community's general plan

10. According to the above paragraph, rehabilitation of structures may take place if 10.____

    A. new conservation and rehabilitation techniques are used
    B. salvaging all the buildings in the entire area is hopeless
    C. the community wishes to preserve historic structures
    D. the existing buildings are structurally sound

11. As used in the above paragraph, the word blighting means MOST NEARLY 11.____

    A. ruining   B. infrequent   C. recurrent   D. traditional

Questions 12-13.

DIRECTIONS: Questions 12 and 13 are to be answered SOLELY on the basis of the following paragraphs.

   We must also find better ways to handle the relocation of people uprooted by projects. In the past, many renewal plans have foundered on this problem, and it is still the most difficult part of the community development. Large-scale replacement of low-income residents -- many ineligible for public housing -- has contributed to deterioration of surrounding communities. However, thanks to changes in housing authority procedures, relocation has been accomplished in a far more satisfactory fashion. The step-by-step community development projects we advocate in this plan should bring further improvement.

   But additional measures will be necessary. There are going to be more people to be moved; and, with the current shortage of apartments, large ones especially, it is going to be tougher to find places to move them to. The city should have more freedom to buy or lease housing that comes on the market because of normal turnover and make it available to relocatees.

12. According to the above paragraphs, one of the reasons a neighborhood may deteriorate is that 12.____

    A. there is a scarcity of large apartments
    B. step-by-step community development projects have failed
    C. people in the given neighborhood are uprooted from their homes
    D. a nearby renewal project has an inadequate relocation plan

13. From the above paragraphs, one might conclude that the relocation phase of community renewal has been improved. 13.____

    A. by changes in housing authority procedures
    B. by development of step-by-step community development projects
    C. through expanded city powers to buy housing for relocation
    D. by the addition of huge sums of money

Questions 14-15.

DIRECTIONS: Questions 14 and 15 are to be answered SOLELY on the basis of the following paragraphs.

   Provision of decent housing for the lower half of the population (by income) was thus taken on as a public responsibility. Public housing was to assist the poorest quarter of urban families while the 221(d)(3) Housing Program would assist the next quarter. But limited funds meant that the supply of subsidized housing could not stretch nearly far enough to help this half of the population. Who were to be left out in the rationing process which was accomplished by the sifting of applicants for housing on the part of public and private authorities?

Discrimination on the grounds of race or color is not allowed under Federal law. In all sections of the country, encouragingly, housing programs are found which follow this law to the letter. Yet, housing programs in some cities still suffer from the residue of racial segregation policies and attitudes that for years were condoned or even encouraged.

Some sifting in the 221(d)(3) Housing Program follows the practice of many public housing authorities, the imposition of requirements with respect to character. This is a delicate matter. To fill a project overwhelmingly with broken families, alcoholics, criminals, delinquents, and other problem tenants would hardly make it a wholesome environment. Yet the total exclusion of such families is hardly an acceptable alternative. To the extent this exclusion is practiced, the very people whose lives are described in order to persuade lawmakers and the public to instigate new programs find the door shut in their faces when such programs come into being. The proper balance is difficult to achieve, but society's neediest families surely should not be totally denied the opportunities for rejuvenation in subsidized housing.

14. From the above paragraphs, it can be assumed that the 221(d)(3) Housing Program

   A. served a population earning more than the median income
   B. served a less affluent population than is served by public housing
   C. excludes all problem families from its projects
   D. is a subsidized housing program

15. According to this text, the provision of housing for the poor

   A. has not been completely accomplished with public monies
   B. is never influenced by segregationist policies
   C. is limited to providing housing for only the neediest families
   D. is primarily the responsibility of the Federal government

16. Five hundred persons attended a public hearing at which a proposed public housing project was being considered. Less than half favored the project while the majority opposed the project.
   According to the above statement, it is REASONABLE to conclude that

   A. the proposal stimulated considerable community interest
   B. the public housing project was disapproved by the city because a majority opposed it
   C. those who opposed the project lacked sympathy for needy persons
   D. the supporters of the project were led by militants

17. A vacant lot close to a polluted creek is for sale. Two buyers compete. One owns an adjacent factory which provides 300 high paying unskilled jobs. He needs to expand or move from the city. If he expands, he will provide 300 additional jobs. The other is a community group in a changing residential area close by. They hope to stabilize the neighborhood by bringing in new housing. They would build an apartment building with 100 dwelling units on the lot.
   According to the above paragraph, it is REASONABLE to conclude that

   A. jobs are more important than housing
   B. there is conflict between the factory owners and the neighborhood group
   C. the neighborhood group will not succeed in stabilizing the area by constructing new housing
   D. the polluted creek should be cleaned up

18. The housing authority faces every problem of the private developer, and it must also assume responsibilities of which private building is free. The authority must account to the community; it must conform to federal regulations; it must provide durable buildings of good standard at low cost; it must overcome the prejudices against public operations, of contractors, bankers, and prospective tenants. These authorities are being watched by anti-housing enthusiasts for the first error of judgment or the first evidence of high costs, to be torn to bits before a Congressional committee.
On the basis of this statement, it would be MOST correct to state that

    A. private builders do not have the opposition of contractors, bankers, and prospective tenants
    B. Congressional committees impede the progress of public housing by petty investigations
    C. a housing authority must deal with all the difficulties encountered by the private builder
    D. housing authorities are no more immune from errors in judgment than private developers

19. Another factor that has considerably added to the city's housing crisis has been the great influx of low-income workers and their families seeking better employment opportunities during wartime and defense boom periods. The circumstances of these families have forced them to crowd into the worst kind of housing and have produced on a renewed scale the conditions from which slums flourish and grow.
On the basis of this statement, one would be justified in stating that

    A. the influx of low-income workers has aggravated the slum problem
    B. the city has better employment opportunities than other sections of the country
    C. the high wages paid by our defense industries have made many families ineligible for tenancy in public housing projects
    D. the families who settled in the city during wartime and the defense build-up brought with them language and social customs conducive to the growth of slums

20. Much of the city felt the effects of the general postwar increase of vandalism and street crime, and the greatly expanded public housing program was no exception. Projects built in congested slum areas with a high incidence of delinquency and crime were particularly subjected to the depredations of neighborhood gangs. The civil service watchmen who patrolled the projects, unarmed and neither trained nor expected to perform police duties, were unable to cope with the situation.
On the basis of this statement, the MOST accurate of the following statements is:

    A. Neighborhood gangs were particularly responsible for the high incidence of delinquency and crime in congested slum areas having public housing programs
    B. Civil service watchmen who patrolled housing projects failed to carry out their assigned police duties
    C. Housing projects were not spared the effects of the general postwar increase of vandalism and street crime
    D. Delinquency and crime affected housing projects in slum areas to a greater extent than other dwellings in the same area

21. Another peculiar characteristic of real estate is the absence of liquidity. Each parcel is a discrete unit as to size, location, rental, physical condition, and financing arrangements. Each property requires investigation, comparison of rents with other properties, and individualized haggling on price and terms.
On the basis of this statement, the LEAST accurate of the following statements is:

    A. Although the size, location, and rent of parcels vary, comparison with rents of other properties affords an indication of the value of a particular parcel
    B. Bargaining skill is the essential factor in determining the value of a parcel of real estate
    C. Each parcel of real estate has individual peculiarities distinguishing it from any other parcel
    D. Real estate is not easily converted to other types of assets

21.____

22. In part, at least, the charges of sameness, monotony, and institutionalism directed at public housing projects result from the degree in which they differ from the city's normal housing pattern. They seem alike because their very difference from the usual makes them stand apart.
In many respects, there is considerably more variety between public housing projects than there is between different streets of apartment houses or tenements throughout the city.
On the basis of this statement, it would be LEAST accurate to state that:

    A. There is considerably more variety between public housing projects than there is between different streets of tenements throughout the city
    B. Public housing projects differ from the city's normal housing pattern to the degree that sameness, monotony, and institutionalism are characteristic of public buildings
    C. Public housing projects seem alike because their deviation from the usual dwellings draws attention to them
    D. The variety in structure between public housing projects and other public buildings is related to the period in which they were built

22.____

23. The amount of debt that can be charged against the city for public housing is limited by law. Part of the city's restricted housing means goes for cash subsidies it may be required to contribute to state-aided projects. Under the provisions of the state law, the city must match the state's contributions in subsidies; and while the value of the partial tax exemption granted by the city is counted for this purpose, it is not always sufficient.
On the basis of this statement, it would be MOST accurate to state that:

    A. The amount of money the city may spend for public housing is limited by annual tax revenues
    B. The value of tax exemptions granted by the city to educational, religious, and charitable institutions may be added to its subsidy contributions to public housing projects
    C. The subsidy contributions for state-aided public housing projects are shared equally by the state and the city under the provisions of the state law
    D. The tax revenues of the city, unless supplemented by state aid, are insufficient to finance public housing projects

23.____

24. Maintenance costs can be minimized and the useful life of houses can be extended by building with the best and most permanent materials available. The best and most permanent materials in many cases are, however, much more expensive than materials which require more maintenance. The most economical procedure in home building has been to compromise between the capital costs of high quality and enduring materials and the maintenance costs of less desirable materials.
On the basis of this statement, one would be justified in stating that:

   A. Savings in maintenance costs make the use of less durable and less expensive building materials preferable to high quality materials that would prolong the useful life of houses constructed from them
   B. Financial advantage can be secured by the home builder if he judiciously combines costly but enduring building materials with less desirable materials which, however, require more maintenance
   C. A compromise between the capital costs of high quality materials and the maintenance costs of less desirable materials makes it easier for a home builder to estimate construction expenditures
   D. The most economical procedure in home building is to balance the capital costs of the most permanent materials against the costs of less expensive materials that are cheaper to maintain

25. Personnel selection has been a critical problem for local housing authorities. The pool of qualified workers trained in housing procedures is small, and the colleges and universities have failed to grasp the opportunity for enlarging it. While real estate experience makes a good background for management of a housing project, many real estate men are deplorably lacking in understanding of social and governmental problems. Social workers, on the other hand, are likely to be deficient in business judgment.
On the basis of this statement, it would be MOST accurate to state that:

   A. Colleges and universities have failed to train qualified workers for proficiency in housing procedures
   B. Social workers are deficient in business judgment as related to the management of a housing project
   C. Real estate experience makes a person a good manager of a housing project
   D. Local housing authorities have been critical of present methods of personnel selection

KEY (CORRECT ANSWERS)

1. B
2. C
3. B
4. B
5. D

6. B
7. B
8. D
9. D
10. D

11. A
12. D
13. A
14. D
15. A

16. A
17. B
18. C
19. A
20. C

21. B
22. B
23. C
24. B
25. A

THE HOUSING CODE

CONTENTS

		Page
I.	Definitions	1
II.	Background of Housing Codes in the United States	5
III.	Objectives of a Housing Code	6
IV.	Limitations	6
V.	Content	7
VI.	Administrative Elements of a Housing Code	8
VII.	Substantive Provisions of a Housing Code	12

THE HOUSING CODE

Any housing code, regardless of who promulgates it, is basically an environmental health protection code. The hygiene of housing, correspondingly, is the area of environmental health that deals with man's most intimate living environment – his home and his neighborhood. Into the fabric of housing hygiene is woven a wide variety of health, safety, economic, social, and political factors.

Early housing codes primarily considered protecting only man's physical health; hence, they were enforced only in slum areas. More recently the realization has been made that if urban blight and its associated human suffering are to be controlled; the housing codes must consider both physical and mental health and must be administered uniformly throughout the community.

In preparing or revising the housing code, local officials must maintain a level of standards that will not merely be "minimal." These standards should maintain a living environment that contributes positively to healthful individual and family living. The fact that a small portion of housing fails to meet a desirable standard is hardly a legitimate reason for retrogressive modification or abolition of a standard. A housing code is merely a means to an end. The end is the eventual elimination of all substandard conditions within the home and neighborhood. This end cannot be reached if the community adopts an inadequate housing code. The adoption of a housing ordinance that establishes low standards for existing housing serves only to legalize and perpetuate an unhealthy living environment. Wherever local conditions are such that immediate enforcement of some standards within the code would cause undue hardship upon some individuals, it is better to provide a time interval for compliance than to eliminate an otherwise satisfactory standard.

I. Definitions

The following definitions of terms have been excerpted from "APHA - CDC Recommended Housing Maintenance and Occupancy Ordinance" and will be used throughout this manual.

1. **Accessory Building or Structure** shall mean a detached building or structure in a secondary or subordinate capacity from the main or principal building or structure on the same premises.

2. **Appropriate Authority** shall mean that person within the governmental structure of the corporate unit who is charged with the administration of the appropriate code.

3. **Approved** shall mean approved by the local or state authority have such administrative authority?

4. **Ashes** shall mean the residue from the burning of combustible materials.

5. **Attic** shall mean any story situated wholly or partly within the roof, and so designed, arranged or built as to be used for business, storage, or habitation.

6. **Basement** shall mean the lowest story of a building, below the main floor and wholly or partially lower than the surface of the ground.

7. **Building** shall mean a fixed construction with walls, foundation and roof, such as a house, factory, or garage.

8. **Bulk Container** shall mean any metal garbage, rubbish, or refuse container having a capacity of two (2) cubic yards or greater and which is equipped with fittings for hydraulic or mechanical emptying, unloading or removal.

9. **Cellar** shall mean a room or group of rooms totally below the ground level and usually under a building.

10. **Central Heating System** shall mean a single system supplying heat to one (1) or more dwelling unite(s) or more than one (1) rooming unit.

11. **Chimney** shall mean a vertical masonry shaft of reinforced concrete, or other approved noncombustible, heat-resisting material enclosing one (1) or more flues, for the purpose of removing products of combustion from solid, liquid, or gaseous fuel.

12. **Dilapidated** shall mean no longer adequate for the purpose or use for which it was originally intended.

13. **Dormitory** shall mean a building or a group of rooms in a building used for institutional living and sleeping purposes by four (4) or more persons.

14. **Dwelling** shall mean any enclosed space wholly or partly used or intended to be used for living, sleeping, cooking, and eating; provided that temporary housing as hereinafter defined shall not be classified as a dwelling. Industrialized housing and modular construction which conform to nationally accepted industry standards and used or intended for use for living, sleeping, cooking, and eating purposes shall be classified as dwellings.

15. **Dwelling Unit** shall mean a room or group of rooms located within a dwelling forming a single habitable unit with facilities used or intended to be used by a single family for living, sleeping, cooking, and eating purposes.

16. **Egress** shall mean an arrangement of exit facilities to assure a safe means of exit from buildings.

17. **Extermination** shall mean the control and elimination of insects, rodents, or other pests by eliminating their harborage places; by removing or making inaccessible materials that may serve as their food; by poisoning, spraying, fumigating, trapping, or by any other recognized and legal pest elimination methods approved by the local or state authority having such administrative authority.

18. **Fair Market Value** shall mean a price at which both buyers and sellers are willing to do business.

19. **Family** shall mean one or more individuals living together and sharing common living, sleeping, cooking, and eating facilities (See also Household).

20. **Flush Water Closet** shall mean a toilet bowl which is flushed with water which has been supplied under pressure and equipped with a water sealed trap above the floor level.

21. **Garbage** shall mean the animal and vegetable waste resulting from the handling, preparation, cooking, serving, and nonconsumption of food.

22. **Grade** shall mean the finished ground level adjacent to a required window.

23. **Guest** shall mean an individual who shares a dwelling unit in a non-permanent status for not more than thirty (30) days.

24. **Habitable Room** shall mean a room or enclosed floor space used or intended to be used for living, sleeping, cooking, or eating purposes, excluding bathrooms, water closet compartments, laundries, furnace rooms, pantries, kitchenettes and utility rooms of less than fifty (50) square feet of floor space, foyers, or communicating corridors, stairways, closets, storage spaces and workshops, hobby and recreation areas.

25. **Health Officer** shall mean the legally designated health authority of the (Name of Corporate Unit) or his authorized representative. (If the legally designated health authority has a title other than "Health Officer" the title of this authority should be substituted for "Health Officer" in this section and all other sections of this ordinance.)

26. **Heated Water** shall mean water heated to a temperature of not less than 120°F at the outlet.

27. **Heating Device** shall mean all furnaces, unit heaters, domestic incinerators, cooking and heating stoves and ranges, and other similar devices.

28. **Household** shall mean one or more individuals living together in a single dwelling unit and sharing common living, sleeping, cooking, and eating facilities (See also Family).

29. **Infestation** shall mean the presence within or around a dwelling of any insects; rodents, or other pests.

30. **Kitchen** shall mean any room used for the storage and preparation of foods and containing the following equipment: sink or other device for dishwashing, stove or other device for cooking, refrigerator or other device for cool storage of food, cabinets or shelves for storage of equipment and utensils, and counter or table for food preparation.

31. **Kitchenette** shall mean a small kitchen or an alcove containing cooking facilities.

32. **Lead-based Paint** shall mean any paint containing more lead than the level established by the U.S. Consumer Product Safety Commission as being the "safe" level of lead in residential paint and paint products.

33. **Meaning of Certain Words** Whenever the words "dwelling," "dwelling unit," "rooming units," "premises," and "structure" are used in the ordinance they shall be construed as though they were followed by the words "or any part thereof." Words used in the singular include the plural, and the plural the singular, the masculine gender includes the feminine and the feminine the masculine.

34. **Multiple Dwelling** shall mean any dwelling containing more than two dwelling units.

35. **Occupant** shall mean any individual, over one (1) year of age, living, sleeping, cooking, or eating in or having possession of a dwelling unit or a rooming unit; except that in dwelling units a guest shall not be considered an occupant.

36. **Operator** shall mean any person who has charge, care, control, or management of a building, or part thereof, in which dwelling units or rooming units are let.

37. **Ordinary Summer Conditions** shall mean a temperature 10°F below the highest recorded temperature in the locality for prior ten (10) year period.

38. **Ordinary Winter Conditions** shall mean a temperature 15°F above the lowest recorded temperature in the locality for prior ten (10) year period.

39. **Owner** shall mean any person who alone or jointly or severally with others:
    (a) shall have legal title to any premises, dwelling or dwelling unit, with or without accompanying actual possession thereof, or
    (b) shall have charge, care, or control of any premises, dwelling or dwelling unit, as owner or agent of the owner, or as executor, administrator, trustee or guardian of the estate of the owner.

40. **Permissible Occupancy** shall mean the maximum number of individuals permitted to reside in a dwelling unit, rooming unit, or dormitory.

41. **Person** shall mean and include any individual, firm, corporation, association, partnership, cooperative, or governmental agency.

42. **Plumbing** shall mean and include all of the following supplied facilities and equipment: gas pipes, gas burning equipment, water pipes, garbage disposal units, waste pipes, water closets, sinks, installed dishwashers, lavatories, bathtubs, shower baths, installed clothes washing machines, catch basins, drains, vents, and any other similar supplied fixtures, and the installation thereof, together with all connections to water, sewer, or gas lines.

43. **Premises** shall mean a platted lot or part thereof or unplatted lot or parcel of land or plot of land, either occupied or unoccupied by any dwelling or nondwelling structure, and includes any such building, accessory structure, or other structure thereon.

44. **Privacy** shall mean the existence of conditions which will permit an individual or individuals to carry out an activity commenced without interruption or interference, either by sight or sound by unwanted individuals.

45. **Properly Connected** shall mean connected in accordance with all applicable code and ordinances of this (Name of Corporate Unit) as from time to time enforced; provided, however, that the application of this definition shall not require the alteration or replacement of any connection in good working order and not constituting a hazard to life or health.

46. **Rat Harborage** shall mean any conditions or place where rats can live, nest, or seek shelter.

47. **Ratproofing** shall mean a form of construction which will prevent the ingress or egress of rats to or from a given space or building, or from gaining access to food, water, or harborage. It consists of the closing and keeping closed of every opening in foundations, basements, cellars, exterior and interior walls, ground or first floors, roofs, sidewalk gratings, sidewalk openings, and other places that may be reached and entered by rats by climbing, burrowing or other methods, by the use of materials impervious to rat gnawing and other methods approved by the (Appropriate Authority).

48. **Refuse** shall mean all putrescible and nonputrescible solids (except body wastes) including garbage, rubbish, ashes, and dead animals.

49. **Refuse Container** shall mean a watertight container that is constructed of metal, or other durable material impervious to rodents, that are capable of being serviced without creating

insanitary conditions, or such other containers as have been approved by the (Appropriate Authority). Openings into the container such as covers and doors shall be tight fitting.

50. **Rooming House** shall mean any dwelling other than a hotel or motel or that part of any dwelling, containing one (1) or more rooming units, or one (1) or more dormitory rooms and in which persons either individually or as families are housed with or without meals being provided.

51. **Rooming Unit** shall mean any room or group of rooms forming a single habitable unit used or intended to be used for living and sleeping, but not for cooking purposes.

52. **Rubbish** shall mean nonputrescible solid wastes (excluding ashes) consisting of either:
    (a) combustible wastes such as paper, cardboard, plastic containers, yard clippings, and wood; or
    (b) noncombustible wastes such as cans, glass, and crockery.

53. **Safety** shall mean the condition of being reasonably free from danger and hazards which may cause accidents or disease.

54. **Space Heater** shall mean a self contained heating appliance of either the convection type or the radiant type and intended primarily to heat only a limited space or area such as one room or two adjoining rooms.

55. **Supplied** shall mean paid for, furnished by, provided by, or under the control of the owner, operator, or agent.

56. **Temporary Housing** shall mean any tent, trailer, mobile home or any other structure used for human shelter which is designed to be transportable and which is not attached to the ground, to another structure, or to any utility system on the same premises for more than thirty (30) consecutive days.

57. **Toxic Substance** shall mean any chemical product applied on the surface of or incorporated into any structural or decorative material which constitutes a potential hazard to human health at acute

58. **Variance** shall mean a difference between that which is required or specified and that which is permitted.

II. Background of Housing Codes in the United States

To assist municipalities with the development of legislation necessary to regulate the quality of housing, the Committee on the Hygiene of Housing, American Public Health Association, prepared and in 1952, published a proposed housing ordinance. This provided a prototype on which such legislation might be based and has served as the basis for countless housing codes enacted in the United States since that time. Some municipalities enacted it without change. Others made revision by omitting some portions, modifying others, and some times adding new provisions.

One must keep in mind when considering the adoption of any model code that the code is, as stated, merely a model. The community should read and consider each element within the model code to determine its applicability to that community. As previously stated, however, a housing code is merely a means to an end. The end is the eventual elimination of all substandard conditions within the home and the neighborhood. This end cannot be reached if the community adopts an inadequate housing code.

III. Objectives of a Housing Code

The Housing Act of 1949 gave new impetus to existing local, state, and Federal housing programs directed towards the elimination of poor housing and the production of sound and decent housing. In passing this legislation, Congress defined a new national objective by declaring that the general welfare and security of the nation and the health and living standards of its people ... require a decent home and a suitable living environment for every American family. This mandate generated an awareness that the quality of housing and residential environment has an enormous influence upon the physical and mental health and the social well-being of each individual and, in turn, upon the economic, political, and social conditions in every community. Consequently, public agencies, units of government, professional organizations, and others sought ways to ensure that the quality of housing and the residential environment did not depreciate or deteriorate.

It soon became apparent that a new type of legislation was needed, namely, ordinances that regulate the supplied facilities and the maintenance and occupancy of dwellings and dwelling units, or as they are more commonly called, "housing codes." The objective of a housing code is to establish minimum standards essential to make dwellings safe, sanitary, and fit for human habitation by governing the condition and maintenance, the supplied utilities and facilities, and the occupancy.

IV. Limitations

A housing code is limited in its effectiveness by several factors. First, if the housing code does not contain *standards that adequately protect the health and well-being of the individuals*, it cannot be effective. The best trained soldier, if armed only with a pea shooter, can accomplish little positive action in a battle. Similarly, the best trained housing inspector, if not armed with an adequate housing code, can accomplish little good in the battle against urban blight.

A second factor affecting the quality of the housing administration effort is the *budget of the housing group*. If the housing effort is directed, because of limitations of funds and personnel, to the fire-fighting efforts of complaint answering, then the community can expect to lose the battle against urban blight. It is only through a systematic enforcement effort by an adequately sized staff of properly trained inspectors that the battle can be won.

A third factor that can affect the housing effort is the *attitude of the political bodies within the area*. A properly administered housing program will require the upgrading of substandard housing throughout the community. Frequently, this results in political pressures being exerted to prevent the enforcement of the code in certain areas of the city. If the housing effort is backed properly by all political elements, blight can be controlled and eventually eliminated within the community. If, however, the housing program is not permitted to choke out the spreading influence of substandard conditions, urban blight will spread like a cancer, engulfing greater and greater portions of the city. Similarly, an effort directed only at the most serious blocks in the city will merely upgrade those blocks while the blight spreads elsewhere. If a cancer is to be controlled, it must be cut out in its entirety. If urban blight is to be controlled, it also must be cut out in its entirety.

A fourth element that limits the ability of a housing program is *whether or not the housing program is supported fully by the other departments within the city*. Regardless of which city agency administers the housing program, the other city agencies must support the activities of the housing program. In addition, great effort should be expended to obtain the support and cooperation of the community as a whole towards the housing effort. This can be accomplished through public awareness and public information programs. These two programs should never be undersold. They can provide considerable support or considerable resistance to the efforts of the program.

A fifth limitation to an effective housing program is an *inadequately or improperly trained inspectional staff*. The housing inspector should have considerable training and considerable capabilities if the effort is to accomplish much good. He should have a basic knowledge and general understanding of the principles involved in many related areas. He should have the capability of evaluating whether a serious or a minor problem exists in matters ranging from a structural stability of a building to the health and sanitary aspects relating to the structure. A housing inspector cannot be expected to accomplish his job properly unless he is given sufficient training so as to prepare him to be able to make basic judgments regarding the severity of problems. Since the housing inspector is a generalized inspector, it is not intended that he should become an expert in all areas such as building, electrical, or health inspection. It is merely intended that he should be able to distinguish whether a problem warrants immediate referral to another department or whether it can be handled through routine channels.

A sixth item that frequently restricts the effectiveness of a housing administration effort is *the fact that many housing groups fail to do a complete job of evaluation of the housing problems*. In many cases, the inspectional effort is restricted to merely evaluating what conditions exist with little or no thought given to why these conditions exist. If a housing effort is to be successful, it must consider why the homes deteriorated. Was it because of environmental stresses within the neighborhood that need to be eliminated or was it because of apathy developed on the part of the occupants? In either case, if the causative agent is not removed, then the inspector faces an annual problem of maintaining the quality of that residence. It is only by eliminating the causes of deterioration that the quality of the neighborhood can be maintained. These, then, are a few of the principal limitations that affect the quality of a housing administration effort.

V. Content

What then are the general items that should be included in a housing code? Although all comprehensive housing codes or ordinances contain a number of common elements, the provisions of any two or more communities on the same element or elements will usually vary to some extent. This is true whether the codes be national or state models, those of a northern, eastern, southern, or western municipality, or even of two or more communities within the same state or region. These variations stem from differences in local policies, preferences, and to a lesser extent, needs. They are also influenced by the standards set by the related provisions of the diverse building, electrical, and plumbing codes in use in the municipality.

Within any housing code there are generally five major sections. These sections are:

A **Definitions of terms** used in the code.

B **Administrative provisions** showing who is authorized to administer the code and the basic methods and procedures that must be followed in implementing and enforcing the sections of the code. The administrative sections deal with items such as what are reasonable hours of inspections; when service of violation notices is and is not required; how to notify either the absentee owner when he can or cannot be contacted in person or through a legally responsible agent, or the resident-owner or tenant; how to process and conduct hearings; what rules to follow in processing dwellings alleged to be unfit for human habitation; how to occupy or use dwellings finally declared fit.

C **Substantive provisions** specifying the various types of health, building, electrical, heating, plumbing, maintenance, occupancy, and use conditions that constitute violations of the housing code. These provisions can also be and often are grouped into three main categories, namely, (1) minimum facilities and equipment for dwelling units, (2) adequate maintenance of dwellings and dwelling units as well as their facilities and equipment, and (3) the occupancy conditions of dwellings and dwelling units.

D **Court and penalty sections** outlining the basis for court action and the penalty or penalties to which the alleged violator will be subjected if he is proved guilty of violating one or more provisions of the code.

E **Enabling, conflict, and unconstitutionality clauses** providing for the date a new or amended code will take effect, prevalence of more stringent provision when there is a conflict of two codes, severability of any part of the ordinance that might be found unconstitutional and retention of all other parts in full course and effect. In any city following the format of the "APHA - CDC Recommended Housing Maintenance and Occupancy Ordinance," the Health Officer or other supervisor in charge of housing inspections will also adopt appropriate housing rules and regulations from time to time to clarify or further refine the provisions of the ordinance. This has been done, for example, by the Commissioners of Health in Baltimore, Maryland and Milwaukee, Wisconsin, and by the District of Columbia's Department of Licenses and Inspections. In contrast, some municipalities such as Fort Worth, Texas; St. Louis, Missouri; and Chicago, Illinois, have tended to make their housing codes broader in the first place and subsequently have relied more on amendments to their ordinances rather than on numerous rules and regulations. Either method has its advantages, or so local practice will often help determine which is used.

Where the rules and regulations method is used care should be taken that the department is not overburdened with a number of minor rules and regulations. Similarly, a basic housing ordinance that encompasses all rules and regulations might have difficulty because any amendments to it require action by the political element of the community. Some housing groups, in attempting to obtain amendments to the ordinance, have had the entire ordinance thrown out by the political bodies.

VI. Administrative Elements of a Housing Code

The administrative procedures and powers of the housing inspection agency its supervisors and staff which are outlined in a housing code are similar to its other provisions in that all are based upon the police power of the state to legislate for public health and safety. In addition, the administrative provisions, and to a lesser extent, the court and penalty provisions outline how the police power is to be exercised in administering and enforcing the code.

Generally, the administrative elements deal with the procedures to follow for ensuring that the constitutional doctrines of reasonableness, equal protection under the laws, and due process of law are observed. They must also guard against violation of its prohibitions against unlawful search and seizure, impairment of obligations of contract, and unlawful delegation of authority. These factors encompass items of great importance to housing inspection supervisors such as the inspector's right of entry, reasonable hours of inspection, proper service, and the validity of the provisions of the housing codes they administer. All are described and discussed generally, in light of United States Supreme Court and state Supreme Court tests and decisions, in the publication entitled, "The Constitutionality of Housing Codes." This publication is a clear and excellent source of information about the constitutional administration of housing codes.

A. **Determination of Legal Owner of Record**

In some communities the importance of ascertaining the legal owner of record is not fully understood by the housing inspection supervisors and inspectors. Consequently, they lose cases in court because they have not taken action against the proper party. This problem often arises in connection with "land contract of sale" properties, where the legal deed never passes to the purchaser until he has paid for the property completely. In these cases, the person who is selling the property is the rightful owner and the action should be taken against him.

The method of obtaining the name and address of the legal owner of a property in violation varies from place to place. Ordinarily a check of the city tax records will suffice unless there is reason to believe these are not up to date on the property in question. In the latter case, a further check of county or parish records will turn up the legal owner if state law requires him to register his deed there. If it does not, the advice of the municipal law department should be sought about the next steps to follow.

B. **Due Process Requirements**

Every notice, complaint, summons, or other type of legal paper concerning alleged housing code violations in a given dwelling or dwelling unit must be legally served on the proper party. This might be the owner, his agent, or the tenant, as required by the code, in order to be valid and to prevent harassment of innocent parties. It is quite customary to require that the notice(s) to correct existing violations and any subsequent notices or letters to the violator be served by certified or registered mail with return receipt requested. The receipt serves as proof of service if the case has to be taken to court.

Due process requirement also calls for clarity and specificity with respect to the alleged violations, both in the violation notices and the court complaint-summons. For this reason, special care must be taken to be complete and accurate in testing the violations and charges. To illustrate, rather than direct the violator "to repair all windows where needed" he should be told exactly which windows and what repairs are involved. Unless he is so advised, his attorney has a built-in defense against the city's case.

The chief limitation on the due process requirement, with respect to service of notices, lies in cases involving immediate threats to health and safety. In these instances, the inspection agency or its representative may, without notice or hearing, issue an order citing the existence of the emergency and requiring such action to be taken as is deemed necessary to meet the emergency.

C. **Hearings and the Condemnation Power**

The purpose of a hearing is to give the alleged violator an opportunity to be heard, if he wishes, before further action is taken by the housing inspection agency. These hearings may be very informal, involving meetings between a representative of the agency and the person ordered to take corrective action. They may also be formal hearings at which the agency head presides and the city and the defendant both are entitled to and usually are represented by counsel and expert witnesses. Each type will be discussed below.

1. **Informal Hearings** – A violation notice may raise questions in the mind of the violator or may be served on him at a time when personal hardships or other factors prevent him from meeting the terms of the notice. Therefore, many housing codes afford him an opportunity to have a hearing at which he may discuss his questions or problems and seek additional time or some modification of the order. Administered in a firm but understanding manner, these hearings serve as invaluable aids in relieving needless fears of those involved, in showing how the inspection program is designed to help them, and in winning their voluntary compliance.

2. **Formal Hearings.** – These are quasi-judicial hearings—even though the prevailing court rules of evidence do not control—from which an appeal may be taken to court. All witnesses must therefore be sworn, and a stenographic record of the proceedings must be made.

   The formal hearing is used chiefly as the basis for determining whether a dwelling is or is not fit for human habitation, occupancy, or use. In the event it is proved "unfit," the building is condemned as such and the owner is given a designated amount of time either to rehabilitate it completely or to demolish it. Where local funds are available or the new Federal demolition grant program is in effect, if the owner fails to obey the order within the time specified, the municipality may demolish his building and put a lien against the property to cover demolition costs.

   This type of "condemnation" hearing is a very effective means of stimulating prompt and appropriate corrective action when it is administered fairly and firmly. This is particularly true if the community funds are available for demolition action when the owner proves reluctant or unwilling to obey the order.

   In some places, such as Oakland, California, the housing inspection agency is permitted only to order unfit buildings repaired or vacated until they are repaired. In others, such as Jersey City, New Jersey, the local ordinance also empowers the housing inspection agency to order these buildings demolished by the city if the owners fail to repair or demolish.

D. **Special Features for Coping with Common Problems**

   1. **Limitation of Occupancy Notification** – This technique was pioneered by Wilmington, Delaware. It makes it mandatory for property owners in the community to obtain legal notice from the housing inspection agency of the maximum number of persons that may occupy each of their dwelling or rooming units. It also requires these owners to have a residence, place of business, or an agent for their properties within the community. The agent should be empowered to take remedial action on any of the properties found in violation. In addition, if the property is sold, the new owner must obtain a new Limitation of Occupancy Notification. The fee charged is nominal.

   2. **Request Inspections** – California and Pennsylvania are among the states that permit their municipalities to offer a request inspection service. In return for a fee, the housing inspector will inspect a property for violations of the housing code before its sale so that the buyer can learn its condition in advance. Some communities require owners to notify prospective purchasers of any outstanding notice of violations they have against their property before the sale. If they fail to do so and their properties are in violation, the code holds them liable to civil action by the purchaser and quasi-criminal action by the inspection agency as housing code violators.

3. **Tickets for Minor Offenses** – Denver, Colorado, have used this method of token fines to prod minor violators and first offenders into correcting without the city resorting to court action. There are mixed views about this technique because it is so akin to formal police action. The inspection agency's primary function is to achieve compliance rather than to punish a criminal for a crime that cannot be "corrected" once the damage has been done. Nevertheless, if the action stimulates compliance and reduces the amount of court action needed to achieve it, the ticket technique will undoubtedly spread.

E. **Other Administrative Aids: Forms and Form Letters**

There is tremendous diversity in these aids, yet many small communities have little information about them. The reason for this is that no one in the nation has developed a "housing inspection library" of standard forms and letters.

Before describing a fairly typical set of forms and form letters, it should be stressed that inspectional forms to be used for legal notices must (a) satisfy legal standards of the code, (b) be meaningful to the owner and sufficiently explicit about the extent and location of particular defects, (c) be adaptable to statistical compilation for the governing body reports, and (d) be written in a manner that will facilitate clerical and other administrative usage.

1. **The Daily Report Form** – This form gives the inspection agency an accurate basis for reporting, evaluating, and, if necessary, improving the productivity and performance of its inspectors.

2. **Complaint Form** – This form helps in obtaining full information from the complainant and thus makes the relative seriousness of the problem clear and reduces the number of crank complaints.

3. **No Entry Notice** – This advises occupant or owner that inspector was there and notifies him he must call and make an appointment or face legal action.

4. **Inspection Report Form** – This is the most important form in the agency. It comes in countless varieties ranging from manual, to key punch, to "automated" and from almost complete write-in to almost complete check-off types. If it is designed properly, it will (a) ensure more productivity and more thoroughness by the inspectors, (b) reduce the time spent in writing reports, (c) locate all violations correctly, and (d) reduce time required for typing violation notices. Forms may vary widely in sophistication from a very simple form to those whose components are identified by number for use in processing the case by automation. Some forms are a combined inspection report and notice form in triplicate so that the first page can be used as the notice of violation, the second as the office record, and the third as the guide for reinspection. A covering form letter notifies the violator of the time allowed to correct the conditions listed in the report-notice.

5. **Violation Notice** – This is the legal notice to the owner or tenant that the specified housing code violations in his property or dwelling unit exist and must be corrected within the indicated amount of time. It may be in the form of a letter that includes the list of alleged violations or has a copy of these attached. It may be a standard notice form, or it may be a combined report-notice. Regardless of the type used, each should make the location and nature of all violations clear and specify the exact section of the code that covers each one. The notice must advise the violator of his right to a hearing. It should also indicate that he has a right to be represented by counsel and that failure to obtain counsel will not be accepted as grounds for postponing a hearing or court case.

6. **Hearing Forms** – These should include a form letter notifying violator of date and time set for his hearing, a standard summary sheet on which the supervisor can record the facts presented at an informal hearing, and a hearing decision letter for notifying all concerned of the hearing results. The latter should include the names of the violator, inspector, law department, and any other city official or agency that may be involved in the case.

7. **Reinspection Form Letters or Notices** – These have the same characteristics as the Violation Notice previously referred to except that they cover the follow-up orders given to the violator who has failed to comply with the original notice within the time specified. Some agencies may use two or three types of these form letters to accommodate different degrees of response by the violator. Whether one or several are used, standardization of these will expedite the processing of cases.

8. **Court Complaint and Summons Forms** – These forms advise the alleged violator of the charges against him and summon him to appear in court at the specified time and place. It is essential that the housing inspection agency work closely with the municipal law department in the preparation of these forms so that each is done in exact accord with the rules of court procedure in the state and community.

9. **Court Action Record Form** – This is not a very prevalent form, but it should be, for it provides an accurate running record of the inspection agency's court actions and their results.

If a housing inspection agency does not include all of these forms and form letters in its basic kit, it should move to introduce the needed additions. Although it will take some time to arrive at the best forms to meet local needs, once they are put into use they will result in marked savings of time.

VII. Substantive Provisions of a Housing Code

A discussion of the substantive provisions of a housing code will be divided into three main categories. Discussions follow on each of these categories

A Minimum Facilities and Equipment for Dwelling Units

What are the minimum facilities and equipment that should be required for a dwelling unit? Keep in mind during this discussion that a dwelling unit must have provisions for preparing at least one regularly cooked meal per day within the unit. Minimum equipment should include a kitchen sink in good working condition and properly connected to the water supply system approved by the appropriate authority. It should provide, at all times, an adequate amount of heated and unheated running water under pressure and should be connected to a sewer system approved by the appropriate authority. Cabinets or shelves, or both, for the storage of eating, drinking, and cooking utensils and food should be provided. These surfaces should be of sound construction and made of material that is easily cleanable and that will not impart a toxic or deleterious effect to the food. In addition, a stove and refrigerator should be provided. Within every dwelling there should be a nonhabitable room that affords privacy and is equipped with a flush water closet in good working condition. Within the vicinity of the flush water closet a lavatory sink should be provided. In no case should a kitchen sink be permitted to substitute as a lavatory sink. In addition, within each dwelling unit there should be provided, within a room that affords privacy, either a bathtub or shower or both, in good working condition. As mentioned in the discussion of the kitchen sink, both the lavatory basin and the bathtub or shower or both should be equipped with an adequate amount of heated and unheated water under pressure. Each should be connected to an approved sewer system. Obviously, within each dwelling unit two or more means of egress should be provided to safe and open space at ground level. Provisions should be incorporated within the housing code to meet the safety requirements of the state and community involved. The housing code should spell out minimum standards for lighting and ventilation within each room in the structure. In addition, minimum thermal standards should be provided. Although most codes merely provide the requirement of a given temperature at a given height above floor level, the community should give consideration to the use of "effective temperatures." The effective temperature is a means of incorporating not only absolute temperature in degrees but also humidity and air movement. This mechanism gives a better indication of the comfort index of the room.

B Adequate Maintenance of Dwellings and Dwelling Units and of Their Facilities and Equipment

The code should spell out provisions that no person shall occupy or let for occupancy any dwelling or dwelling units that do not comply with stated requirements. Generally, these requirements specify that the structure be in sound condition and good repair regarding foundation, roof, exterior walls, doors, and window space and window condition; that it be damp-free, watertight and reasonably weathertight; that all structural surfaces be sound and in good repair. These provisions basically state that any necessary repairs should be made before the unit is relet to new occupants.

C The Occupancy Conditions of Dwellings and Dwelling Units

Occupancy provisions set maximum density standards within dwelling units. Generally, they require a given quantity of square footage of space for sleeping area. Requirements in this section restrict the number of basic families permitted within anyone dwelling unit. They state, in addition, the minimum ceiling heights, and closet space.

The housing code is the basic tool of the housing inspector. This code spells out what he may and may not do. It sets the requirements he will enforce and provides him with his basis for action. A housing effort can be no better than the code allows.

BUILDING ASPECTS OF A HOUSING INSPECTION

CONTENTS

		Page
I.	Background Factors	1
II.	Housing Construction Terminology	1
III.	Structure	4
IV.	Discussion of Inspection Techniques	15
V.	Noise as an Environmental Stress	17

BUILDING ASPECTS OF A HOUSING INSPECTION

The principle function of a house is to furnish protection from the elements. In its current stage, however, our civilization requires that a home provide not only shelter but also privacy, safety, and reasonable protection of our physical and mental health. A living facility that fails to offer these essentials through adequately designed and properly maintained interiors and exteriors cannot be termed "healthful housing."

I. Background Factors

In this chapter, a building will be considered in terms of its major components: heating, plumbing, and electrical systems. Each of these items will be examined in detail in future chapters. Attention will be given in this chapter to the portions of a building not visible upon completion of the ceiling, roof, and interior and exterior walls in order to give the reader an understanding of generally accepted construction practices. Emphasis, however, will be placed upon the visible interior and exterior parts of a completed dwelling that have a bearing on the soundness, state of repair, and safety of the dwelling both during intended use and in the event of a fire. These are some of the elements that the housing inspector must examine when making a thorough housing inspection.

II. Housing Construction Terminology

(Key to Component Parts Numbered in Figure 1)

A Fireplace

1. **Chimney** - A vertical masonry shaft of reinforced concrete or other approved non-combustible, heat resisting material enclosing one or more flues. It removes the products of combustion from solid, liquid, or gaseous fuel.

2. **Flue Liner** - The flue is the hole in the chimney. The liner, usually of terra cotta, protects the brick from harmful smoke gases.

3. **Chimney Cap** - This top is generally of concrete. It protects the brick from weather.

4. **Chimney Flashing** - Sheet-metal flashing provides a tight joint between chimney and roof.

5. **Firebrick** - An ordinary brick cannot withstand the heat of direct fire, and so special firebrick is used to line the fireplace.

6. **Ash Dump** - A trap door to let the ashes drop to a pit below, from where they may be easily removed.

7. **Cleanout Door** - The door to the ash pit or the bottom of a chimney through which the chimney can be cleaned.

8. **Chimney Breast** - The inside face or front of a fireplace chimney.

9. **Hearth** - The floor of a fireplace that extends into the room for safety purposes.

B Roof

10. **Ridge** - The top intersection of two opposite adjoining roof surfaces.

11. **Ridge Board** - The board that follows along under the ridge.

12. **Roof Rafters** - The structural members that support the roof.

13. **Collar Beam** - Really not a beam at all. A tie that keeps the roof from spreading. Connects similar rafters on opposite side of roof.

14. **Roof Insulation** - An insulating material (usually rock wool or fiberglas) in a blanket form placed between the roof rafters for the purpose of keeping a house warm in the winter, cool in the summer.

15. **Roof Sheathing** - The boards that provide the base for the finished roof.

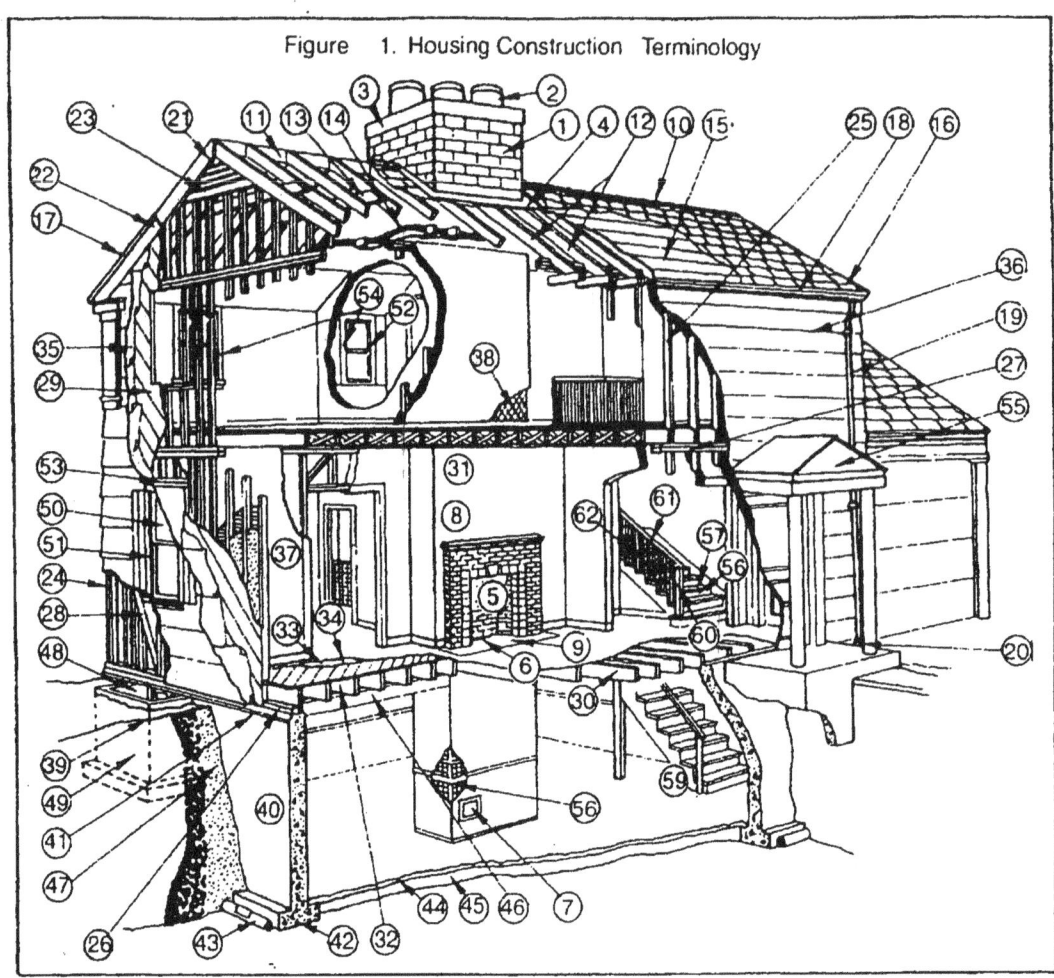

Figure 1. Housing Construction Terminology

16 **Roofing** - The wood, asphalt, or asbestos shingles - or tile, slate or metal - that form the outer protection against the weather.

17 **Cornice** - A decorative element made up of molded members usually placed at or near the top of an exterior or interior wall.

18 **Gutter** - The trough that gathers rainwater from a roof.

19 **Downspouts** - The pipe that leads the water down from the gutter.

20 **Storm Sewer Tile** - The underground pipe that receives the water from the downspouts and carries it to the sewer.

21 **Gable** - The triangular end of a building with a sloping roof.

22 **Barage Board** - The fascia or board at the gable just under the edge of the roof.

23 **Louvers** - A series of slanted slots arranged to keep out rain, yet allow ventilation.

C **Walls and Floors**

24 **Corner Post** - The vertical member at the corner of the frame, made up to receive inner and outer covering materials.

25 **Studs** - The vertical wood members of the house, usually 2 X 4's generally spaced every 16 inches.

26 **Sill** - The board that is laid first on the foundation, and on which the frame rests.

27 **Plate** - The board laid across the top ends of the studs to hold them even and rigid.

28 **Corner Bracing** - Diagonal strips to keep the frame square and plumb.

29 **Sheathing** - The first layer of outer wall covering nailed to the studs.

30 **Joist** - The structural members or beams that hold up the floor or ceiling, usually 2 X 10's or 2 X 12's spaced 16 inches apart.

31 **Bridging** - Cross bridging or solid. Members at the middle or third points of joist spans to brace one to the next and to prevent their twisting.

32 **Subflooring** - The rough boards that are laid over the joist. Usually laid diagonally.

33 **Flooring Paper** - A felt paper laid on the rough floor to stop air infiltration and, to some extent, noise.

34 **Finish Flooring** - Usually hardwood, of tongued and grooved strips.

35 **Building Paper** - Paper placed outside the sheathing, not as a vapor barrier, but to prevent water and air from leaking in. Building paper is also used as a tarred felt under shingles or siding to keep out moisture or wind.

36 **Beveled Siding** - Sometimes called clapboards, with a thick butt and a thin upper edge lapped to shed water.

37 **Wall Insulation** - A blanket of wool or reflective foil placed inside the walls.

38 **Metal Lath** - A mesh made from sheet metal onto which plaster is applied.

D **Foundation and Basement**

39 **Finished Grade Line** - The top of the ground at the foundation.

40 **Foundation Wall** - The wall of poured concrete (shown) or concrete blocks that rests on the footing and supports the remainder of the house.

41 **Termite Shield** - A metal baffle to prevent termites from entering the frame.

42 **Footing** - The concrete pad that carries the entire weight of the house upon the earth.

43 **Footing Drain Tile** - A pipe with cracks at the joints to allow underground water to drain in and away before it gets into the basement.

44 **Basement Floor Slab** - The 4- or 5-inch layer of concrete that forms the basement floor.

45 **Gravel Fill** - Placed under the slab to allow drainage and to guard against a damp floor.

46 **Girder** - A main beam upon which floor joists rest. Usually of steel, but also of wood.

47 **Backfill** - Earth, once dug out, that has been replaced and tamped down around the foundation.

48 **Areaway** - An open space to allow light and air to a window. Also called a light well.

49 **Area Wall** - The wall, of metal or concrete, that forms the open area.

E **Windows and Doors**

50 **Window** - An opening in a building for admitting light and air. It usually has a pane or panes of glass and is set in a frame or sash that is generally movable for opening and shutting.

51 **Window Frame** - The lining of the window opening.

52 **Window Sash** - The inner frame, usually movable, that holds the glass.

53 **Lintel** - The structural beam over a window or door opening.

54 **Window Casing** - The decorative strips surrounding a window opening on the inside.

F Stairs and Entry

55 **Entrance Canopy** - A roof extending over the entrance door.

56 **Furring** - Falsework or framework necessary to bring the outer surface to where we want it.

57 **Stair Tread** - The horizontal strip where we put our foot when we climb up or down the stairs.

58 **Stair Riser** - The vertical board connecting one tread to the next.

59 **Stair Stringer** - The sloping board that supports the ends of the steps.

60 **Newel** - The post that terminates the railing.

61 **Stair Rail** - The bar used for a handhold when we use the stairs.

62 **Balusters** - Vertical rods or spindles supporting a rail.

III. Structure

A Foundation

The word **foundation** is used to mean:
1. Construction below grade such as footings, cellar or basement walls.
2. The composition of the earth on which the building rests.
3. Special construction such as pilings and piers used to support the building.

The foundation bed may be composed of solid rock, sand, gravel, or unconsolidated sand or clay. Rock, sand, or gravel are the most reliable foundation materials. Unconsolidated sand and clay, though found in many sections of the country, are not as desirable, because they are subject to sliding and settling.

The footing (see Figure 2) distributes the weight of the building over a sufficient area of ground so as to ensure that the foundation walls will stand properly. Footings are usually constructed of a masonry-type material such as concrete; however, in the past wood and stone have been used. Some older houses have been constructed without footings.

Although it is usually difficult to determine the condition of a footing without excavating the foundation, a footing in a state of disrepair or lack of a footing will usually be indicated either by large

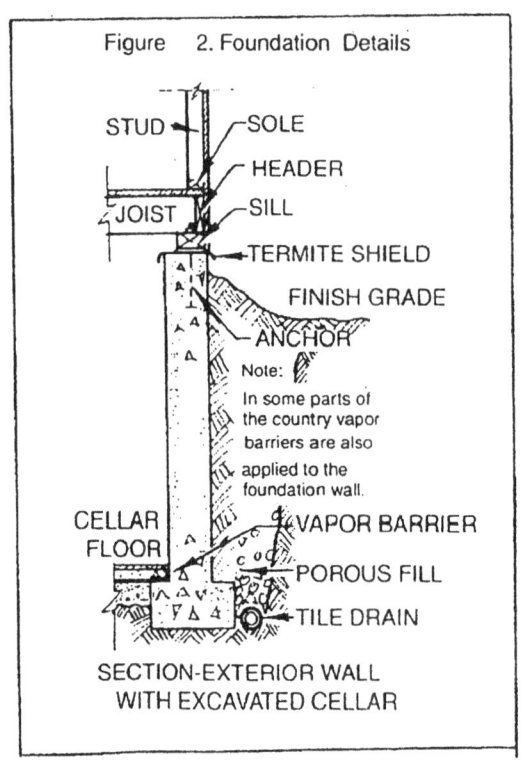

Figure 2. Foundation Details

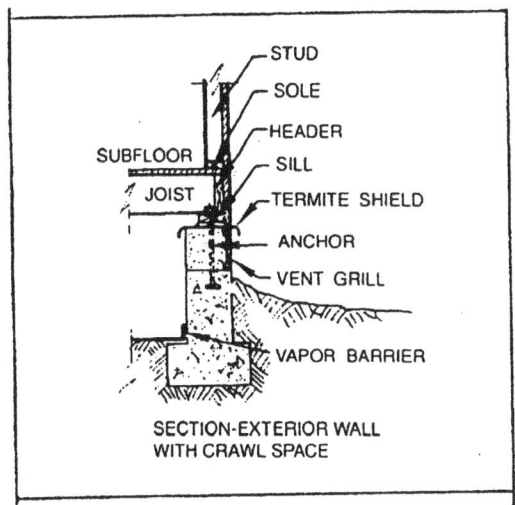

Section—Exterior Wall with Crawl Space

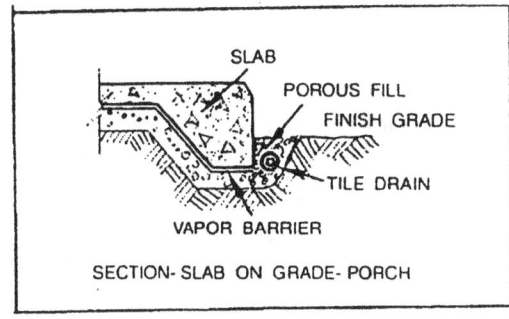

Section—Slab on Grade—Porch

cracks or by settlement in the foundation walls (see Figure 3).

Foundation wall cracks are usually diagonal, starting from the top, the bottom, or the end of the wall. Cracks that do not extend to at least one edge of the wall may not be caused by foundation problems. Such wall cracks may be due to other structural problems and should also be reported.

The foundation walls support the weight of the structure and transfer this weight to the footings. The foundation walls may be made of stone, brick, concrete, or concrete blocks and should be moisture proofed with either a membrane of water-proof material or a coating of portland cement mortar. The membrane may consist of plastic sheeting or a sandwich of standard roofing felt joined and covered with tar or asphalt. The purpose of waterproofing the foundation walls is to prevent water from penetrating the wall material and leaving the basement or cellar walls damp.

Holes in the foundation walls are a common finding in many old houses. These holes may be caused by missing bricks or blocks. Holes and cracks in a foundation wall are undesirable because they make a convenient entry for rats and other rodents and also indicate the possibility of further structural deterioration. These holes should not be confused with adequately installed vents in the foundation wall that permit ventilation and prevent moisture entrapment.

The basement or cellar floor should be made of concrete placed on at least 6 inches of gravel. The purpose of a concrete floor is to protect the basement or cellar from invasion by rodents or from flooding. The gravel distributes ground water movements under the concrete floor, reducing the possibility of the water's penetrating the floor. A waterproof membrane, such as plastic sheeting, should be laid before the concrete is placed for additional protection against flooding.

The basement or cellar floor should be gradually but uniformly sloped towards a drain or a series of drains from all directions. These drains permit the basement or cellar floor to be drained if it becomes flooded.

Evidence of ineffective waterproofing or moisture proofing will be indicated by water or moisture marks on the floor and walls.

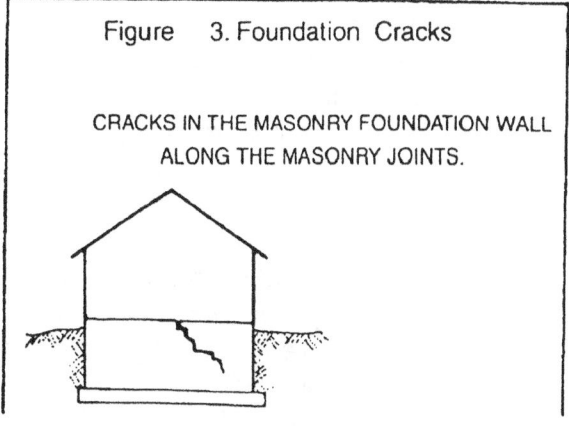

Figure 3. Foundation Cracks

CRACKS IN THE MASONRY FOUNDATION WALL ALONG THE MASONRY JOINTS.

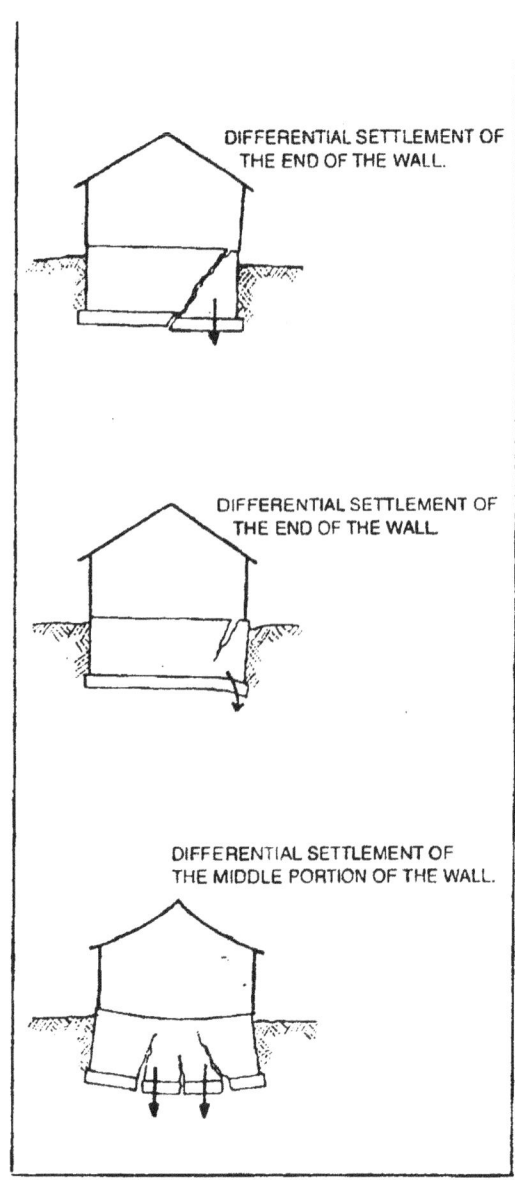

Cellar doors, hatchways, and basement windows should be weathertight and rodent proof. A hatchway can be inspected by standing at the lower portion with the doors closed; if daylight can be seen, the door probably needs repair.

B Framing

Many different types of house-framing systems are found in various sections of the country; however, the majority of the members in each framing system are the same. They include:

1. **Foundation Sills:** (see Figure 4 and 5). The purpose of the sill is to provide support or a bearing surface for the outside walls of the building. The sill is the first part of the frame to be placed and rests directly on the foundation wall. It is bolted to the foundation wall by sill anchors. It is good practice to protect the sill against termites by extending the foundation wall to at least 18 inches above the ground and using a non-corroding metal shield continuously around the outside top of the foundation wall.

2. **Flooring Systems:** (see Figure 5). The flooring system is composed of a combination of girders, joists, sub-flooring, and finished flooring that may be made up of concrete, steel, or wood. Joists are laid perpendicular to the girders, at about 16 inches on centers, and are the members to which the sub-flooring is attached. When the subfloor is wood, it may be nailed at either right angles or diagonally to the joists.

   As shown in Figure 5, a girder is a member that in certain framing systems supports the joists and is usually a larger section than the joists it supports. Girders are found in framing systems where there are no interior bearing walls or where the span between bearing walls is greater than the joists are capable of spanning. The most common application of a girder is to support the first floor in residences. Often a board known as a ledger is applied to the side of a wood girder or beam to form a ledge for the joists to rest upon. The girder, in turn, is supported by wood posts or steel "lally columns" which extend from the cellar or basement floor to the girder.

3. **Studs:** (see Figure 4 and 5). Wall studs are almost always 2 by 4

inches; studs 2 by 6 inches are occasionally used to provide a wall thick enough to permit the passage of waste pipes. There are two types of walls or partitions: bearing and nonbearing. A bearing wall is constructed at right angles to and supports the joists. A nonbearing wall or partition acts as a screen or enclosure; hence, the headers in it are often parallel to the joists of the floor above.

In general, studs like joists are spaced 16 inches on center. In light construction such as garages and summer cottages where plaster is omitted, or some other material is used for a wall finish, wider spacing on studs is common.

Openings for windows or doors must be framed in studs. This framing consists of horizontal members called "headers," and vertical members called "trimmers" (see Figure 1).

Since the vertical spaces between studs can act as flues to transmit flames in the event of a fire, "fire stops" are important in preventing or retarding fire from spreading through a building by way of air passages in walls, floors, and partitions. Fire stops are wood obstructions placed between studs or floor joists to prevent fire from spreading in these natural fluespaces.

4 **Interior Wall Finish:** Many types of materials are used for covering interior walls and ceilings, but the principal types are plaster and dry-wall construction. Plaster is a mixture, usually lime, sand, and water, applied in two or three coats to lath to form a hard-wall surface. Dry-wall finish is a material that requires little, if any, water for application. More specifically, dry-wall finish may be gypsum board, plywood, fiberboard, or wood in various sizes and forms.

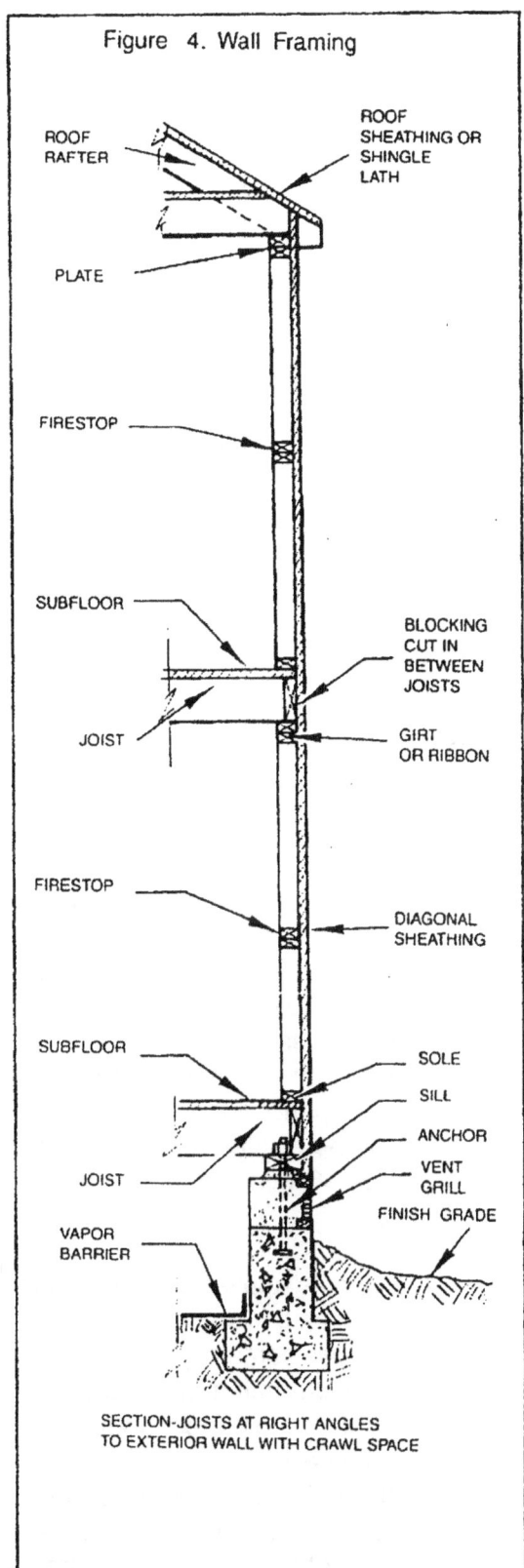

Figure 4. Wall Framing

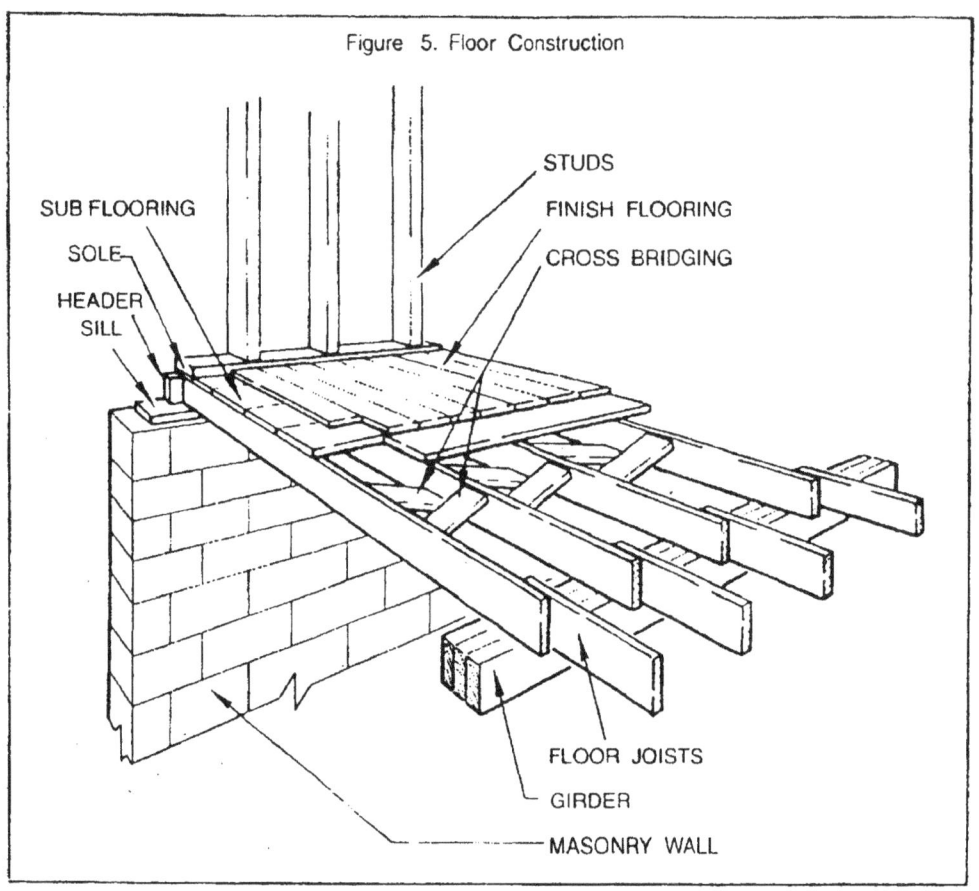

Figure 5. Floor Construction

Gypsum board is a sheet material composed of a gypsum filler faced with paper. Sheets are usually 4 feet wide and can be obtained in lengths up to 12 feet. In dry-wall construction, gypsum boards are fastened to the studs either vertically or horizontally and then painted. The edges along the length of the sheet are recessed to receive joint cement and tape.

A plaster finish requires a base upon which plaster can be spread. Wood lath at one time was the plaster base most commonly used, but today gypsum-board lath is more popular. It has paper faces with a gypsum filler. Such lath is 16 by 48 inches and 1/2 or 3/8 inches thick.

It is applied horizontally across the studs. Gypsum lath may be perforated to improve the bond and thus lengthen the time the plaster can remain intact when exposed to fire. The building codes in some cities require that gypsum lath be perforated. Expanded-metal lath may also be used as a plaster base. Expanded-metal lath consists of sheet metal slit and expanded to form openings to hold the plaster. Metal lath is usually 27 by 96 inches and is fastened to the studs.

Plaster is applied over the base to a minimum thickness of 1/2 inch. Because some drying may take place in wood-framing members after the house is completed, some shrinkage can be expected, which, in turn, may cause plaster cracks to develop around openings and in corners. Strips of lath imbedded in the plaster at these locations prevent cracks.

On the inside face of studs that form an exterior wall, vapor barriers are used to prevent condensation on the wall. The vapor barrier is an asphalted paper or metal foil through which moisture-laden air cannot travel.

5 **Stairways:** (see Figure 6). The general purpose of the standards for stairway dimensions is to ensure that there is adequate headroom, width, and uniformity in riser and tread size of every step to accommodate the expected traffic on each stairway safely.

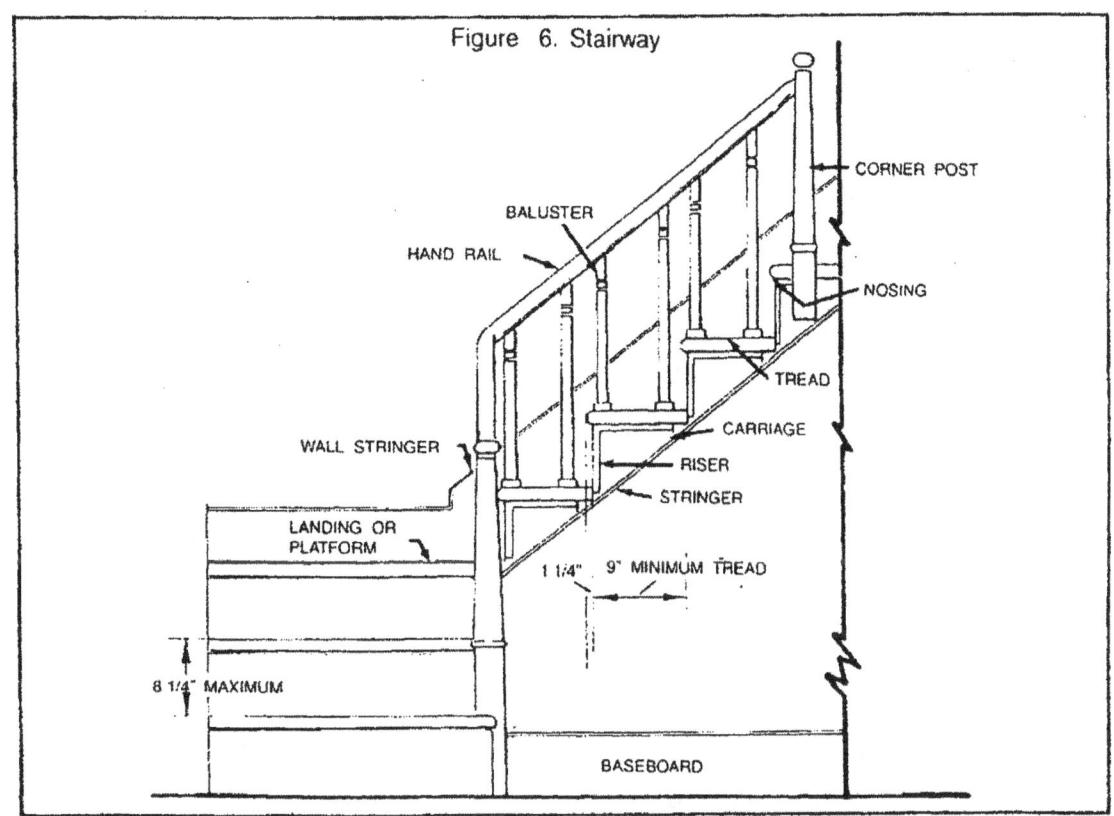

Figure 6. Stairway

Interior stairways should be not less than 44 inches in width. The width of a stairway may be reduced to 36 inches in one- and two-family dwellings. Stairs with closed risers should have maximum risers of 8 1/4 inches and a minimum tread of 9 inches plus 1 1/4-inch nosing. Basement stairs are often constructed with open risers. These stairs should have maximum risers of 8 1/4 inches and minimum treads of 9 inches plus 1/2-inch nosing. The headroom in all parts of the stair enclosure should be no less than 80 inches.

Exterior stairway dimensions should be the same as those called for in interior stairways, except that the headroom requirement does not apply.

6 **Windows:** The four general classifications of windows for residences are:

a Double-hung sash window that moves up or down, balanced by weights hung on chains or ropes, or springs on each side.

b Casement window sash is hinged at the side and can be hung so that it will swing outward or inward.

c Awning window - usually has two or more glass panes that are hinged at the top and swing about a horizontal axis.

d Sliding window - usually has two or more glass panes that slide past one another on a horizontal track.

The principal parts of a double-hung window (see Figure 4-7) are the lights, the top rail-framing members, bars or muntins that separate the lights, stiles - side-framing members, bottom rail, sash weights, and sash cords or chains. (All rails are horizontal, all stiles vertical.) The casement window's principal parts include: top and bottom rails, muntins, butt hinges, and jamb. All types of windows should open freely and close securely.

The exterior sill is the bottom projection of a window. The drip cap is a separate piece of wood projecting over the top of the window and is a component of the window casing.

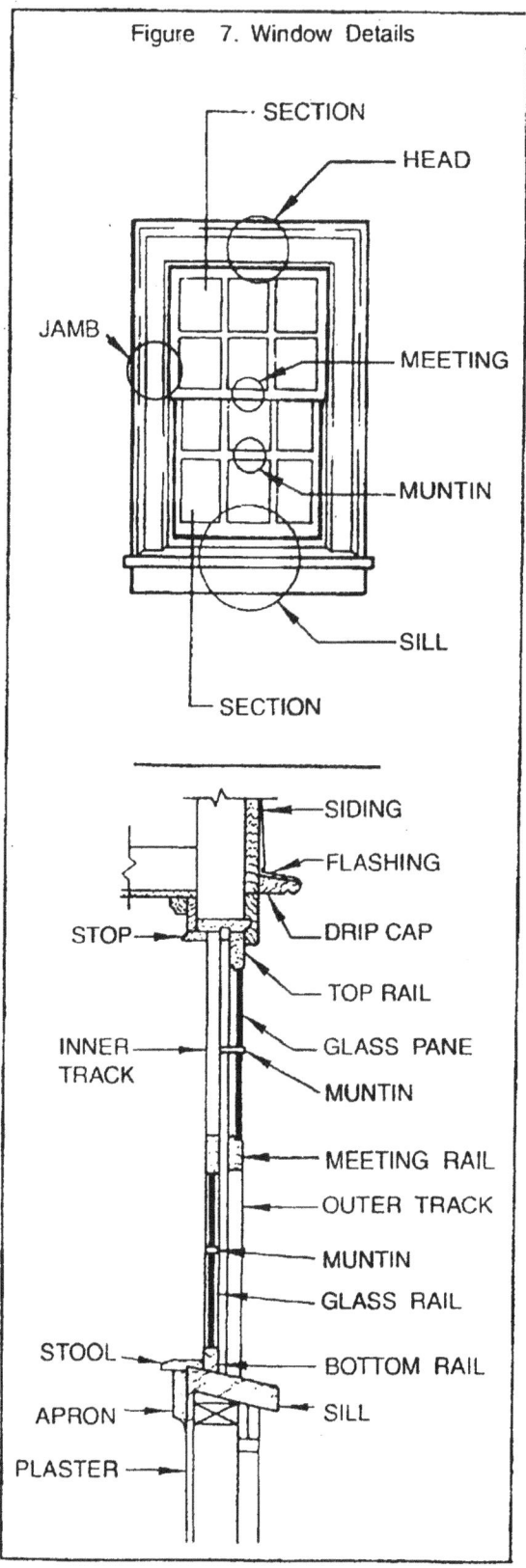

Figure 7. Window Details

7 **Doors:** There are many styles of doors both for exterior and interior use. Interior doors should offer a rea-

sonable degree of privacy. Exterior doors must, in addition to offering privacy, protect the interior of the structure from the elements. The various parts of a door have the same definitions as the corresponding parts of a window.

The most common types of doors are:

a **Batten door**: This consists of boards nailed together in various ways. The simplest is two layers nailed to each other at right angles, usually with each layer at 45 degrees to the vertical.

Another type of batten door consists of vertical boards nailed at right angles to several (two to four) cross strips called ledgers, with diagonal bracing members nailed between ledgers. If vertical members corresponding to ledgers are added at the sides, the verticals are called frames.

Batten doors are often found in cellars and other places where appearance is not a factor and economy is desired.

b **Flush doors**: Solid flush doors are perfectly flat, usually on both sides, although occasionally they are made flush on one side and paneled on the other. Flush doors sometimes are solid planking, but they are commonly veneered and possess a core of small pieces of white pine or other wood. These pieces are glued together with staggered end joints. Along the sides, top, and bottom are glued 3/4-inch edge strips of the same wood, used to create a smooth surface that can be cut or planed. The front and back faces are then covered with a 1/8-to 1/4-inch layer of veneer.

Solid flush doors may be used on both the interior and exterior.

c **Hollow-core doors**: These, like solid flush doors, are perfectly flat, but unlike solid doors, the core consists mainly of a grid of crossed wooden slats or some other type of grid construction. Faces are 3-ply plywood instead of one or two plies of veneer, and the surface veneer may be any species of wood, usually hardwood. The edges of the core are solid wood and are made wide enough at the appropriate places to accommodate locks and butts. Doors of this kind are considerably lighter than solid flush doors.

Hollow-core doors are usually used as interior doors.

d **Paneled doors**: Most doors are paneled, with most panels consisting of solid wood or plywood, either "raised" or "flat," although exterior doors frequently have one or more panels of glass, in which case they are called "lights." One or more panels may be employed although the number seldom exceeds eight. Paneled doors may be used both on the interior or exterior.

In addition to the various types of wood doors, metal is often used as a veneer or for the frame.

In general, the horizontal members are called rails and the vertical members are called stiles. Every door has a top and bottom rail, and some may have intermediate rails. There are always at least two stiles, one on each side of the door. The frame of a doorway is the portion to which the door is hinged. It consists of two side jambs and a head jamb, with an integral or attached stop against which the door closes.

Exterior door frames are ordinarily of softwood plank, with side rabbitted to receive the door in the same way as casement windows. At the foot is a sill, made of hardwood to withstand the wear of traffic, and sloped down and out to shed water.

Interior door frames are similar to exterior, except that they are often set directly on the hardwood flooring without a sill.

Building codes throughout the country call for doors in various locations within the structure to be fire resistant. These doors are often covered with metal or some other fire-resistant materials, and some are completely constructed of metal. Fire-resistant doors are usually located between a garage and a house, stairwells and hallways, all boiler rooms. The fire resistance rating required for various doors differs with local fire codes

C Roof Framing (see Figures 1, 4, 8, and 9)

Rafters serve the same purpose for the roof as joists do for floors, i.e., providing support for sheathing and roofing material. Rafters are usually spaced 20 inches on center.

1. **Collar Beam:** Collar beams are ties between rafters on opposite sides of the roof. If the attic is to be used for rooms, the collar beam may double as the ceiling joist.

2. **Purlin:** A purlin is the horizontal member that forms the support for the rafters at the intersection of the two slopes of a gambrel roof.

3. **Ridge Board:** A ridge board is a horizontal member against which the rafters rest at their upper ends; it forms a lateral tie to make them secure.

4. **Hip:** Like a ridge except that it slopes. The intersection of two adjacent, rather than two opposite, roof planes.

5. **Roof Boards:** The manner in which roof boards are applied depends upon the type of roofing material. Roof boards may vary from tongue-and-groove lumber to plywood panels.

6. **Dormer:** The term dormer window is applied to all windows in the roof of a building, whatever their size and shape.

D Exterior Walls and Trim (see Figure 4 and 9)

Exterior walls are enclosure walls whose purpose is to make the building weathertight. In most one- to three-story buildings they also serve as bearing walls. These walls may be made of many different materials.

Frequently used framed exterior walls appear to be of brick construction. In this situation, the brick is only one course thick and is called a brick veneer. It supports nothing but itself and is kept from toppling by ties connected to the frame wall.

In frame construction the base material of the exterior walls is called "sheathing." The sheathing material may be square-edge, shiplap, or tongue-and-groove boards.

In recent construction there has been a strong trend toward the use of plywood or composition panels.

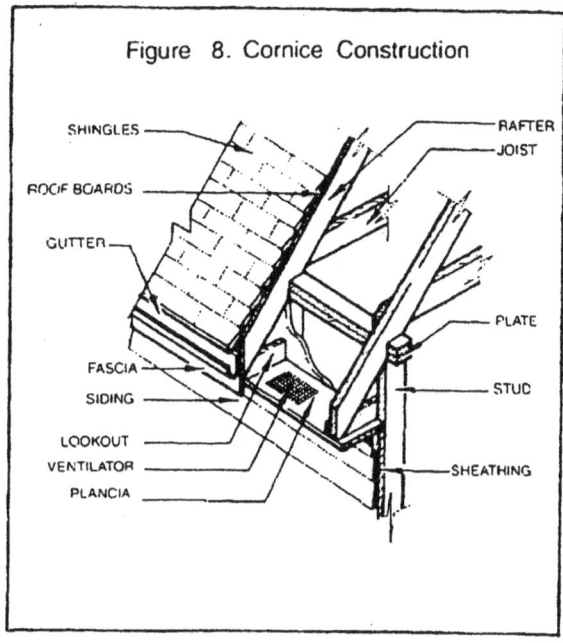

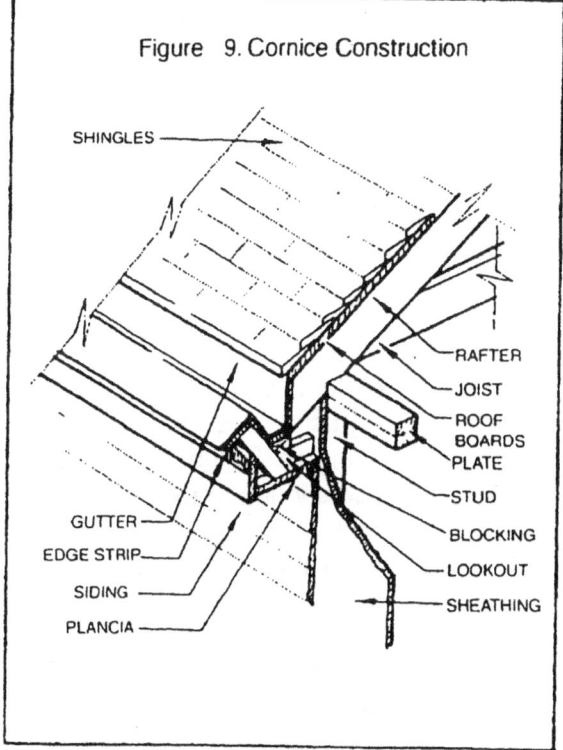

Sheathing, in addition to serving as a base course for the finished siding material, stiffens the frame to resist sway caused by wind. It is for this reason that sheathing has been applied diagonally on frame buildings.

The finished siding may be clapboard, shingles, aluminum, brick asphalt, wood, and so forth, or a combination thereof. Good aluminum siding has a backer board that serves as added insulation and affords rigidity to the siding. Projecting cornices are a decorative trim found at the top of the building's roofline. A parapet wall is that part of the masonry wall that extends up and beyond the roofline and is capped with a noncombustible material. It helps prevent spread of fire, provides a rest for fire department ladders, and helps prevent people on the roof from falling off.

Many types of siding, shingles, and other exterior coverings are applied over the sheathing. Wood siding, cedar, and other wood shingles or shakes, clapboard, common siding (called bevel siding), composition siding, asbestos, cement shingles, asbestos-cement siding, and the aforementioned aluminum siding are commonly used for exterior coverings. Clapboards and common siding differ only in the length of the pieces. Clapboards are 4 feet long while panel siding comes in lengths from 6 to 16 feet. Composition siding is made of felt and asphalt, which are often shaped to look like brick. Asbestos and cement shingles are rigid and produce a covering that is fire resistant. Cedar wood shingles are also manufactured with a backer board that gives insulation and fire-resistant qualities. Asbestos cement siding made of asbestos fiber and portland cement has good fire-resistant qualities and is a rigid covering.

E   Roof Coverings (Flexible Material Class)

   1 **Asphalt Shingle:** The principal damage to asphalt shingle roofs is caused by the action of strong winds on shingles nailed too high. Usually the shingles affected by winds are those in the four or five courses nearest the ridge and in the area

extending about 5 feet down from the edge or rake of the roof.

2. **Asphalt Built-up Roofs:** These may be un-surfaced, the coating of bitumen being exposed directly to the weather, or they may be surfaced having slag or gravel imbedded in the bituminous coating. The use of surfacing material is desirable as a protection against wind damage and the elements. This type of roof should have enough pitch to drain water readily.

3. **Coal Tar Pitch Built-up Roofs:** This type roof must be surfaced with slag or gravel. Coal tar pitch built-up roof should always be used on deck pitched less than 1/2 inch per foot; that is, where waler may collect and stand. This type roof should be inspected on completion, 6 months later, and then at least once a year, preferably in the fall. When the top coating of bitumen shows damage or has become badly weathered, it should be renewed (rigid material class).

4. **Slate Roofs:** The most common problem with slate roofs is the replacement of broken slates. Roofs of this type normally render long service with little or no repair.

5. **Tile Roofs:** Replacement of broken shingle tiles is the main maintenance problem. This is one of the most expensive roofing materials. It requires very little maintenance and gives long service.

6. **Copper Roofs:** Usually are of 16-ounce copper sheeting and applied to permanent structures. When properly installed, they require practically no maintenance or repair. Proper installation allows for expansion and contraction with changes in temperature.

7. **Galvanized Iron Roofs:** Maintenance is done principally by removing rust and keeping roof well painted. Leaks can be corrected by re-nailing, caulking, or replacing all or part of the sheet or sheets in disrepair.

8. **Wood Shingle Roofs:** The most important factors of this type roof are its pitch and exposure, the character of wood, kind of nails used, and preservative treatment given shingles. Creosote and coal tar preservative are satisfactory for both treated and untreated shingles.

9. **Flashing:** Valleys in roofs that are formed by the junction of two downward slopes may be finished, open, or closed. In a closed valley the slates, tiles, or shingles of one side meet those of the other, and the flashing below them may be comparatively narrow. In an open valley, the flashing, which may be made of zinc, copper, or aluminum, is laid in a continuous strip, extending 12 to 18 inches on each side of the valley, while the tiles or slates do not come within 4 to 6 inches of it.

   The ridges built up on a sloping roof where it runs down against a vertical projection, like a chimney or a skylight, should be weather-proofed with flashing.

   Metal flashings are generally used with slate, tile, metal, and wood shingles. Failure of roof flashing is usually due to exposed nails that have come loose. The loose nails allow the flashing to lift with leakage resulting.

10. **Gutters and Leaders:** Gutters and leaders should be of noncombustible materials. They should be securely fastened to the structure and spill into a storm sewer if the neighborhood is so provided. When there is no storm sewer, a concrete or stone block placed on the ground beneath the leader prevents water from eroding the lawn. This store

block is called a splash block. Gutters will not become plugged if protected against clogging of leaves and twigs. Gutters should be checked every spring and fall and then cleaned out when necessary.

IV. Discussion of Inspection Techniques

A serious building defect may often be observed during a housing inspector's routine examination. In many cases it is beyond the scope of the housing inspector's background to analyze the underlying causes and to recommend a course of action that will facilitate repair in an efficient and economical manner. In situations such as this, it is important that the inspector realize his limitations and refer the matter to the proper expert.

A prime example of a technically complex situation that a housing inspector might observe is a leaning, buckling, or bulging foundation or bearing wall. This problem may be the result of a number of hidden or interacting problems. For example, it may be the result of differential building settlement or failure of a structural beam or girder. It is beyond the scope of the housing inspector's responsibilities to discover the cause of the defect, but it is his responsibility to note the problem and refer it to the proper authority. In this case the proper authority would be a building inspector.

In the aforementioned situation where a bulging foundation wall was discovered, this would obviously constitute a violation of the housing ordinance and should be written up as such by the housing inspector. Since the housing inspector is generally not qualified to determine whether the house should be evacuated because it is in danger of imminent collapse, he should seek the advice of a building inspector.

A question that frequently arises is *which violations should be referred to an expert?* Needless to say, circumstances that obviously fall within the jurisdiction of another department should be referred to the department. The housing inspector should discuss with his supervisor any situation in which he feels inadequate to make a decision. In all cases the inspector should inform his supervisor before referring a problem to another agency or expert.

Another reason for referral to other departments is that when a remedial action is completed the other department will be in a better position to determine whether the job is satisfactory.

This principle of referral should be applied to every portion of the inspection, whether it deals with health, heating, plumbing, gas, or electrical as well as structural defects.

Certain structural items should be recognized as unsafe by the housing inspector. For example, a beam that has sagged or slanted may cause a portion of or an entire floor to sag or slope. Where a sagging or sloping floor is found, examine the ceiling of the room below or the basement for a broken or dropped girder or joist.

Doors and windows that are out of level will not close completely. It may be possible to see outside light through openings around window rails and door jambs. If an inspector detects such a situation, the condition of the supporting girders, girts, posts, and studs should be questioned, since this condition is evidence that some of these members may be termite infested or rotted and may be causing the outside wall to sag. Glass panes in doors and windows should be replaced if found to be broken or missing. Windows should also be checked for proper operation, and items such as broken sash cords or chains noted.

If the roof of the structure appears to be sagging, the inspector should make a special effort to examine the rafters, purlin, collar beams, and ridge boards if these members are exposed as in unfinished attics. The condition of the roof boards may be examined while he is in the attic. If light can be seen between these boards the roof is unsound. Evidence of a leaking roof will be indicated by loose plaster or peeling or stained paint and wall paper. Areas of the roof where flashing occurs, such as around the chimney, are frequent origins of roof leaks. It is essential that the leak be found and repaired, not only to prevent the entrance of moisture into the building, but also to prevent the loosening of the plaster, rotting of timbers, and extension of damage to the remainder of the house.

Gutters and rain leaders should be placed around the entire building to insure proper drainage of water. This will lessen the possibility of seepage of water through siding and window frames, and entrance of water into the cellar or basement. Lack of or leaking gutters may result in rotting of the siding or erosion of the exposed portion of the cellar or basement walls. This situation commonly exists where the mortar between bricks or concrete blocks in foundation walls is found to be heavily eroded. Gutters should be free from dirt and leaves.

The exterior siding should be in sound, weathertight condition. Peeled or worn paint on wood siding will expose the bare wood to the elements and result in splitting and warping of siding. This condition will eventually lead to the entrance of rain water with resultant rotting of the sheathing and studs as well as inside dampness and falling plaster. Sound and painted siding will prevent major repairs and expenses in the future. This condition will often be particularly prevalent on the north face of the structure.

Roof and chimneys should be inspected for tilting, missing bricks, deterioration of flashing, and pointing of chimney bricks. In addition, roof covering should be checked for broken spots and missing shingles or tiles. Roof doors should be metal clad, self-closing, tight fitting, and unlockable. The roof should also be examined for weather-tightness and broken TV antennas.

Porches should be carefully examined for weakened treads, missing or cracked boards, holes, and holes covered with tin plates, railing rigidity, missing posts, handrail rigidity, condition of the columns that support the porch roof, and the condition of the porch roof itself. The open section beneath the porch should be inspected for broken lattice-work. Check under the porch for accumulation of dirt and debris that can offer a harborage for vermin and rodents.

Loose plaster and missing or peeling wallpaper or paint should be noted. Bugs and cockroaches eat the paste from the wallpaper while leaving behind loose paper.

The basic parts of a stairway that a housing inspector should be able to identify correctly are the following:

A   Riser

B   Tread

C   Nosing

D   Handrail

E   Balustrade and Balusters, the Vertical Members that Support the Handrail, and

F   The Soffit, Underpart of the Stairway.

In the examination of a stairway (be careful to turn the light on) initially check the underside, if visible, to see if it is intact. Then proceed slowly up the stairs placing full weight on each tread and checking for loose, wobbling, or uneven treads and risers. Regardless of the size of the treads or risers they should all be of uniform size. For all stairs that rise 3 or more feet, a handrail should be present and in a sound and rigid condition.

Any fireplace should conform to the requirements of the local code. An unused fireplace that has its opening covered with wallpaper or other material should have a solid seal behind the paper. Operable fireplaces should have a workable damper and a fire screen, and should be clean.

Garages and accessory structures should be inspected in the same manner as the main building.

Sidewalks and driveways, whether constructed of flagstone, concrete, or asphalt, should be checked for creaking, buckling, and other conditions dangerous to pedestrian travel.

Stone, brick, or concrete steps should be inspected for cracks, deterioration, and pointing.

Fences should be in a sound condition and painted. Fire escapes should be checked for paint condition, loose or broken treads and rails, proper operating condition, and proper connection to the house.

V. Noise as an Environmental Stress

People feel comfortable in an environment with a low-level, soothing, steady, unobstrusive level of sound, typical of the natural undisturbed environment. All of us have experienced the anguish that noise can cause, whether it be noise from a neighbor's television, the grinding of truck gears while asleep, the persistent whine of a fan motor, or the sound of children racing down the halls. These annoyances experienced in the home are producing public demands for noise control legislation.

Not only is noise disturbing, but studies also indicate that extreme noise can cause deafness and perhaps interfere with other bodily functions.

While few existing housing ordinances contain enforceable noise provisions, noise problems must be considered by the building inspector because they intimately affect and are affected by his decisions. As a housing inspector, you can help residents by suggesting corrective noise measures that can be taken; you can refer them to agencies, if needed, for corrective action; you can help them to understand that their noisy environment can place limitations on their behavior, capabilities, and satisfaction with their home.

Noise is unwanted sound. Noise can travel through air or through the building structure. The first stage of noise control is the control of sound at its source. If attempts to quiet the source are not completely successful, then other, more expensive corrective measures will be required.

Although a visual examination of a dwelling may detect some sources of noise leaks (see Figure 10) such as wide gaps or cracks at ceiling, floor, or adjoining wall edges, it is usually inadequate since it fails to detect sources of noise leaks hidden from the eye. A far more effective test is to be alert for the operation of some noisy device like a vacuum cleaner in a closed room and listen near the other side of the wall for any noise leakage. The ear is a reasonably good sensing device. If a noise leak is noticed, the partition may be surveyed at critical points with a bright flashlight while an observer looks for light leakage in a darkened room on the other side. Detection of any light leakage in the darkened room will signify a noise leak.

Noise carried as vibration by a building structure is called structure-borne noise. Detecting structure-borne noise caused by the operation of mechanical equipment is somewhat more difficult (see Figure 11). With noisy equipment in operation, the inspector can sometimes locate noise leaks or structure-borne noise paths by conducting similar hearing tests along with pressing the ear against various room surfaces or using fingertips to sense the vibration of these surfaces.

A Airborne Noise

The sources of airborne noise that cause the most frequent disturbances in the home are audio instruments such as televisions, radios, phonographs, or pianos; adults and children speaking loudly, singing, crying and shouting; household appliances such as garbage disposals, dishwashers, vacuum cleaners, clothes washers, and dryers; plumbing noises such as pipes knocking, toilets flushing, and water running.

The disturbing influences of airborne noise are generally limited to the areas near the noise source. For example, a phonograph may cause annoyance in rooms of a neighbor's apartment adjacent to the phonograph but rarely in rooms farther removed unless doors or passageways are left open. Sound absorption materials such as carpeting, acoustical tile, drapery, and upholstered furniture in the intervening rooms may often provide a significant reduction in the disturbing noise before it reaches rooms where quiet is desired.

Under no conditions should sound-absorptive materials be used on the surfaces of walls and ceilings for the sole purpose of preventing the transmission of sound as structure-borne noise. To do so would be a complete waste of effort. To illustrate, imagine the noise conducted by a wall constructed solely of drapery or acoustical tile attached to studs. The noise level in the room would be reduced, but sound produced in the room would pass through the wall to adjoining rooms with little, if any, reduction in noise level. Sound absorptive materials should be used in and near areas of high noise levels to limit airborne noise at the source of the noise and reduce the effects of noise along corridors.

The transmission of noise from one completely enclosed room to an adjoining room separated by a partition wall may be either direct transmission through the wall, indirect transmission through other walls, ceilings, and floors common to both rooms, or through corridors adjacent to such rooms.

In some older wood frame houses, the open troughs between studs and joists are efficient sound transmission paths. This noise transmission by indirect paths is known as "flanking transmission" (see Figure 10 and 11). In addition to the flanking paths, there may be noise leaks particularly along the ceiling, floor, and sidewall edges of the wall. In order to obtain the highest sound insulation performance, a partition wall must be of airtight construction. Care must be exercised to seal all openings, gaps, holes, joints, and penetrations of piping and conduits with a nonsetting caulking compound. Even hairline cracks, particularly at adjoining wall, floor, and ceiling edges, transmit a substantially greater amount of noise than would normally be expected on the basis of the size of the crack.

Figure 10. Flanking Transmission of Airborne Noise

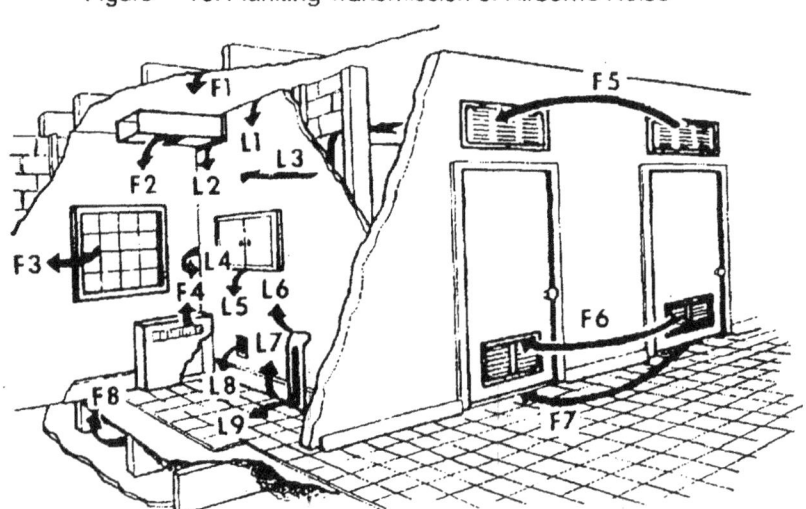

FLANKING NOISE PATHS	NOISE LEAKS
F1 Open plenums over walls, false ceilings	L1 Poor seal at ceiling edges
F2 Unbaffled duct runs	L2 Poor seal around duct penetrations
F3 Outdoor path, window to window	L3 Poor mortar joints, porous masonry block
F4 Continuous unbaffled inductor Units	L4 Poor seal at sidewall, filler panel, etc.
F5 Hall path, open vents	L5 Back-to-back cabinets, poor workmanship
F6 Hall path, louvered doors	L6 Holes, gaps at wall penetrations
F7 Hall path, openings under doors	L7 Poor seal at floor edges
F8 Open troughs in floor-ceiling structure	L8 Back-to-back electrical outlets
	L9 Holes, gaps at floor penetrations

Other points to consider are these: leaks are (a) batten strip A/O post connections of prefabricated walls, (b) under-floor pipe or service chases, (c) recessed, spanning light fixtures, (d) ceiling and floor cover plates of movable walls, (e) unsupported A/O unbacked wall-board joints (f) edges and backing of built-in cabinets and appliances, (g) prefabricated, hollow metal, exterior curtain walls.

It is often helpful to use one sound to drown out another disturbing noise; for example, music on the radio can be used to drown out the noise of traffic. The use of sound to drown out noise is particularly useful in masking noises that occur infrequently, such as accelerating or braking vehicles, periodic mechanical equipment noise, barking dogs, laughter, or shouting.

B **Structure-Borne Noise**

Structure-borne noise occurs when wall, floor, or other building elements are set into vibration by direct contact with vibrating sources such as mechanical equipment or domestic appliances. A small, vibrating pipe firmly attached to a plywood or gypsum wall panel will amplify the vibration noise. An illustration of this amplification of structure-borne noise is provided by the sound board of a piano. The major sources of structure-borne noise are the impact of walking on wood floors or of slamming doors, plumbing system noises, heating and air-conditioning system noises, noise from mechanical equipment or appliances, and vibration from sources outside the building. If the vibration is severe enough, it may have adverse effects not only on the occupants of a building but also on the building structure. Household appliances such as refrigerators, washing machines, sewing machines, clothes dryers, televisions, and pianos should be vibration isolated from the floor by means of rubber mounts placed under them if disturbing structure-borne noise is to be avoided. Residents should also be cautioned against locating these noise sources along party walls and in particular against mounting these appliances and kitchen cabinets directly on party walls so that the walls act as sounding boards in adjoining apartments. Window air-conditioners should be completely vibration isolated from the surrounding window frame by rubber gaskets and padding. The importance of isolating a vibrating source from the structure in the control of equipment noise cannot be overemphasized.

Another source of disturbing structure-borne noise is squeaking of wood floors. Some squeaks can be eliminated by lubricating the tongues of wood floor boards with mineral oil applied sparingly to the openings between adjacent boards. Loose finish flooring may be securely fastened to subflooring by surface nailing into the

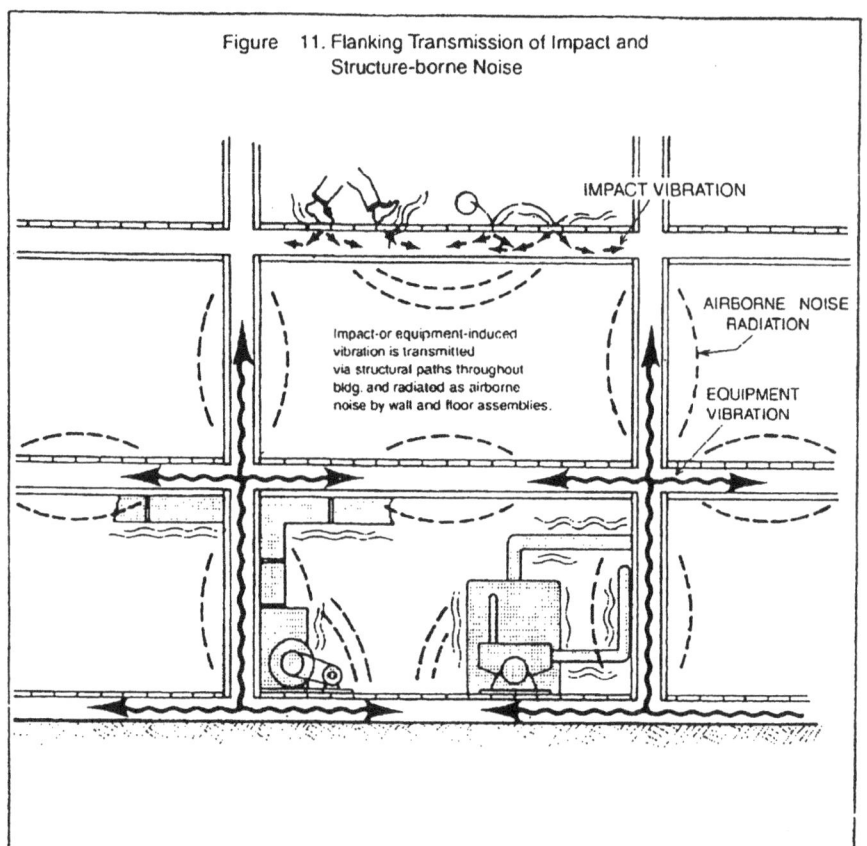

Figure 11. Flanking Transmission of Impact and Structure-borne Noise

subfloor and preferably the joists. Ring-type nails or sawtooth staples properly spaced should be used in nailing finish flooring to subflooring. In an exposed joist structure, where finish flooring is warped, driving screws up through the subfloor and into the finish floor will be effective in drawing the layers of flooring tightly together to reduce noise.

Of course, noise caused by the impact of walking or scraping can be substantially reduced by the use of carpets. In the case of door slams, the impact noise may be eliminated by the use of door closers or rubber bumpers.

The noisy hammering of a plumbing system is usually caused by the sudden interruption of water-flow, for example, by a quick closing or opening of a tap.

Air chambers can be built into the plumbing system to reduce water hammer. The air pockets, rubber inserts, or spring elements in air chambers act to reduce noise. Air chambers are explained in Chapter 6.

Defective, loose, or worn valve stems create intense chattering of the plumbing system. The defective device can frequently be found without difficulty, since immediate use of the device causes the vibration, which generally occurs at some low-flow-velocity setting and diminishes or disappears at a higher flow setting. For example, if a chattering noise occurs when a particular faucet or tap is opened partially and diminishes when fully opened, the faucet more than likely has some loose or defective parts and should be repaired.

Noise can be a very complex problem. The housing inspector is not expected to be an acoustics expert. Nor is he expected to be able to analyze and solve the noise problems that an acoustics consultant would normally handle. He can, however, help teach the public that the annoyances and stress caused by noise can be partially alleviated by a simple awareness of common noise problems found in many residences.

Although the housing inspector is not an expert in the fields of zoning, plumbing, building, and electrical systems, he should be familiar with the applicable code in each of the respective fields. Familiarization with these codes will better enable him to recognize violations.

PLUMBING ELEMENTS OF A HOUSING INSPECTION

CONTENTS

	PAGE
I. Background Factors	1
II. Definitions	1
III. Main Features of an Indoor Plumbing System	3
IV. Elements of a Plumbing System	3

PLUMBING ELEMENTS OF A HOUSING INSPECTION

Plumbing may be defined as practice, materials, and fixtures used in the installation, maintenance, and alteration of all piping, fixtures, appliances, and appurtenances in connection with sanitary or storm drainage facilities, the venting system, and the public or private water supply systems. **Plumbing** does not include the trade of drilling water wells, installing water softening equipment, or the business of manufacturing or selling plumbing fixtures, appliances, equipment, or hardware. A plumbing system consists of three separate parts: an adequate potable water supply system; a safe, adequate drainage system; and ample fixtures and equipment.

I. Background Factors

The generalized inspector of housing is concerned with a safe water supply system, an adequate drainage system, and ample and proper fixtures and equipment. This chapter covers the major features of a residential plumbing system and the basic plumbing terms the inspector must know and understand to identify properly housing code violations involving plumbing and the more complicated defects that he will refer to the appropriate agencies.

II. Definitions

1. **Air Chambers** — Air Chambers are pressure absorbing devices that eliminate water hammer. They should be installed as close as possible to the valves or faucet and at the end of long runs of pipe.

2. **Air Gap (Drainage System)** — The unobstructed vertical distance through the free atmosphere between the outlet of a water pipe and the flood level rim of the receptacle into which it is discharging.

3. **Air Gap (Water Distribution System)** — The unobstructed vertical distance through the free atmosphere between the lowest opening from any pipe or faucet supplying water to a tank, plumbing fixture, or other device and the flood level rim of the receptacle.

4. **Air Lock** — An air lock is a bubble of air which restricts the flow of water in a pipe.

5. **Backflow** — Backflow is the flow of water or other liquids, mixtures, or substances into the distributing pipes of a potable water supply from any source or sources other than the intended source. Back siphonage is one type of backflow.

6. **Back Siphonage** — Back siphonage is the flowing back of used, contaminated, or polluted water from a plumbing fixture or vessel into a potable water supply due to a negative pressure in the pipe.

7. **Branch** — A branch is any part of the piping system other than the main, riser, or stack.

8. **Branch Vent** — A vent connecting one or more individual vents with a vent stack.

9. **Building Drain** — The building (house) drain is the part of the lowest piping of a drainage system that receives the discharge from soil, waste, or other drainage pipes inside the walls of the building (house) and conveys it to the building sewer beginning 3 feet outside the building wall.

10. **Cross Connection** — Any physical connection or arrangement between two otherwise separate piping systems, one of which contains potable water and the other either water of unknown or questionable safety or steam, gas, or chemical whereby there may be a flow from one system to the other, the direction of flow depending on the pressure differential between the two systems. (See Backflow and Back siphonage.)

11. **Disposal Field** — An area containing a series of one or more trenches lined with coarse aggregate and conveying the effluent from the septic tank through vitrified clay pipe or

perforated, non-metallic pipe, laid in such a manner that the flow will be distributed with reasonable uniformity into natural soil.

12 **Drain** — A drain is any pipe that carries waste water or water-borne waste in a building (house) drainage system.

13 **Flood Level Rim** — The top edge of a receptacle from which water overflows.

14 **Flushometer Valve** — A device that discharges a predetermined quantity of water to fixtures for flushing purposes and is closed by direct water pressures.

15 **Flush Valve** — A device located at the bottom of the tank for flushing water closets and similar fixtures.

16 **Grease Trap** — See Interceptor

17 **Hot Water** — Hot water means potable water that is heated to at least 120°F and used for cooking, cleaning, washing dishes, and bathing.

18 **Insanitary** — Contrary to sanitary principles — injurious to health.

19 **Interceptor** — A device designed and installed so as to separate and retain deleterious, hazardous, or undesirable matter from normal wastes and permit normal sewage or liquid wastes to discharge into the drainage system by gravity.

20 **Leader** — An exterior drainage pipe for conveying storm water from roof or gutter drains to the building storm drain, combined building sewer, or other means of disposal.

21 **Main Vent** — The principal artery of the venting system, to which vent branches may be connected.

22 **Main Sewer** — See Public Sewer.

23 **Pneumatic** — The word pertains to devices making use of compressed air as in pressure tanks boosted by pumps.

24 **Potable Water** — Water having no impurities present in amounts sufficient to cause disease or harmful physiological effects and conforming in its bacteriological and chemical quality to the requirements of the Public Health Service drinking water standards or meeting the regulations of the public health authority having jurisdiction.

25 **P & T (Pressure and Temperature) Relief Valve** — A safety valve installed on a hot water storage tank to limit temperature and pressure of the water.

26 **P Trap** — A trap with a vertical inlet and a horizontal outlet.

27 **Public Sewer** — A common sewer directly controlled by public authority.

28 **Relief Vent** — An auxiliary vent that permits additional circulation of air in or between drainage and vent systems.

29 **Septic Tank** — A watertight receptacle that receives the discharge of a building's sanitary drain system or part thereof and is designed and constructed so as to separate solid from the liquid, digest organic matter through a period of detention, and allow the liquids to discharge into the soil outside of the tank through a system of open-joint or perforated piping, or through a seepage pit.

30 **Sewerage System** — A sewerage system comprises all piping, appurtenances, and treatment facilities used for the collection and disposal of sewage, except plumbing inside and in connection with buildings served, and the building drain.

31 **Soil Pipe** — The pipe that directs the sewage of a house to the receiving sewer, building drain, or building sewer.

32 **Soil Stack** — The vertical piping that terminates in a roof vent and carries off the vapors of a plumbing system.

33 **Stack Vent** — An extension of a solid or waste stack above the highest horizontal drain connected to the stack. Sometimes called a waste vent or a soil vent.

34 **Storm Sewer** — A sewer used for conveying rain water, surface water, condensate, cooling water, or similar liquid waste.

35 Trap — A trap is a fitting or device that provides a liquid seal to prevent the emission of sewer gases without materially affecting the flow of sewage or waste water through it.

36 Vacuum Breaker — A device to prevent backflow (back siphonage) by means of an opening through which air may be drawn to relieve negative pressure (vacuum).

37 Vent Stack — The vertical vent pipe installed to provide air circulation to and from the drainage system and that extends through one or more stories.

38 Water Hammer — The loud thump of water in a pipe when a valve or faucet is suddenly closed.

39 Water Service Pipe — The pipe from the water main or other sources of potable water supply to the water-distributing system of the building served.

40 Water Supply System — The water supply system consists of the water service pipe, the water-distributing pipes, the necessary connecting pipes, fittings, control valves, and all appurtenances in or adjacent to the building or premises.

41 Wet Vent — A vent that receives the discharge of waste other than from water closets.

42 Yoke Vent — A pipe connecting upward from a soil or waste stack to a vent stack for the purpose of preventing pressure changes in the stacks.

III. Main Features of an Indoor Plumbing System

The primary functions of the plumbing system within the house are as follows:

1 To bring an adequate and potable supply of hot and cold water to the users of the dwelling.

2 To drain all waste water and sewage discharged from these fixtures into the public sewer, or private disposal system.

It is, therefore, very important that the housing inspector familiarize himself fully with all elements of these systems so that he may recognize inadequacies of the structure's plumbing as well as other code violations. In order to aid the inspector in understanding the plumbing system, a series of drawings and diagrams has been included at the end of this chapter.

IV. Elements of a Plumbing System

A Supply System

1 Water Service: The piping of a house service line should be as short as possible. Elbows and bends should be kept to a minimum since these reduce the pressure and therefore the supply of water to fixtures in the house.

The house service line should also be protected from freezing. The burying of the line under 4 feet of soil is a commonly accepted depth to prevent freezing. This depth varies, however, across the country from north to south. The local or state plumbing code should be consulted for the recommended depth in your area of the country.

A typical house service installation is pictured in Figure 1.

The materials used for a house service may be copper, cast iron, steel or wrought iron. The connections used should be compatible with the type of pipe used.

a Corporation stop — The corporation stop is connected to the water main. This connection is usually made of brass and can be connected to the main by use of a special tool without shutting off the municipal supply. The valve incorporated in the corporation stop permits the pressure to be maintained in the main while the service to the building is completed.

b Curb stop — The curb stop is a similar valve used to isolate the building from the main for repairs, nonpayment of water bills, or flooded basements.

Since the corporation stop is usually under the street and would necessitate breaking the pavement to reach the valve, the curb stop is used as the isolation valve.

c Curb stop box — The curb stop box is an access box to the curb stop for opening and closing the valve. A long-handled wrench is used to reach the valve.

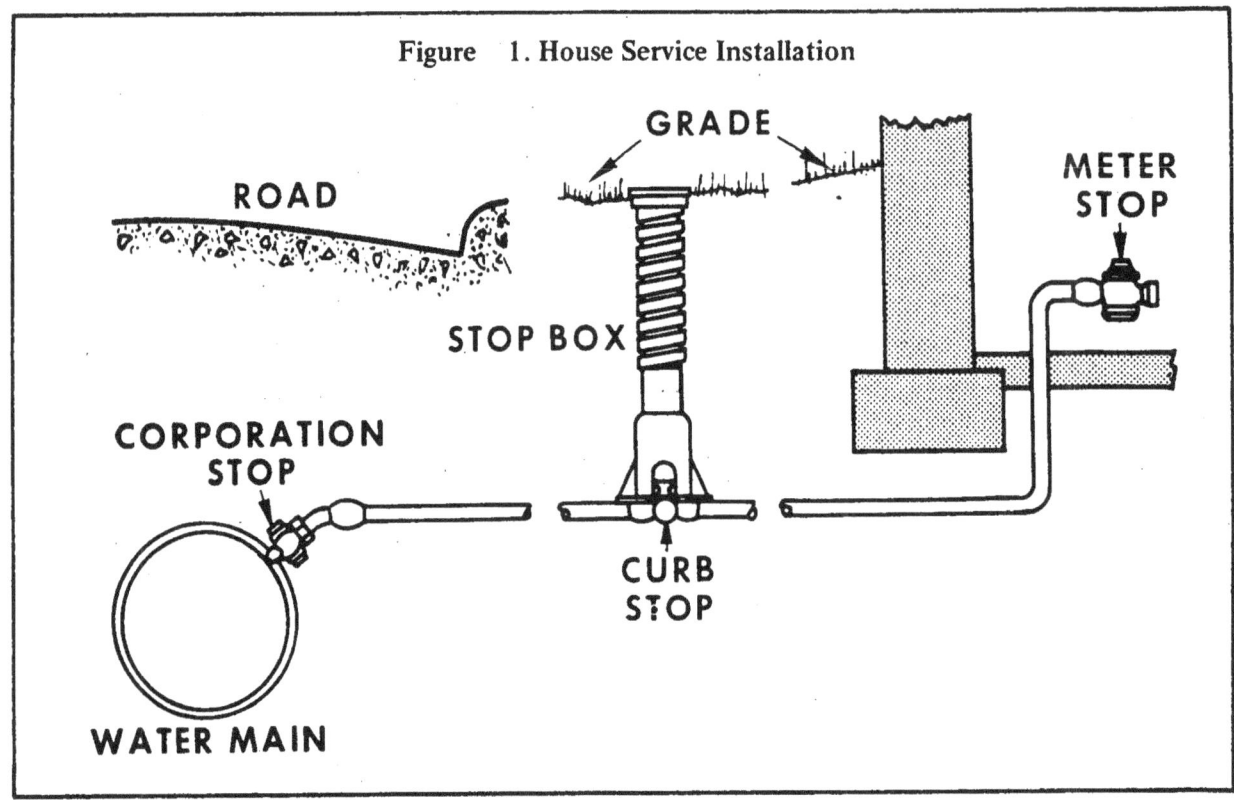

Figure 1. House Service Installation

- d **Meter stop** — The meter stop is a valve placed on the street side of the water meter to isolate the meter for installation or maintenance. Many codes require a gate valve on the house side of the meter to shut off water for house plumbing repairs. The curb and meter stops are not to be used frequently and can be ruined in a short time if used very frequently.

- e **Water meter** — The water meter is a device used to measure the amount of water used in the house. It is usually the property of the city and is a very delicate instrument that should not be abused.

  Since the electric system is usually grounded to the water line, a grounding loop-device should be installed around the meter. Many meters come with a yoke that maintains electrical continuity even though the meter is removed.

2 **Hot and Cold Water Main Lines:** The hot and cold water main lines are usually hung from the basement ceiling and are attached to the water meter and hot-water tank on one side and the fixture supply risers on the other.

These pipes should be installed in a neat manner and should be supported by pipe hangers or straps of sufficient strength and number to prevent sagging.

Hot and cold water lines should be approximately 6 inches apart unless the hot water line is insulated. This is to insure that the cold water line does not pick up heat from the hot water line.

The supply mains should have a drain valve or stop and waste valve in order to remove water from the system for repairs. These valves should be on the low end of the line or on the end of each fixture riser.

- a **The fixture risers** start at the basement main and rise vertically to the fixtures on the upper floors. In a one-family dwelling, riser branches will usually proceed from the main riser to each fixture grouping. In any event the fixture risers should not depend on the branch risers for support but should be supported with a pipe bracket.

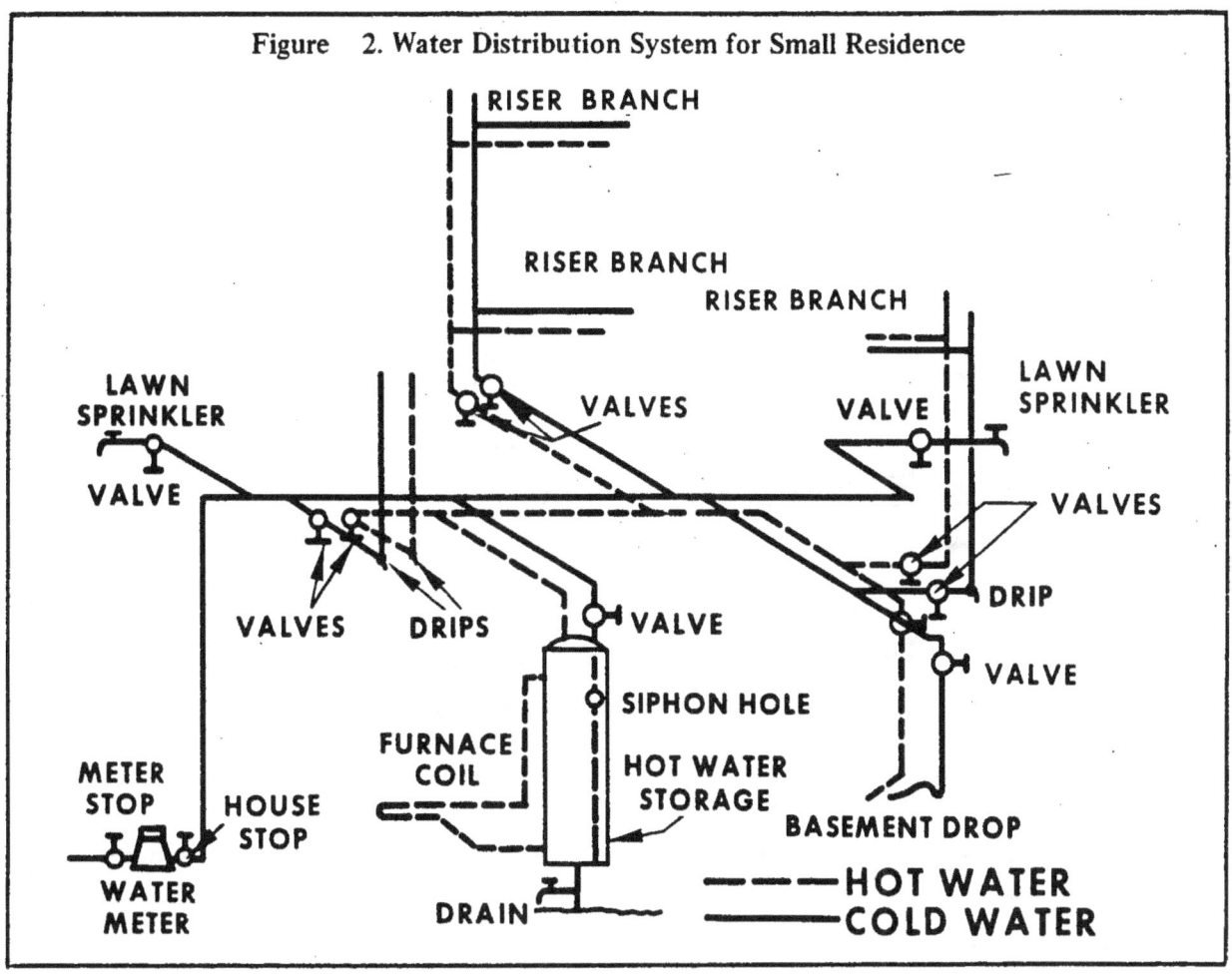

Figure 2. Water Distribution System for Small Residence

b Each fixture is then connected to the branch riser by a separate line. The last fixture on a line is usually connected directly to the branch riser. Figure 2 is a diagram of a typical single-family-residence water supply system.

3 **Hot Water Heaters:** Hot water heaters are usually powered by electricity, fuel oil, gas, or in rare cases, coal or wood. They consist of a space for heating the water and a storage tank for providing hot water over a limited period of time.

All hot water heaters should be fitted with a temperature-pressure relief valve no matter what fuel is used.

This valve will operate when either the temperature or the pressure becomes too high due to an interruption of the water supply or a faulty thermostat.

Figure 3 shows the correct installation of a hot water heater.

4 **Pipe Sizes:** The size of basement mains and risers depends on the number of fixtures supplied. However, a ¾ inch pipe is usually the minimum size used. This allows for deposits on the pipe due to hardness in the water and will usually give satisfactory volume and pressure.

B **Drainage System**

The water supply brought into the house and used is discharged through the drainage system. This system is either a sanitary drainage system carrying just interior waste water or a combined system carrying interior waste and roof runoff. The sanitary system will be discussed first.

1 **Sanitary Drainage System:** The proper sizing of the sanitary drain or house drain depends on the number of fixtures it serves. The usual

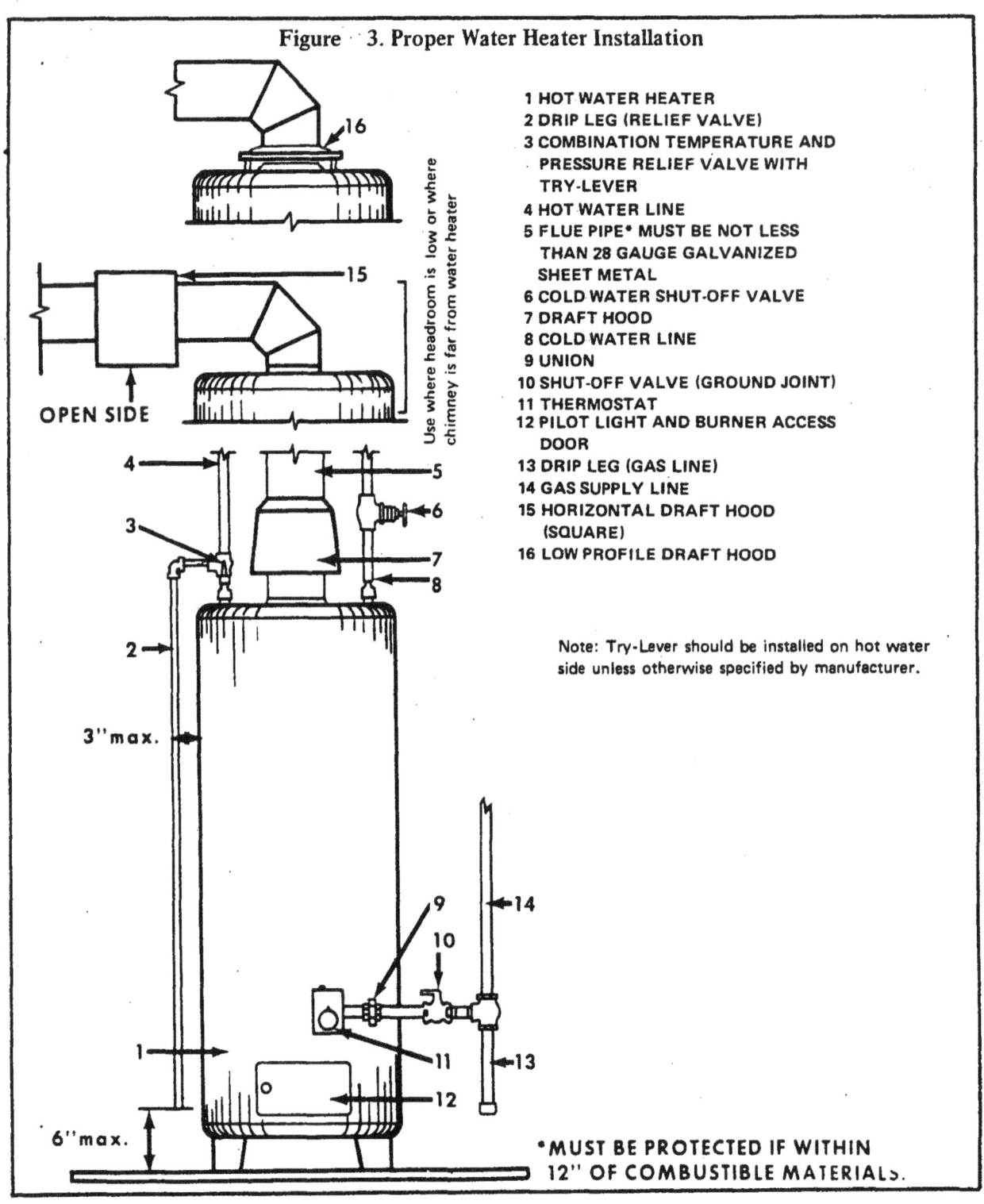

Figure 3. Proper Water Heater Installation

1. HOT WATER HEATER
2. DRIP LEG (RELIEF VALVE)
3. COMBINATION TEMPERATURE AND PRESSURE RELIEF VALVE WITH TRY-LEVER
4. HOT WATER LINE
5. FLUE PIPE* MUST BE NOT LESS THAN 28 GAUGE GALVANIZED SHEET METAL
6. COLD WATER SHUT-OFF VALVE
7. DRAFT HOOD
8. COLD WATER LINE
9. UNION
10. SHUT-OFF VALVE (GROUND JOINT)
11. THERMOSTAT
12. PILOT LIGHT AND BURNER ACCESS DOOR
13. DRIP LEG (GAS LINE)
14. GAS SUPPLY LINE
15. HORIZONTAL DRAFT HOOD (SQUARE)
16. LOW PROFILE DRAFT HOOD

Note: Try-Lever should be installed on hot water side unless otherwise specified by manufacturer.

*MUST BE PROTECTED IF WITHIN 12" OF COMBUSTIBLE MATERIALS.

minimum size is 6 inches in diameter. The materials used are usually cast iron, vitrified clay, plastic, and in rare cases, lead. For proper flow in the drain the pipe should be sized so that it flows approximately one-half full. This ensures proper scouring action so that the solids contained in the waste will not be deposited in the pipe.

a **Sizing of house drain** — The Uniform Plumbing Code Committee has developed a method of sizing of house drains in terms of "fixture units." One "fixture unit" equals approximately 7½ gallons of water per minute. This is the surge flow-rate of water discharged from a wash basin in 1 minute. All other fixtures have been related to this unit.

A table fixture unit values is shown in Table 1.

The maximum number of fixture units attached to a sanitary drain is shown in Table 2.

b **Grade of house drain** — A house drain or building sewer should be sloped toward the sewer to ensure scouring of the drain. Figure 4 shows the results of proper and improper pitch of a house drain.

The usual pitch of a house or building sewer is ¼ inch fall in 1 foot of length.

Table 1. FIXTURE UNIT VALUES

Fixture	Units
Lavatory/wash basin	1
Kitchen sink	2
Bathtub	2
Laundry tub	2
Combination fixture	3
Urinal	5
Shower bath	2
Floor drain	1
Slop sinks	3
Water closet	6
One bathroom group (water closet, lavatory, bathtub, and shower; or water closet, lavatory, and shower)	8
180 square feet of roof drained	1

c **House drain installation** — A typical house drain installation is shown in Figure 5. Typical branch connections to the main are shown in Figure 6.

d **Fixture and branch drains** — A branch drain is a waste pipe that collects the waste from two or more fixtures and conveys it to the building or house sewer. It is sized in the same way as the house sewer, taking into account that all water closets must have a minimum 3-inch diameter drain, and

Table 2. SANITARY DRAIN SIZES

Maximum number of fixture units

Diameter of pipe, in.	Slope 1/8"/Ft.	Slope 1/4"/Ft.	Slope 1/2"/Ft.
1¼	1	1	1
1½	2	2	3
2	5	6	8
3	15	18	21
4	84	96	114
6	300	450	600
8	990	1,392	2,220
12	3,084	4,320	6,912

*A water closet must enter a 3 inch diameter drain and no more than 2 water closets may enter a 3 inch horizontal branch.

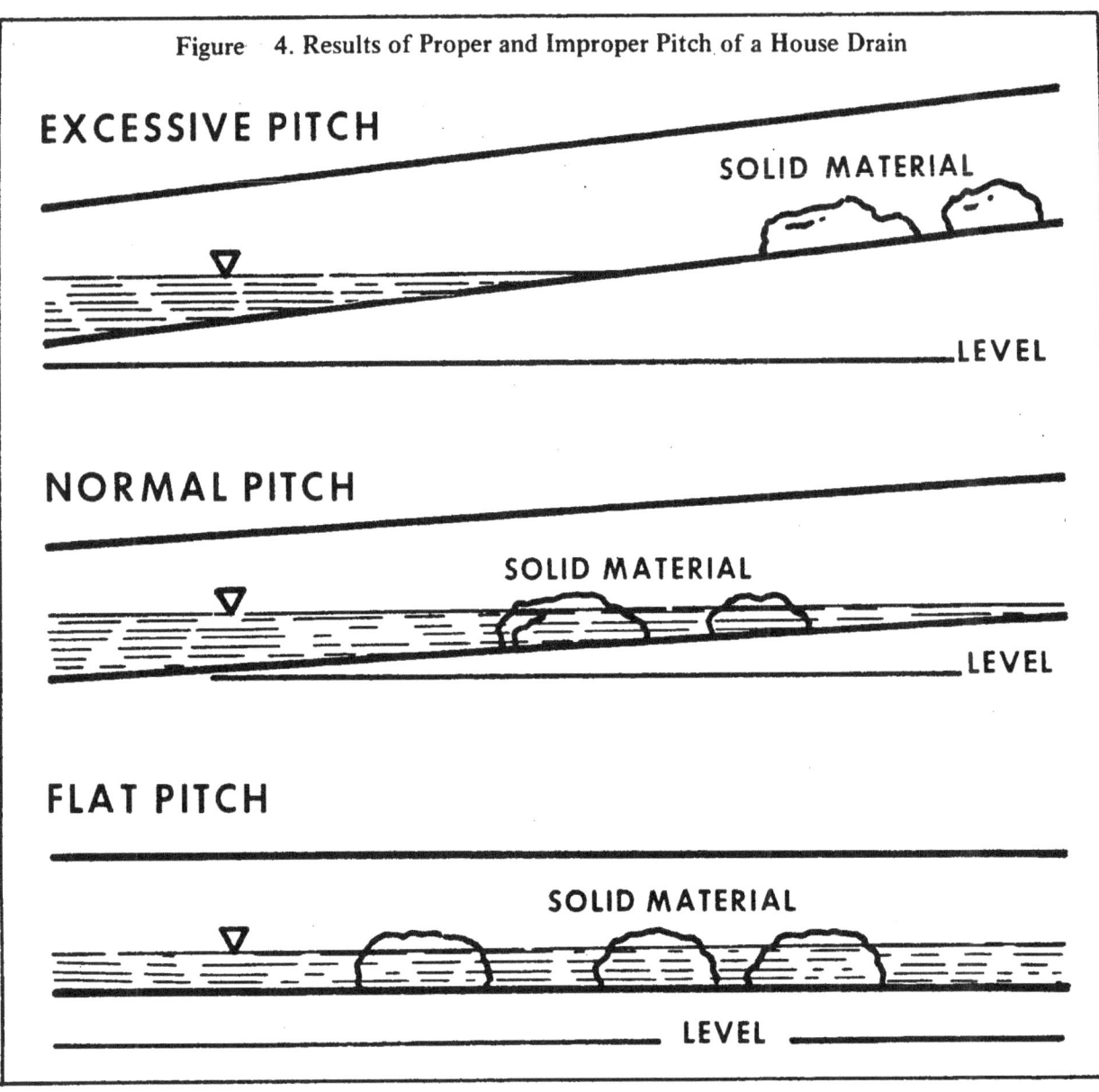

Figure 4. Results of Proper and Improper Pitch of a House Drain

only two water closets may connect into one 3-inch drain.

All branch drains must join the house drain with a "Y"-type fitting as shown in Figure 6. The same is true for fixture drains joining branch drains.

The "Y" fitting is used to eliminate, as much as possible, the deposit of solids in or near the connection. A build-up of these solids will cause a blockage in the drain.

The recommended minimum size of fixture drain is shown in Table 3.

e Traps — A plumbing trap is a device used in a waste system to prevent the passage of sewer gas into the structure and yet not hinder the fixture's discharge to any great extent. All fixtures connected to a household plumbing system should have a trap installed in the line.

Table 3. MINIMUM FIXTURE SERVICE

Fixture	Supply line, in.	Vent line, in.	Drain line, in.
Bathtub	½	1½	1½-2
Kitchen sink	½	1½	1½
Lavatory	3/8	1¼	1¼
Laundry sink	½	1½	1½
Shower	½	2	2
Water closet (tank)	3/8	3	3

Figure 5. Typical House Drain Installation

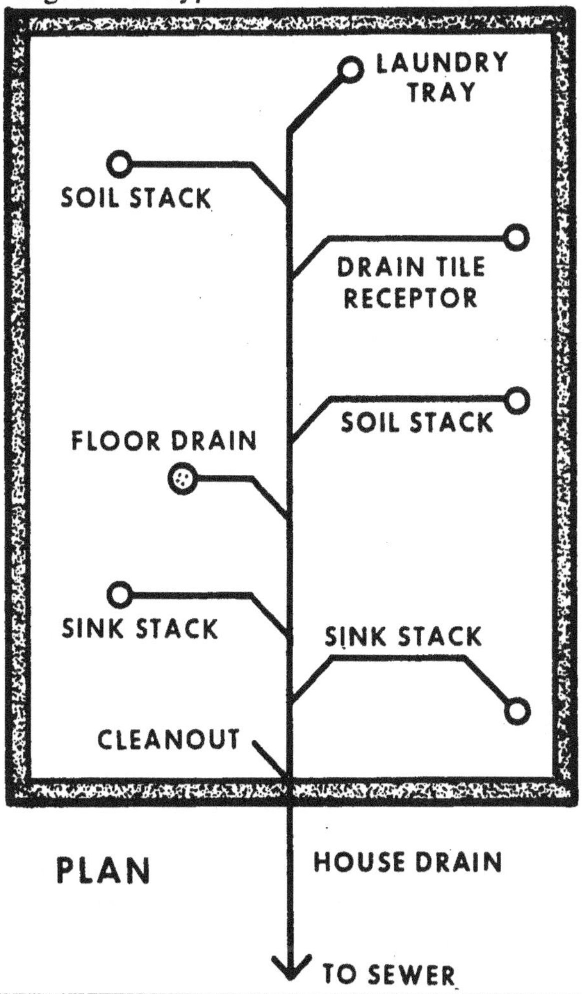

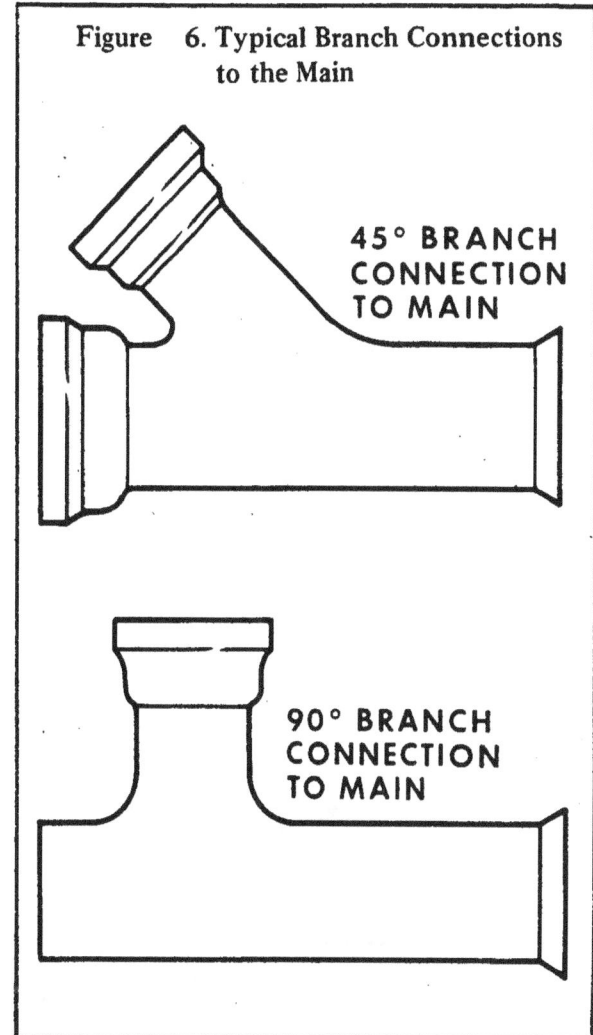

Figure 6. Typical Branch Connections to the Main

The effect of sewer gases on the human body are known; many are extremely harmful. Additionally, certain sewer gases are explosive. A trap will prevent these gases from passing into the structure.

1) "P" trap — The most common trap found today is the "P" trap. Figure 6-7 is a drawing of a "P" trap.

The depth of the seal in a trap is usually 2 inches. A deep seal trap has a 4-inch seal.

As was mentioned earlier, the purpose of a trap is to seal out sewer gases from the structure. Since a plumbing system is subject to wide variations in flow, and this flow originates in many different sections of the system, there is a wide variation in pressures in the waste lines. These pressure differences tend to destroy the water seal in the trap.

To counteract this problem mechanical traps were introduced. It has been found, however, that the corrosive liquids flowing in the system corrode or jam these mechanical traps. It is for this reason that most plumbing codes prohibit mechanical traps.

There are many manufacturers of traps, and all have varied the design somewhat. Figures 8 and 9 show various types of "P" traps. The "P" trap is usually found in lavatories, sinks, urinals, drinking fountains, showers, and other installations that do not discharge a great deal of water.

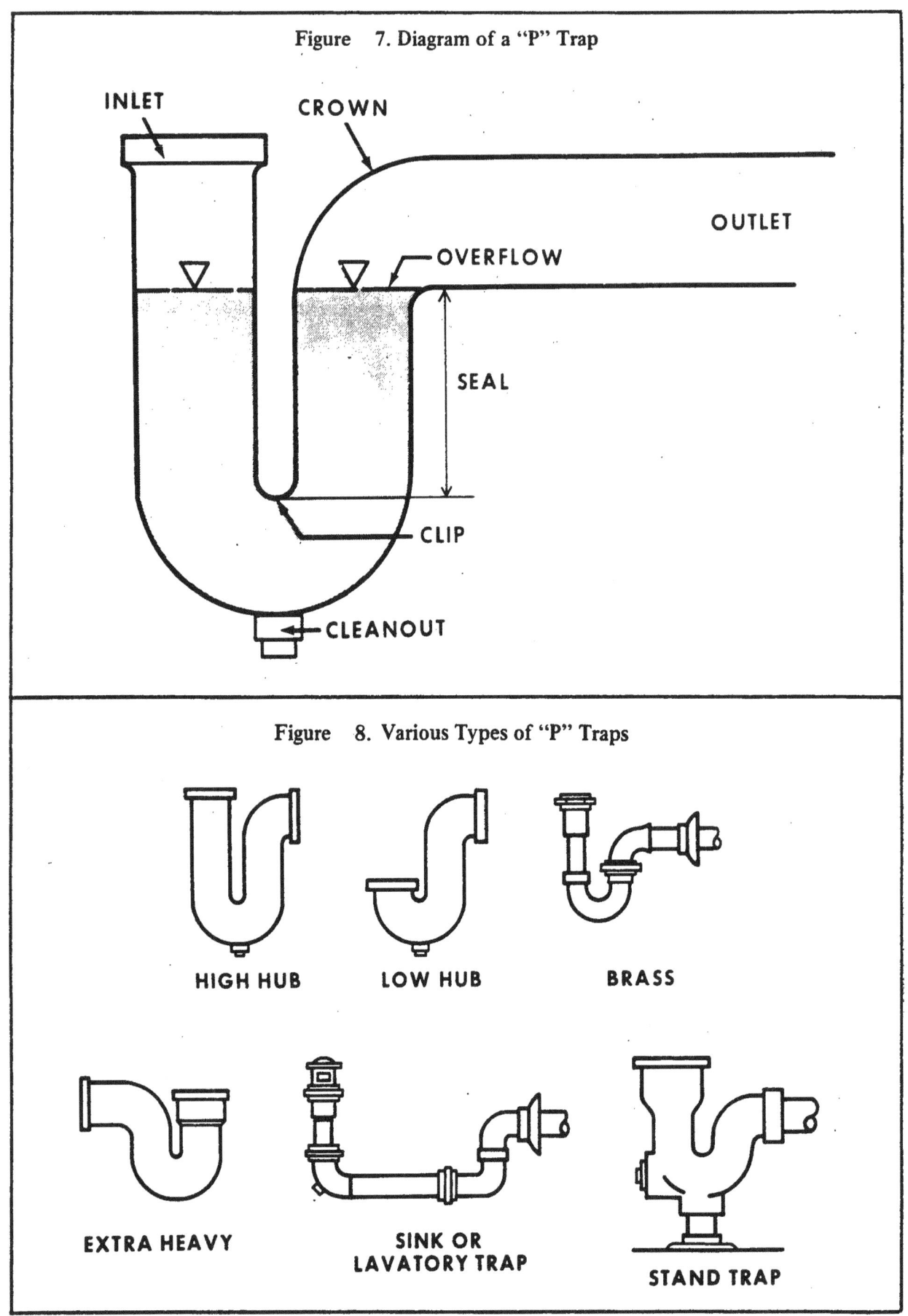

Figure 7. Diagram of a "P" Trap

Figure 8. Various Types of "P" Traps

2) Drum trap — The drum trap is another water seal-type trap. They are usually used in the 4- x 5-inch or 4- x 8-inch sizes. These traps have a greater sealing capacity than the "P" trap and pass large amounts of water quickly. Figure 10 shows a drum trap.

Drum traps are commonly connected to bathtubs, foot baths, sitz baths, and modified shower baths. Figure 11 shows a drum trap connected to a bathtub and shower.

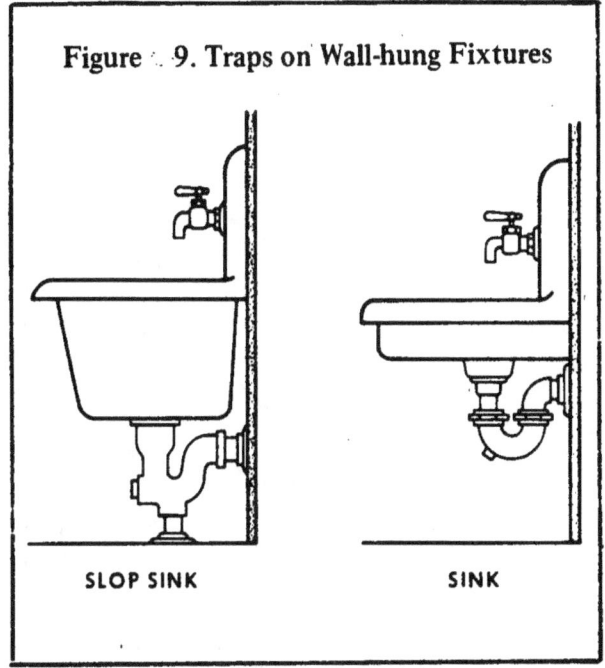

Figure 9. Traps on Wall-hung Fixtures

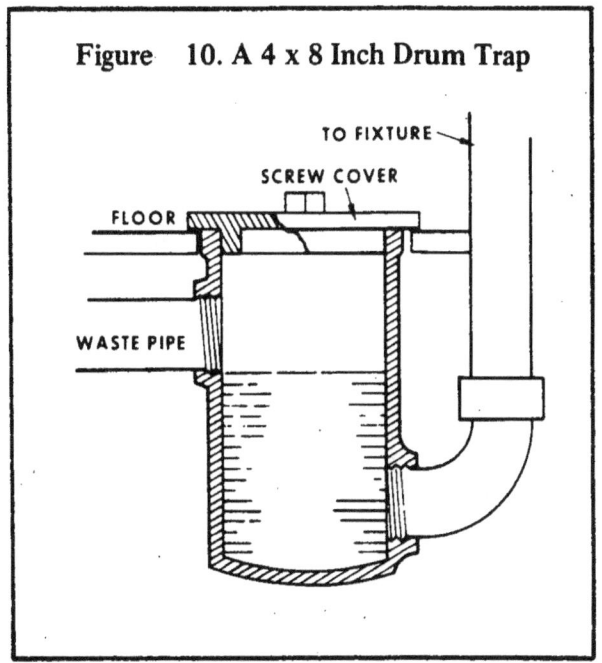

Figure 10. A 4 x 8 Inch Drum Trap

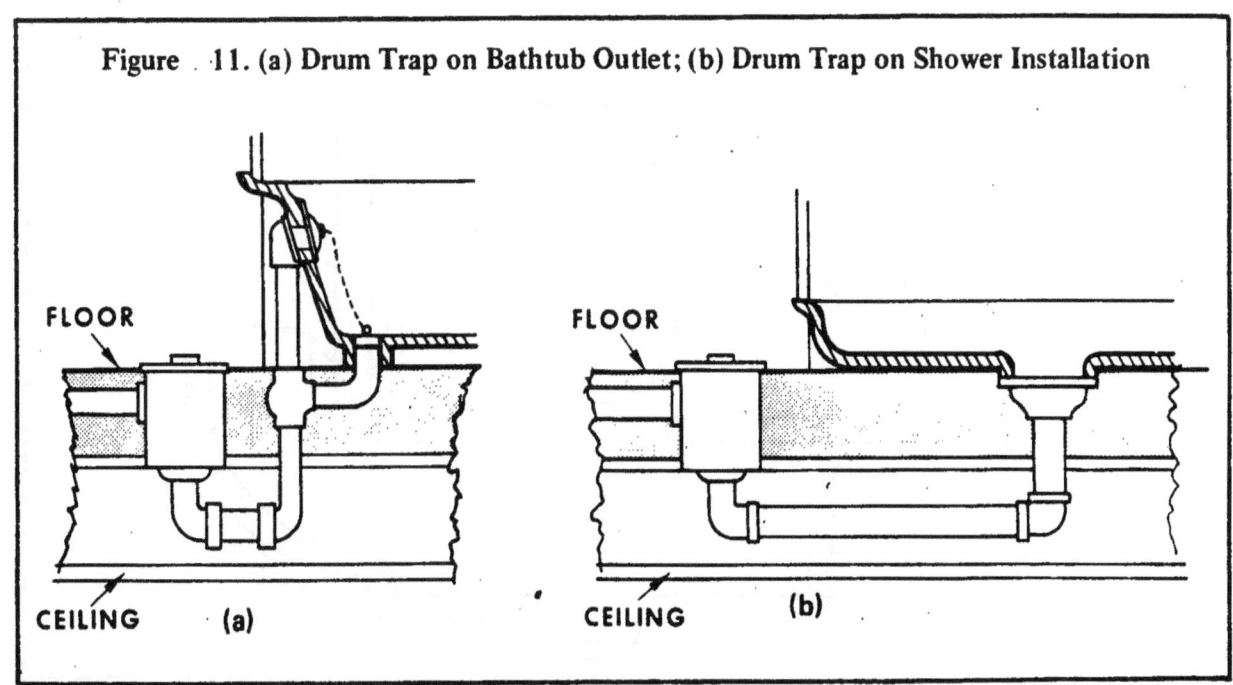

Figure 11. (a) Drum Trap on Bathtub Outlet; (b) Drum Trap on Shower Installation

3) Objectionable traps — The "S" trap and the ¾ "S" trap should not be used in plumbing installations. They are almost impossible to ventilate properly, and the ¾ "S" trap forms a perfect siphon.

The bag trap, an extreme form of "S" trap, is seldom found. Figure 12 shows these types of "S" traps.

Figure 13 shows one type of mechanically sealed trap. Any trap that depends on a moving part for its effectiveness is usually inadequate and has been prohibited by the local plumbing codes.

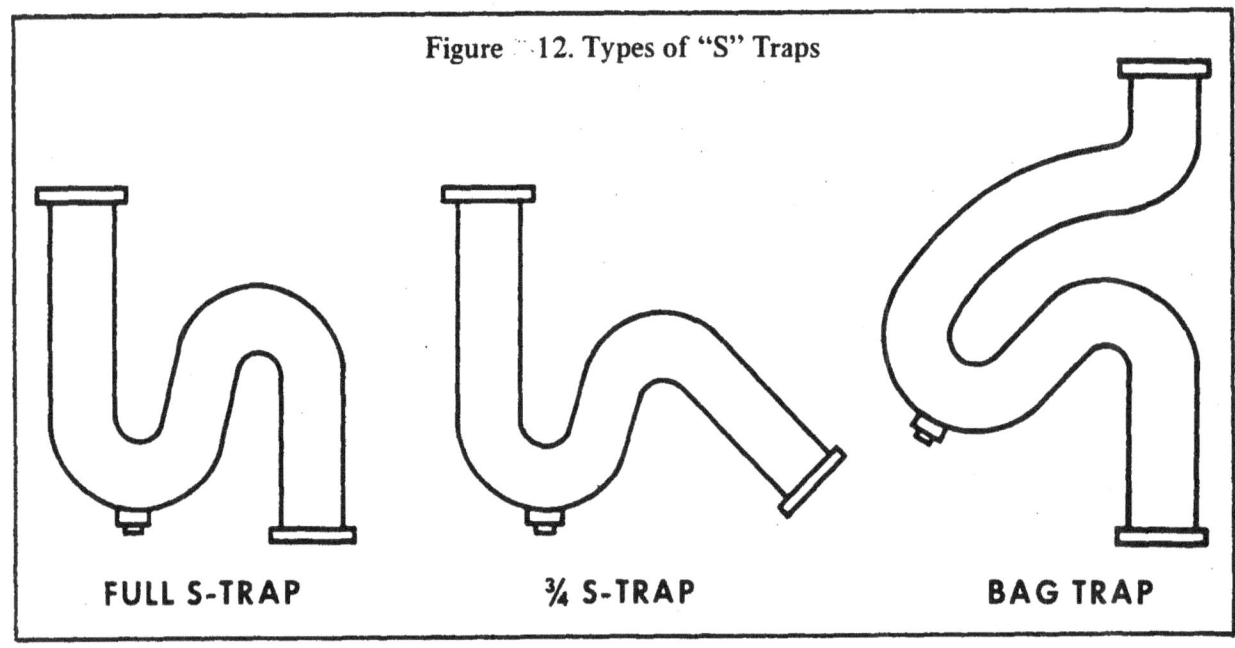

Figure 12. Types of "S" Traps

FULL S-TRAP   **¾ S-TRAP**   **BAG TRAP**

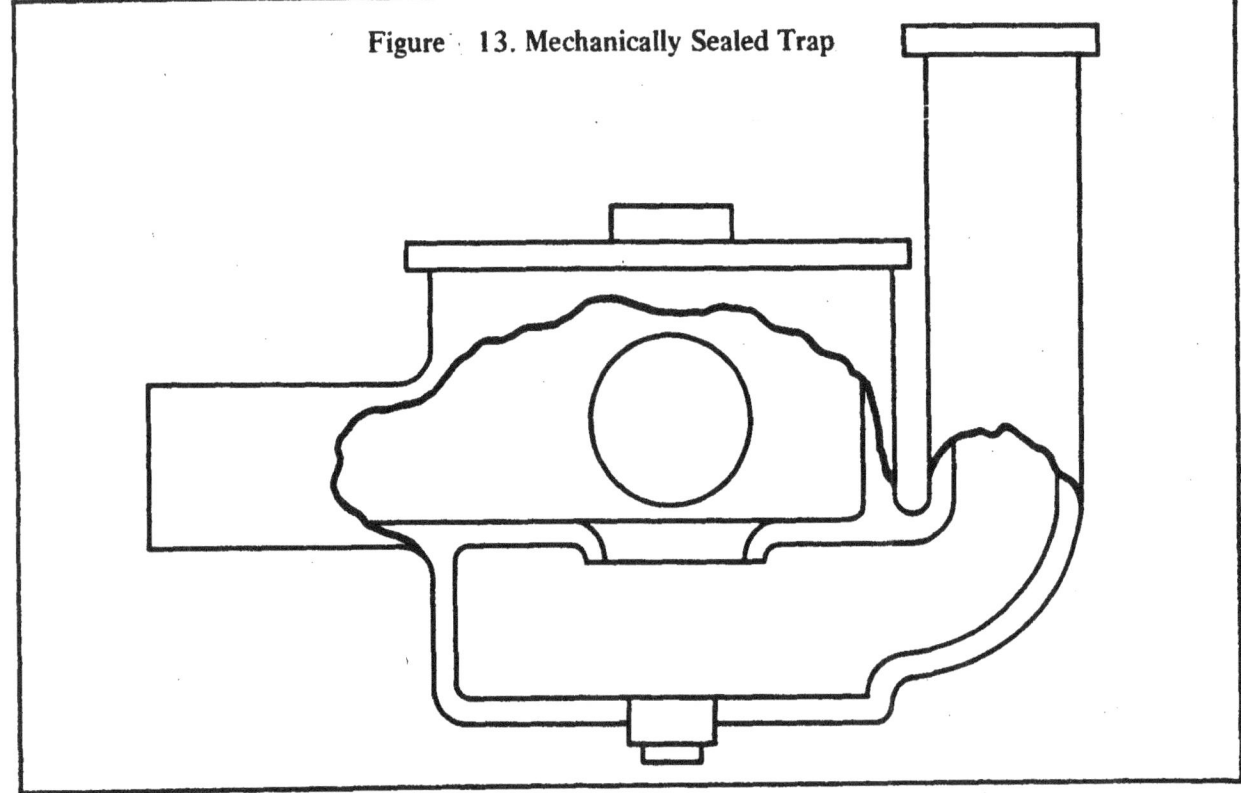

Figure 13. Mechanically Sealed Trap

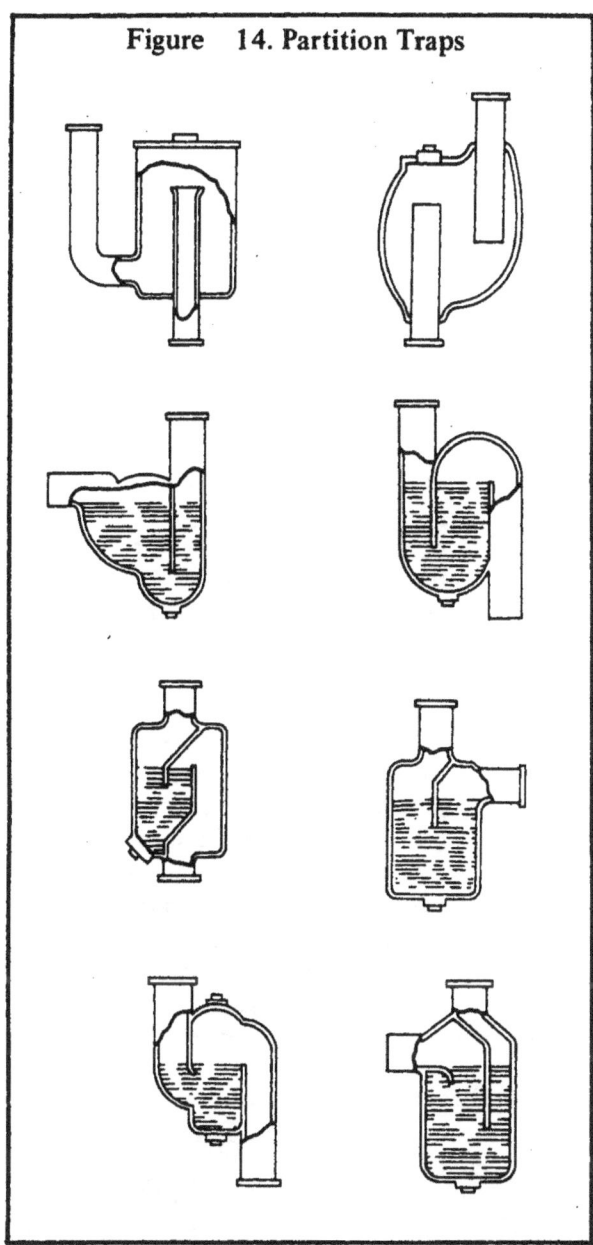

Figure 14. Partition Traps

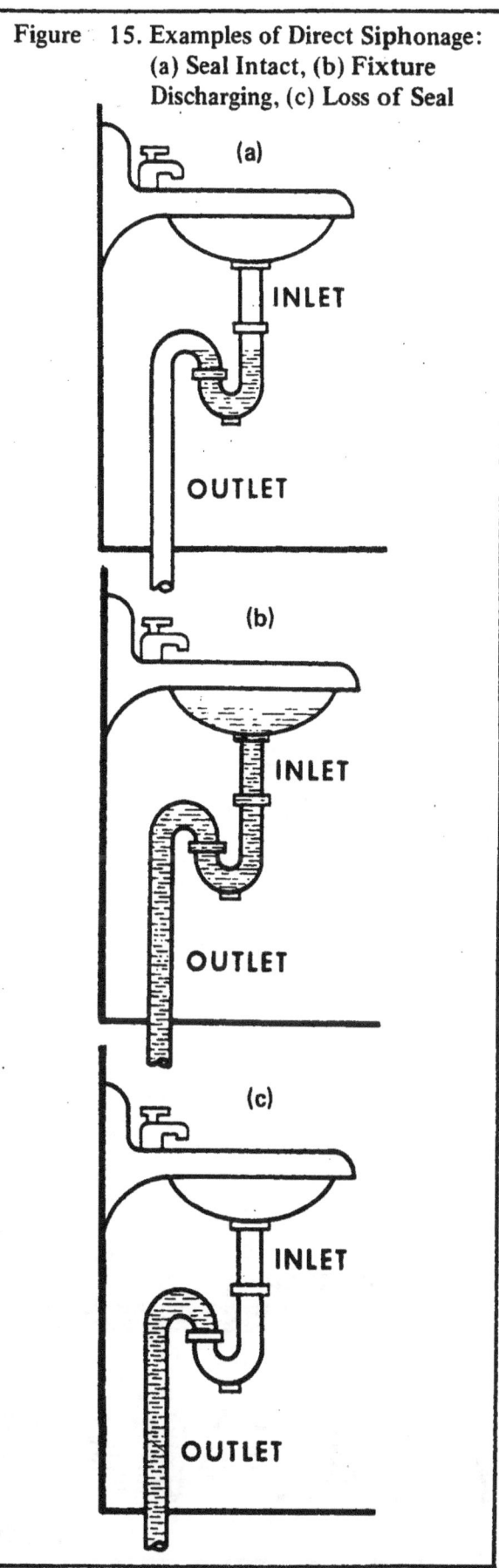

Figure 15. Examples of Direct Siphonage: (a) Seal Intact, (b) Fixture Discharging, (c) Loss of Seal

Figure 14 shows various types of internal partition traps. These traps work, but their design usually results in their being higher priced than the "P" or drum traps.

It should be remembered that traps are used only to prevent the escape of sewer gas into the structure. They do not compensate for pressure variations. Only proper venting will eliminate pressure problems.

f **Ventilation** — A plumbing system is ventilated to prevent trap seal loss, material deterioration, and flow retardation.

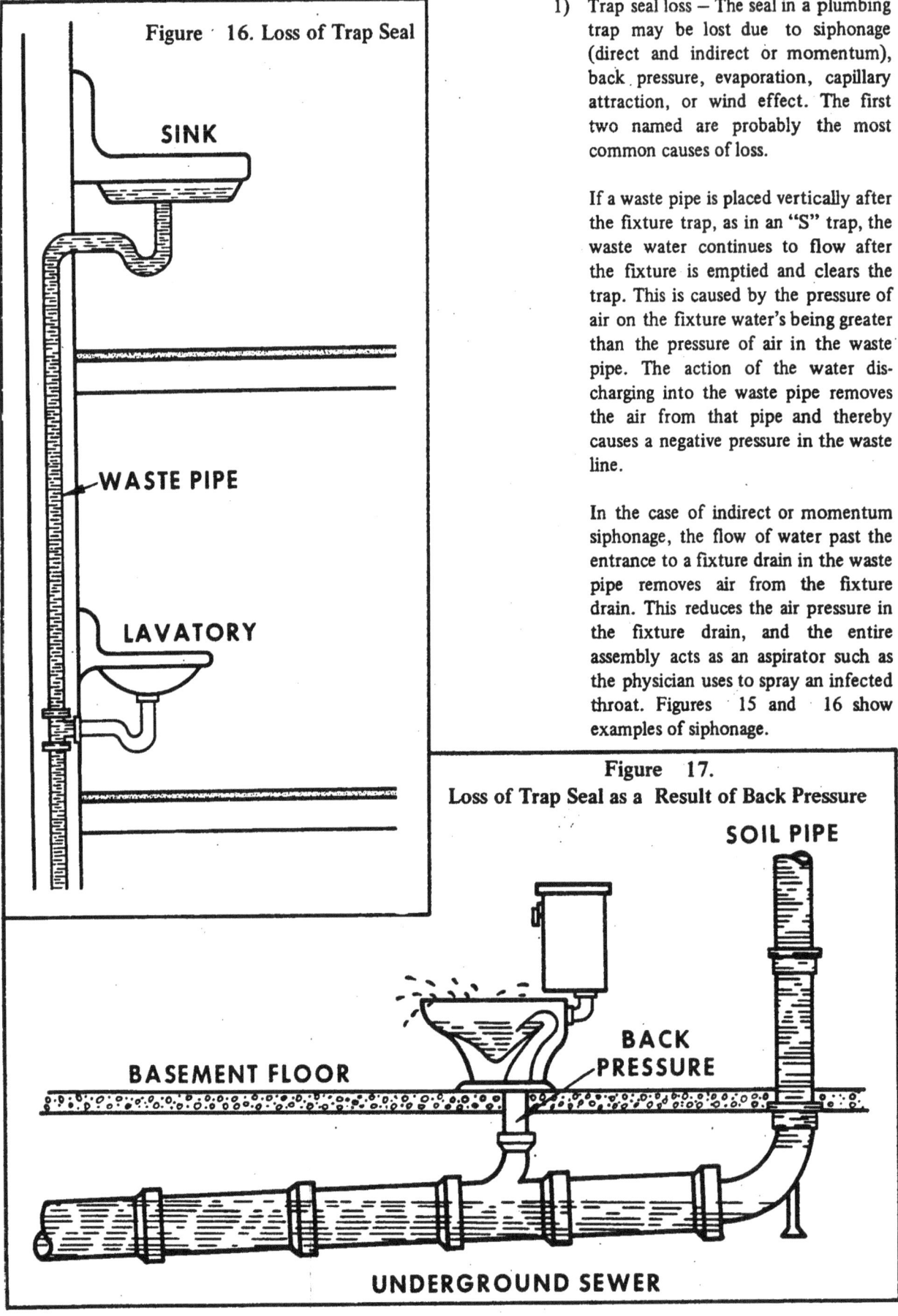

Figure 16. Loss of Trap Seal

Figure 17. Loss of Trap Seal as a Result of Back Pressure

1) Trap seal loss — The seal in a plumbing trap may be lost due to siphonage (direct and indirect or momentum), back pressure, evaporation, capillary attraction, or wind effect. The first two named are probably the most common causes of loss.

If a waste pipe is placed vertically after the fixture trap, as in an "S" trap, the waste water continues to flow after the fixture is emptied and clears the trap. This is caused by the pressure of air on the fixture water's being greater than the pressure of air in the waste pipe. The action of the water discharging into the waste pipe removes the air from that pipe and thereby causes a negative pressure in the waste line.

In the case of indirect or momentum siphonage, the flow of water past the entrance to a fixture drain in the waste pipe removes air from the fixture drain. This reduces the air pressure in the fixture drain, and the entire assembly acts as an aspirator such as the physician uses to spray an infected throat. Figures 15 and 16 show examples of siphonage.

2) Back pressure — The flow of water in a soil pipe varies according to the fixtures being used. A lavatory gives a small flow and a water closet a large flow. Small flows tend to cling to the sides of the pipe, but large ones form a slug of waste as they drop. As this slug of water falls down the pipe the air in front of it becomes pressurized. As the pressure builds it seeks an escape point. This point is either a vent or a fixture outlet. If the vent is plugged or there is no vent, the only escape for this air is the fixture outlet. The air pressure forces the trap seal up the pipe into the fixture. If the pressure is great enough the seal is blown out of the fixture entirely. Figures 17 and 18 illustrate this type of problem.

3) Vent sizing — Vent pipe installation is similar to that of soil and waste pipe. The same fixture unit criteria are used. Table 3 shows minimum vent pipe sizes.

Vent pipes of less than 1¼ inches in diameter should not be used. Vents smaller than this diameter tend to clog and do not perform their function.

4) Individual fixture ventilation — Figure 19 shows a typical installation of a wall-hung plumbing unit. This type of ventilation is generally used for sinks, lavatories, drinking fountains, and so forth.

Figure 20 shows a typical installation of a bathtub or shower ventilation system.

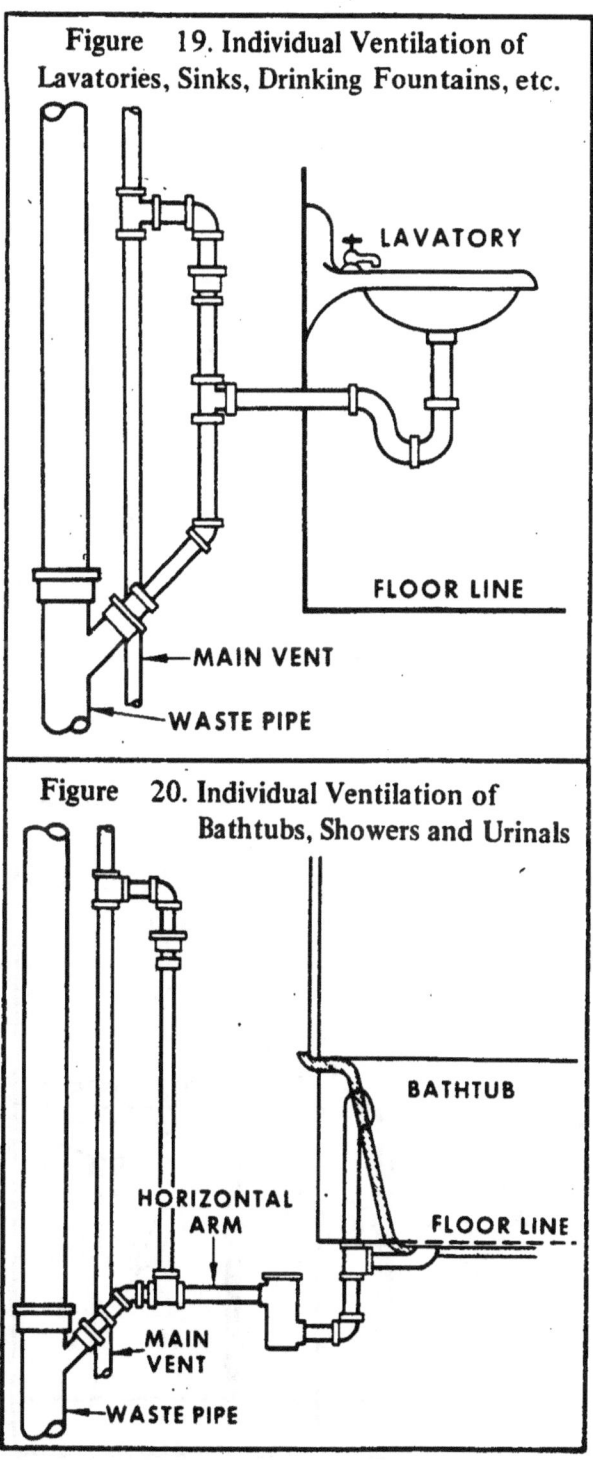

Figure 19. Individual Ventilation of Lavatories, Sinks, Drinking Fountains, etc.

Figure 20. Individual Ventilation of Bathtubs, Showers and Urinals

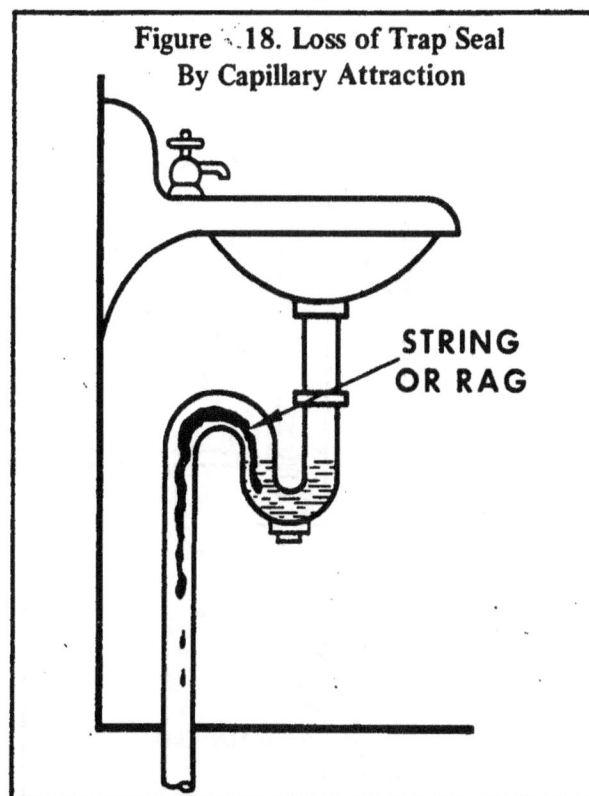

Figure 18. Loss of Trap Seal By Capillary Attraction

Figure 21 shows the proper vent connection for a water closet or slop sink. The water closet can be either a tank type or a flushometer valve type.

5) Unit venting — Figures 22 to 24 picture a back-to-back ventilation system for various common plumbing fixtures. The unit venting system is commonly used in apartment buildings. This type of system saves a great deal of money and space when fixtures are placed back to back in separate apartments.

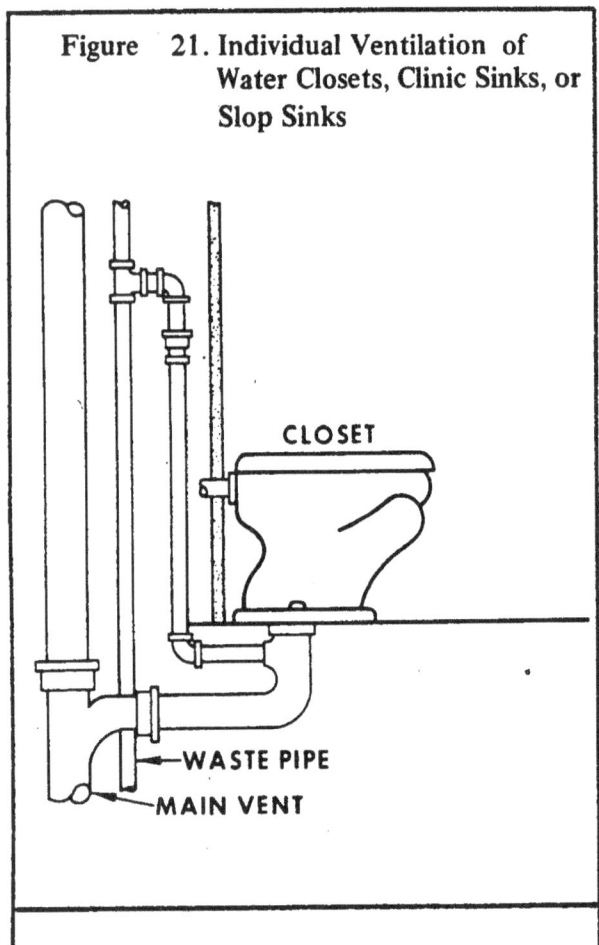

Figure 21. Individual Ventilation of Water Closets, Clinic Sinks, or Slop Sinks

Figure 22. Unit Vent Method of Ventilating Wall-hung Fixture Traps

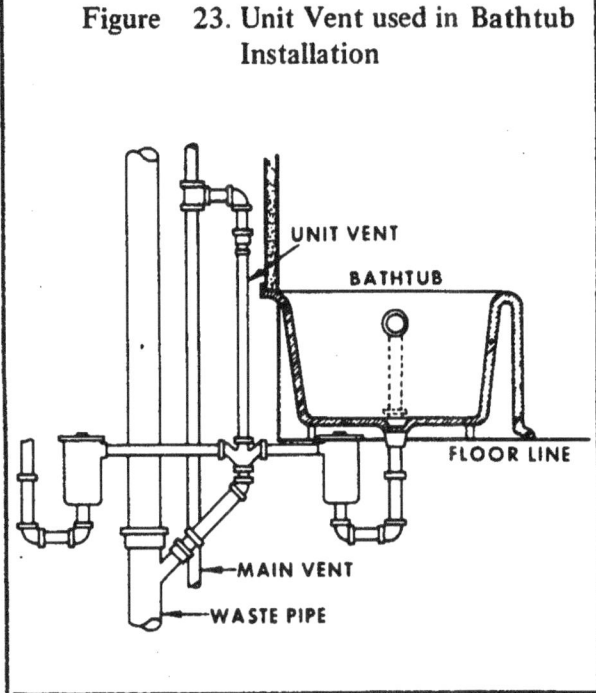

Figure 23. Unit Vent used in Bathtub Installation

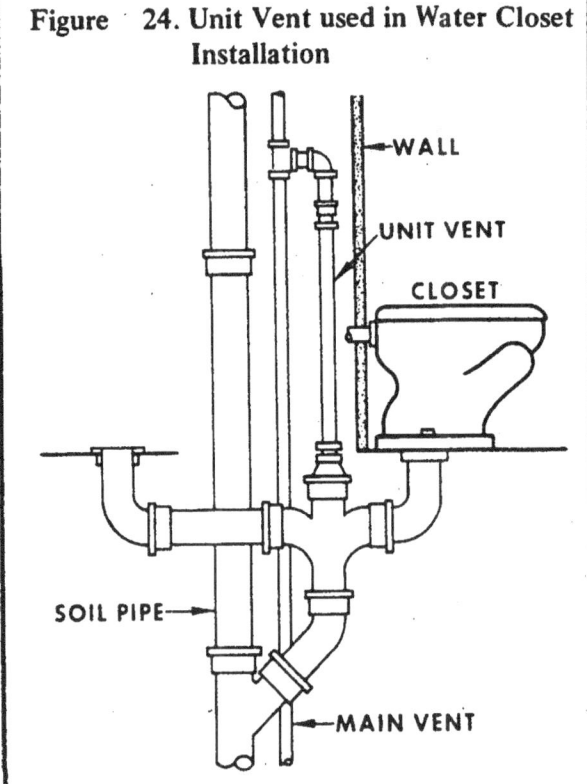

Figure 24. Unit Vent used in Water Closet Installation

Figure 25 shows a double combination "Y" used for joining the fixtures to the common soil pipe. The deflectors are to prevent waste from one fixture flowing back up into the waste in the attached fixture on the other side of the wall.

6) Wet venting — Wet venting of a plumbing system is common in household bathroom fixture grouping. It is exactly what the name implies: the vent pipe is used as a waste line. Figure 26 shows a typical wet-vent installation in a home.

7) Total drainage system — Up to now we have talked about the drain, soil waste, and vent systems of a plumbing system separately. For a working system, however, they must all be connected. Figures 27 through 32 show some typical drainage systems that are found in homes and small apartment buildings.

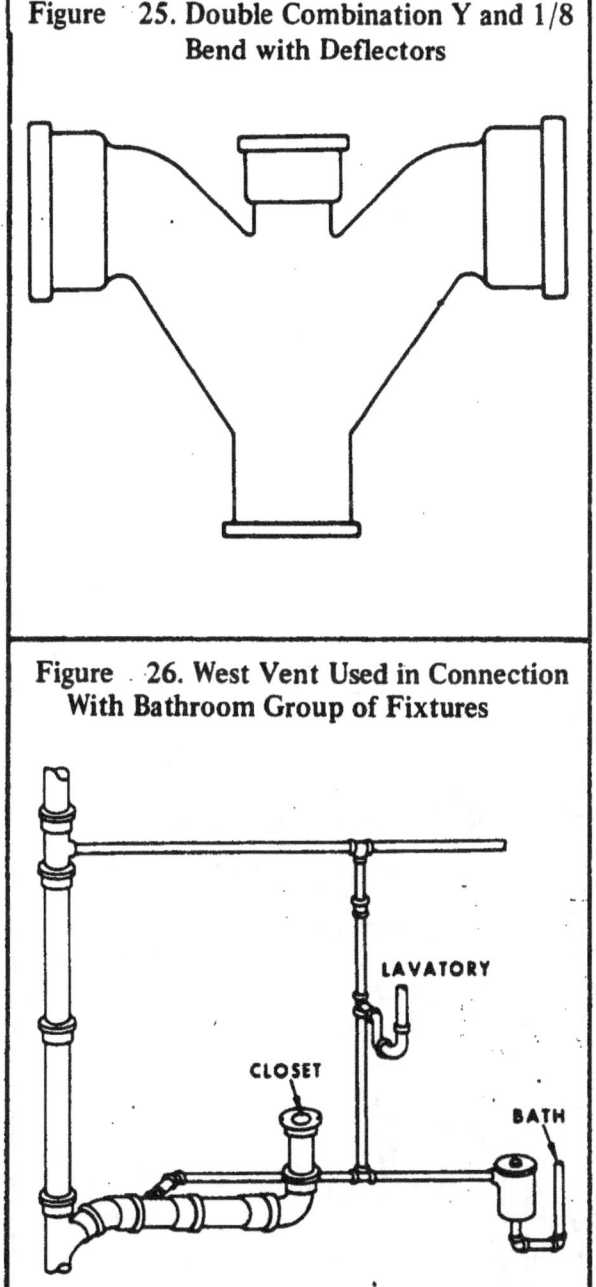

Figure 25. Double Combination Y and 1/8 Bend with Deflectors

Figure 26. West Vent Used in Connection With Bathroom Group of Fixtures

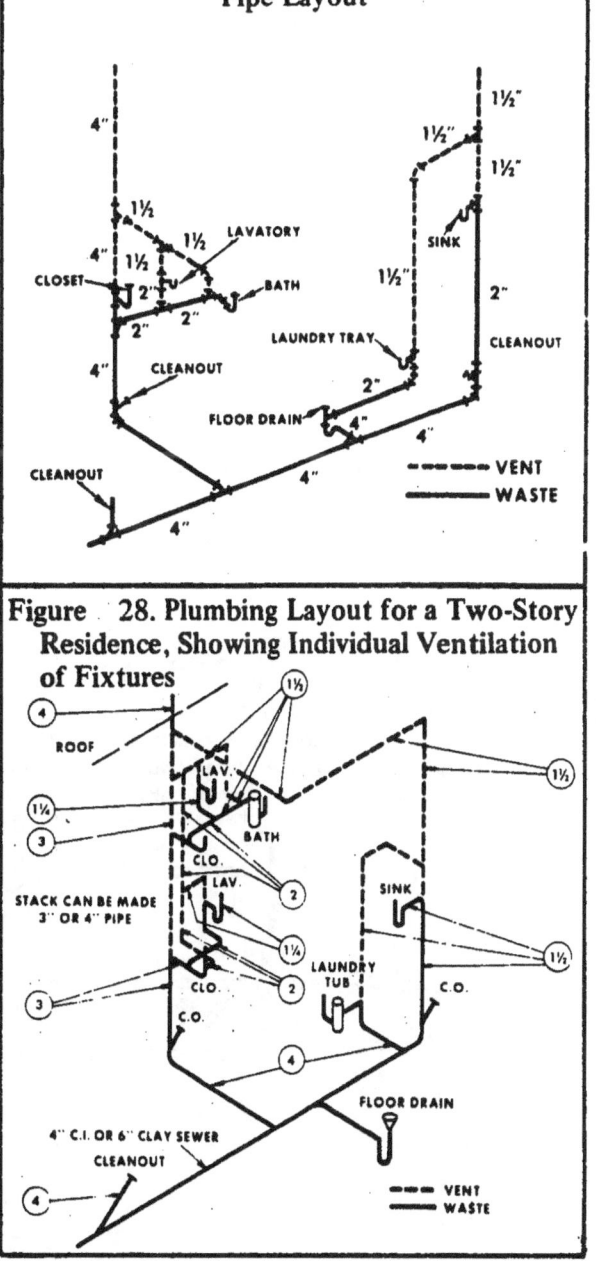

Figure 27. Drain Soil Waste and Vent Pipe Layout

Figure 28. Plumbing Layout for a Two-Story Residence, Showing Individual Ventilation of Fixtures

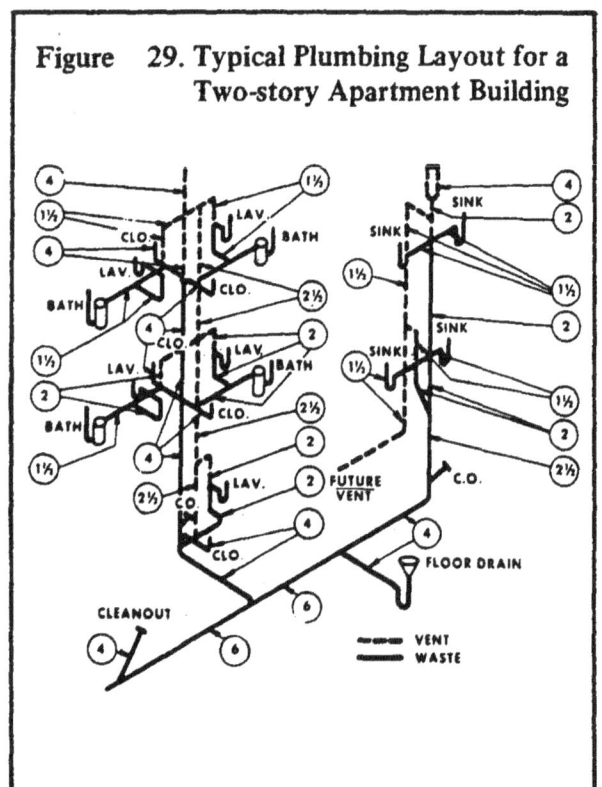

Figure 29. Typical Plumbing Layout for a Two-story Apartment Building

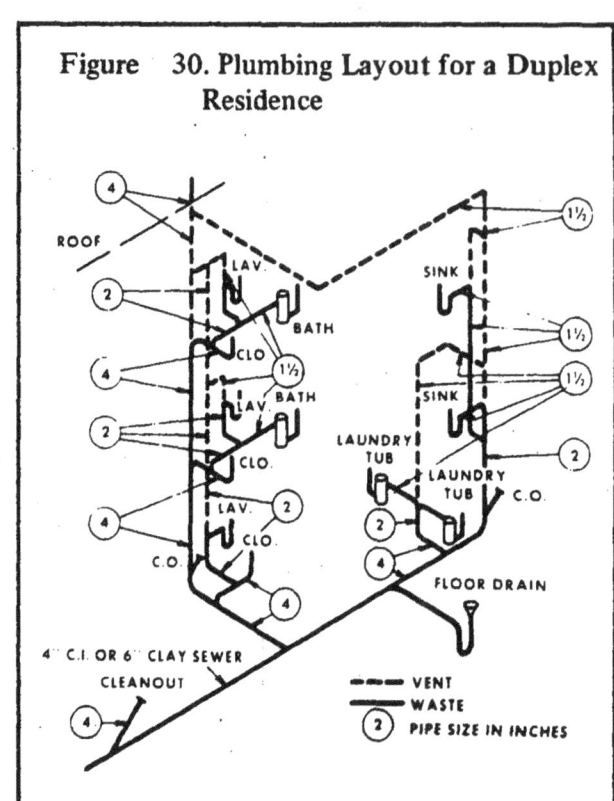

Figure 30. Plumbing Layout for a Duplex Residence

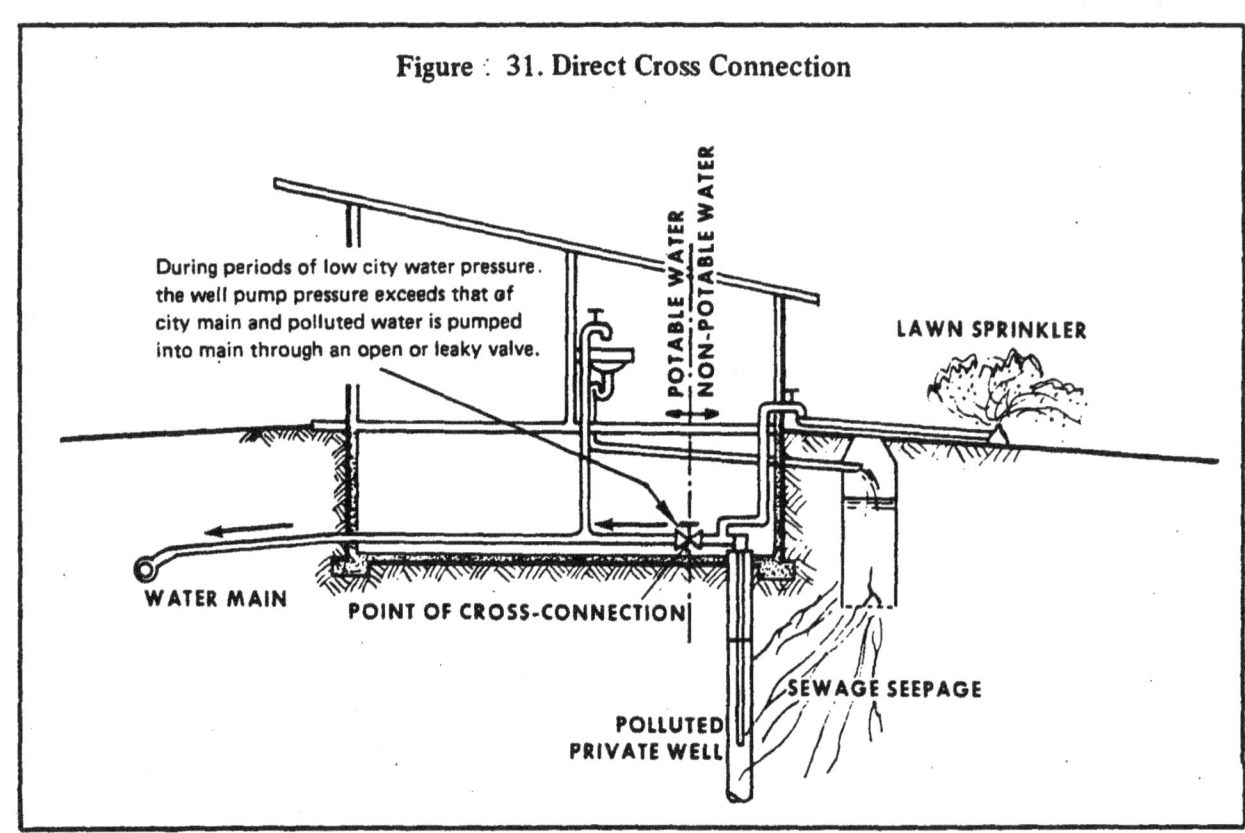

Figure 31. Direct Cross Connection

Figure 32. Cross Connection

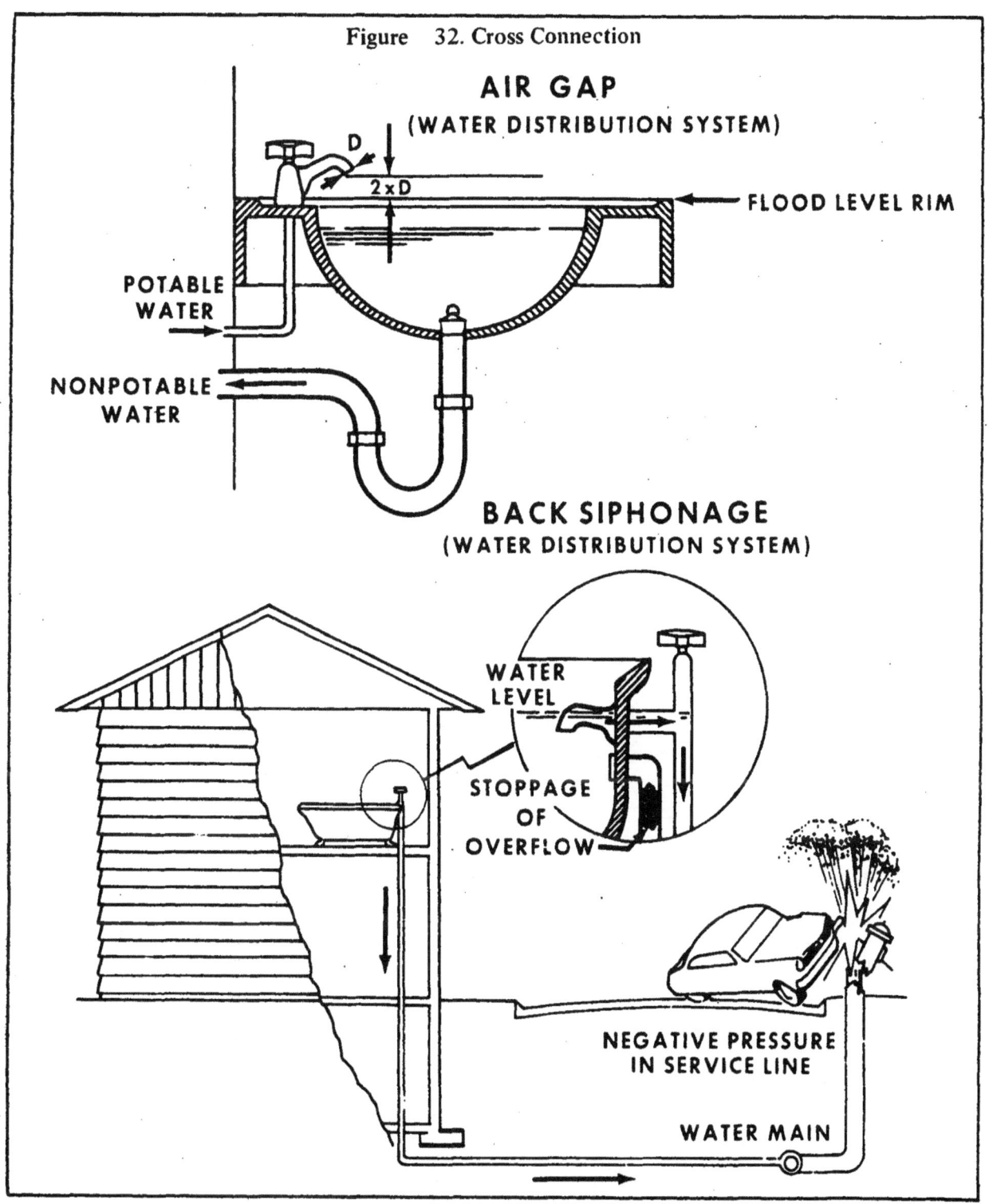

ELECTRICAL ASPECTS OF A HOUSING INSPECTION

TABLE OF CONTENTS

		Page
I.	Definitions	1
II.	Flow of Electric Current	2
III.	Electric Service Entrance	4
IV.	Grounding	6
V.	Two- or Three-Way Electric Services	7
VI.	Residential Wiring Adequacy	8
VII.	Wire Size and Types	8
VIII.	Electric Service Panel	10
IX.	Overcurrent Devices	11
X.	Electric Circuits	13
XI.	Common Electrical Violations	16
XII.	Steps Involved in Actual Inspections	18
XIII.	Wattage Consumption of Electrical Appliances	20
XIV.	Motor Currents	20

ELECTRICAL ASPECTS OF A HOUSING INSPECTION

There are two basic codes concerned with residential wiring that are of importance to the housing inspector. The first is the local electrical code. The purpose of this code is to safeguard persons and buildings and their contents from hazards arising from the use of electricity for light, heat, and power. The electrical code contains basic minimum provisions considered necessary for safety. Compliance with this code and proper maintenance will result in an installation essentially free from hazard but not necessarily efficient, convenient, or adequate for good service or future expansion.

The majority of local electrical codes are modeled after the National Electrical Code, published by the National Fire Prevention Association.

Just because an electrical installation was safe and adequate under the provisions of the electrical code at the time of installation does not indicate that the system is safe and adequate for use today. Hazards often occur because of overloading of wiring systems by methods or usage not in conformity with the code. This occurs because initial wiring did not provide for increases in the use of electricity. For this reason it is recommended that the initial installation be adequate and that reasonable provisions for system changes be made as may be required for future increase in the use of electricity.

The other code that contains electrical provisions is the local housing code. It establishes minimum standards for artificial and natural lighting and ventilation, specifies the minimum number of electric outlets and lighting fixtures per room, and prohibits temporary wiring except under certain circumstances. In addition, the housing code usually requires that all components of the electrical system be installed and maintained in a safe condition so as to prevent fire or electric shock.

This chapter contains electrical terms and major features of a residential wiring system that should be familiar to the housing inspector. It also contains a review of the steps involved in the electrical inspection, as well as commonly found conditions.

I. Definitions

A **Electricity** - is energy that can be used to run household appliances; it can produce light and heat, shocks, and numerous other effects.

B **Current** - the flow of electricity through a circuit.

1 **Alternating current** is an electrical current that reverses its direction of flow at regular intervals: For example, it would alternate 60 times every second in a 60-cycle system. This type of power is commonly found in homes.

2 **Direct current** is an electric current flowing in one direction. This type of current is not commonly found in today's homes.

C **Ampere** - the unit used in measuring intensity of flow of electricity. Symbol for it is "I."

D **Volt** - the unit for measuring electrical pressure or force, which is known as electromotive force. Symbol for it is "E."

E **Watt** - is the unit of electric power. Volts X Amperes = Watts.

F **Circuit** - the flow of electricity through two or more wires from the supply source to one or more outlets and back to the source.

G **Circuit Breaker** - a safety device used to break the flow of electricity by opening the circuit automatically in the event of overloading or used to open or close it manually.

H **Short Circuit** - is a break in the flow of electricity through a circuit due to the load caused by improper connection between hot and neutral wires (have the electrical inspector check for its location).

I **Conductor** - any substance capable of conveying an electric current. In the home, copper wire is usually used.

   1 **Bare conductor** is one with no insulation or covering.

   2 **Covered conductor** is one covered with one or more layers of insulation.

J **Fuse** - a safety device that cuts off the flow of electricity when the current flowing through the fuse exceeds its rated capacity.

K **Ground** - to connect with the earth as to ground an electric wire directly to the earth or indirectly through a water pipe or some other conductor. Usually a green-colored wire is used for grounding the whole electrical system to the earth. A white wire is then usually used to ground individual electrical components of the whole system.

L **Conductor Gauge** - a numerical system used to label electric conductor sizes, given in American Wire Gauge (AWG). The larger the AWG number the smaller the wire size.

M **Hot Wires** - those that carry the electric current or power to the load; they are usually black or red.

N **Service** - the conductor and equipment for delivering energy from the electricity supply system to the wiring system of the premises.

O **Service Drop** - the overhead service connectors from the last pole or other aerial support to and including the splices, if any, connecting to the service entrance conductors at the building or other structure.

P **Insulator** - a material that will not permit the passage of electricity.

Q **Neutral Wire** - the third wire in a three-wire distribution circuit; it is usually white or light gray and is connected to the ground.

R **Service Panel** - main panel or cabinet through which electricity is brought to building and distributed. It contains the main disconnect switch and fuses or circuit breakers.

S **Voltage Drop** - a voltage loss when wires carry current. The longer the cord the greater the voltage drop.

II. Flow of Electric Current

Electricity is usually generated by a generator that converts mechanical energy into electrical energy. The electricity is then run through a transformer where voltage is increased to several hundred thousand volts and in some instances to a million or more volts. This high voltage is necessary in order to increase the efficiency of power transmission over long distances.

This high-transmission voltage is then stepped down (reduced) to normal 115/230-volt household current by a transformer located near the point of use (residence). The electricity is then transmitted to the house by a series of wires called a "service drop." In areas where the electric wiring is underground, the wires leading to the building are buried in the ground.

In order for electric current to flow, it must travel from a higher to a lower potential voltage. In an electrical system the hot wires (black or red) are at a higher potential than the neutral or ground wire (white or green). Therefore, current will flow between the hot wires and the neutral or ground wires.

The voltage is a measure of the force at which electricity is delivered. It is similar to pressure in a water supply system.

Current is measured in amperes and is the quantity of flow of electricity. It is similar to measuring water in gallons per second.

A watt is equal to volts times amperes. It is a measure of how much power is flowing. Electricity is sold in quantities of watt-hours.

The earth, by virtue of moisture contained within the soil, serves as a very effective conductor. Therefore, in power transmission, instead of having both the hot and neutral wires carried by the transmission poles, one lead of the generator is connected to the ground, which serves as a conductor (see Figure 1). Only hot wires are carried by the transmission towers. At the house, or point where the electricity is to be used, the circuit is completed by another connection to ground.

The electric power utility provides a ground somewhere in its local distribution system; therefore, there is a ground wire in addition to the hot wires within the service drop. In Figure 1 this ground can be seen at the power pole that contains the stepdown transformer.

In addition to the ground connection provided by the electric utility, every building is required to have an independent ground, called a "system ground."

The system ground provides for limiting the voltage upon the circuit, which might otherwise occur through exposure to lighting, or for limiting the maximum potential to ground due to normal voltage. Therefore, the system ground's main purpose is to protect the electric system itself and offer limited protection to the user.

The system ground serves the same purpose as the power company's ground, however, being closer to the building, it has a lower resistance.

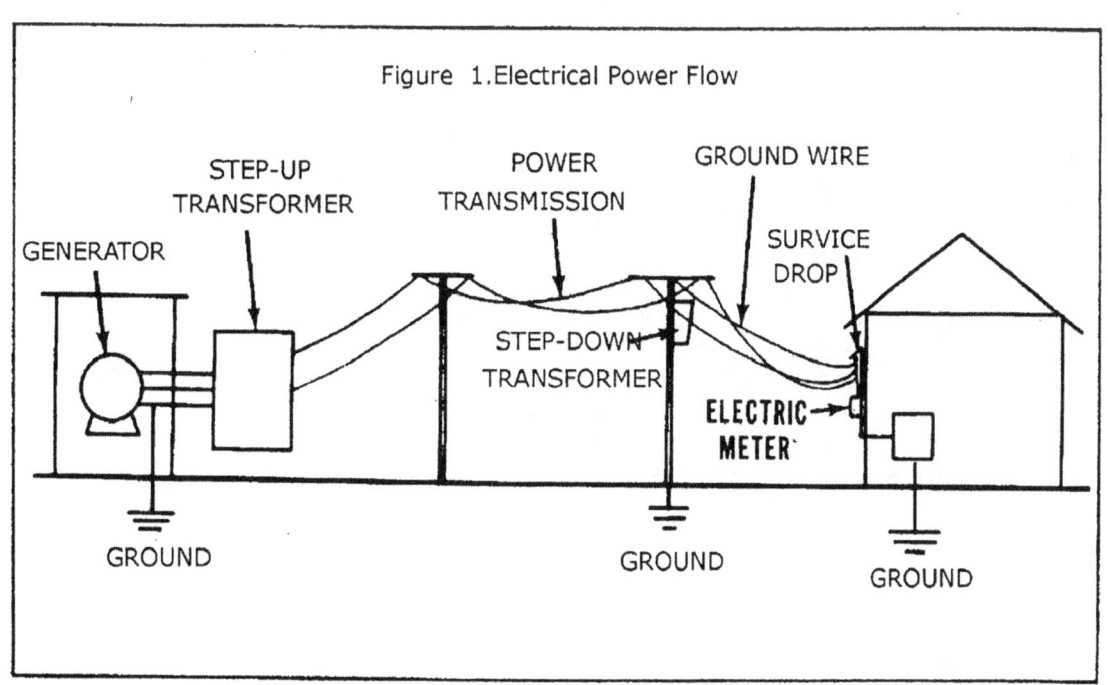

Figure 1. Electrical Power Flow

The "equipment ground," which we will discuss later in this chapter, protects man from potential harm during the use of certain electrical equipment.

The system ground should be a continuous wire of low resistance and of sufficient size to conduct current safely from lightning and overloads.

III. Electric Service Entrance

A Service Drop

The "Entrance Head" (see Figure 2) should be attached to the building at least 10 feet above ground, to prevent accidental contact by people. The conductor should clear all roofs by at least 8 feet and residential driveways by 12 feet. For public streets, alleys, roads, and driveways on other than residential property the clearance must be 18 feet.

The wires or conductor should be of sufficient size to carry the load and not smaller than No. 8 copper or equivalent.

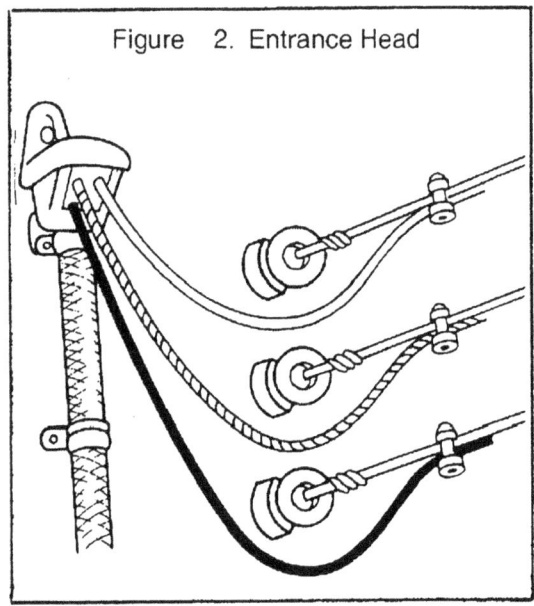

Figure 2. Entrance Head

For connecting wire from the entrance head to the service drop wires, the National Electrical Code requires that the service entrance conductors be installed either (1) below the level of the service head, or (2) below the termination of the service-entrance cable sheath. Drip loops must be formed on individual conductors. This will prevent water from entering the electric service system.

The wires that form "entrance cable" should extend 36 inches from the entrance head, to provide a sufficient length to connect service drop wires to the building with insulators (see Figure 2).

The entrance cable may be a special type of armored outdoor type of wire or it may be enclosed in a conduit. The electric power meter may be located either within or outside the building. In either instance, the meter must be located before the main power disconnect.

Figure 3 shows an armored cable service entrance. The armored cable is anchored to the building with metal straps spaced every 4 feet. The cable is run down the wall and through a hole drilled through the building. The cable is then connected to the service panel, which should be located within 1 foot of where the cable enters the building.

The ground wire need not be insulated. This ground wire may be either solid or stranded copper, or a material with an equivalent resistance.

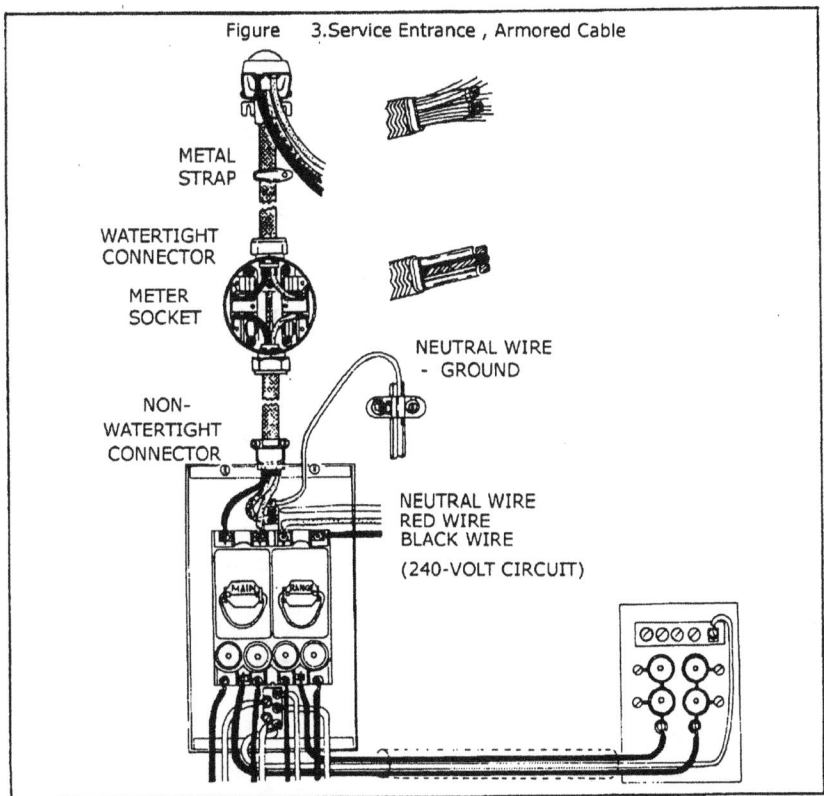

Figure 4 shows the use of thin-wall conduit in a service entrance.

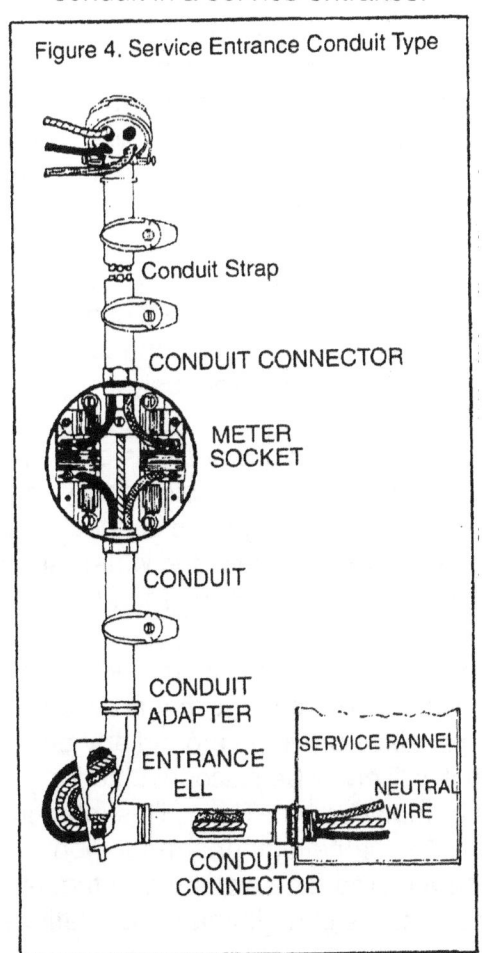

B Underground Service

When wires are run underground they must be protected from moisture and physical damage. The opening in the building foundation where the underground service enters the building must be moisture proof. Local codes should be referred to, concerning allowable materials for this type of service entrance.

C Electric Meter

The electric meter may be located inside or outside the building, as shown in Figure 3 or 4. The meter itself is weatherproof and is plugged into a weatherproof socket (see Figure 5). The electric power company furnishes the meter, the socket may or may not be furnished by the power company.

IV. Grounding

The system ground consists of grounding the neutral incoming wire as well as the neutral wire of the branch circuits. The equipment ground consists of grounding the metal parts of the service entrance, such as the service switch, as well as the service entrance conduit, armor, or cable.

The usual ground connection is to a water pipe of the city water system. The connection should be made to the street side of the cold water meter as shown in Figure 6.

If the water meter is located near the street curb, then the ground connection should be made to the cold water pipe as close as possible to where it enters the building.

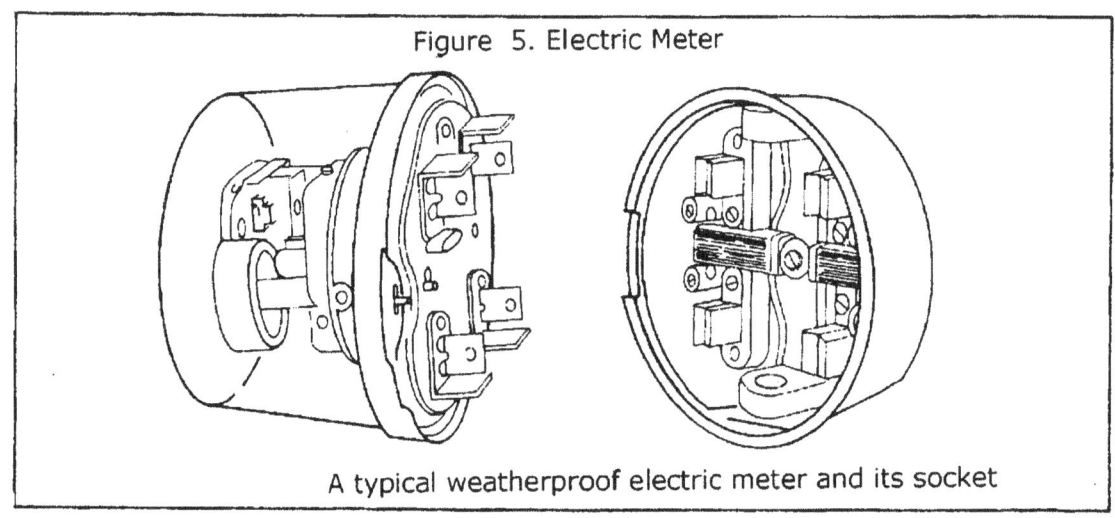

Figure 5. Electric Meter

A typical weatherproof electric meter and its socket

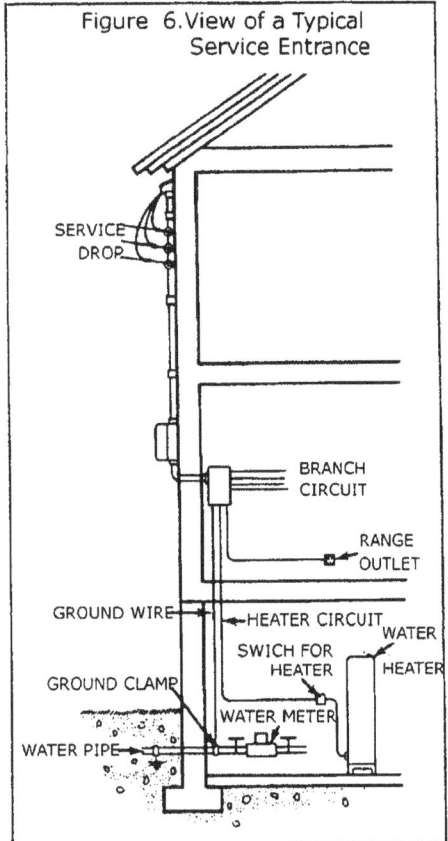

Figure 6. View of a Typical Service Entrance

It is not unusual for a water meter to be removed from a building for service. If the ground connection is made at a point in the water piping system on the building side of the water meter, the ground circuit will be broken upon removal of the meter. This broken ground circuit represents a shock hazard if both sides of the water meter connections should be touched simultaneously.

In some instances the connections between the water meter to pipes are electrically very poor. In this case, if the ground connection is made on the building side of the water meter, there may not be an effective ground.

In order to prevent the two aforementioned situations the code requires that an effective bonding shall be provided around any equipment that is likely to be disconnected for repairs or replacement. This is illustrated in Figure 7. The same jumper arrangement would be required for a water meter that is installed near the curb. In many installations the water meter mounting bracket is designed to serve as an electric jumper.

Often an amateur mechanic, in the process of doing a household repair, will disconnect the house ground. Therefore, the housing inspector should always check the house ground to see if it is properly connected.

Figure 8 shows a typical grounding scheme at the service box of a residence. In this figure, only the grounded neutral wires are shown. The neutral strap is an uninsulated metal strip that is riveted directly to the service box. The ground wires from the service entrance, branch circuits, and house ground are joined by this strip.

When a city water supply is not available for grounding, a substitute must be made. The most common ground is a pipe or rod that is driven into the ground a distance of at least 8 feet. If the pipe is made of steel or iron, it must be 3/4 inch in diameter and galvanized. A copper ground pipe of 1/2 inch diameter is sufficient.

The code requires that a ground rod be entirely independent of and kept at least 6 feet from any other ground of the type used for radio, telephone, or lightning rods.

V. Two- or Three-Wire Electric Services

One of the wires in every installation is grounded. This neutral wire is always white. The hot wires are usually black or red or some other color, but never white.

The potential difference or voltage between the hot wires and the ground or neutral of a normal residential electrical system is 115

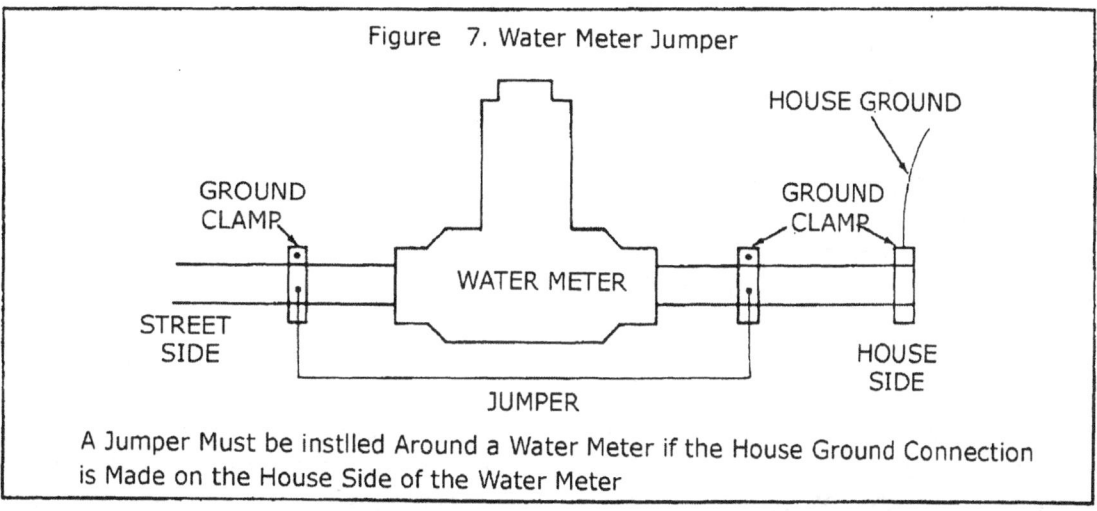

Figure 7. Water Meter Jumper

A Jumper Must be instlled Around a Water Meter if the House Ground Connection is Made on the House Side of the Water Meter

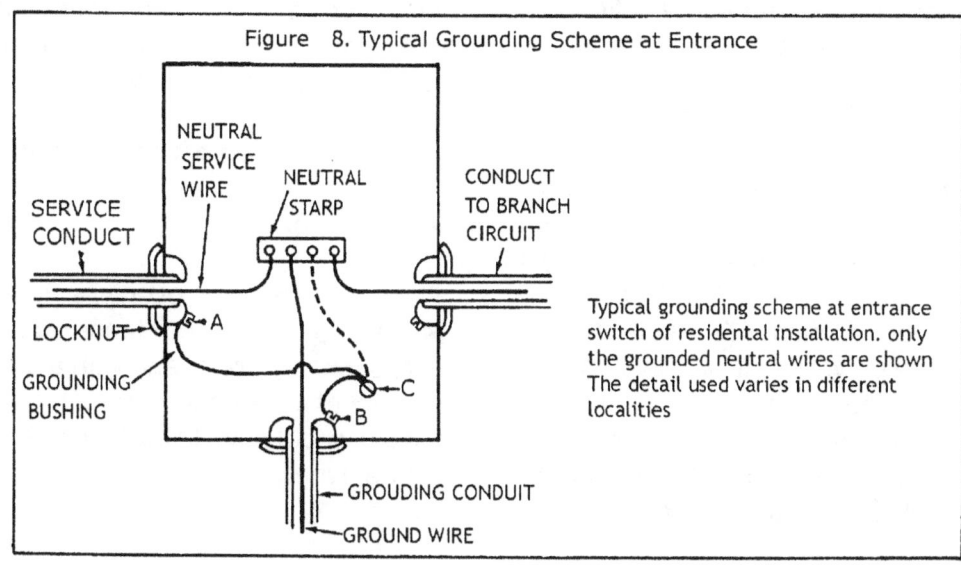

Figure 8. Typical Grounding Scheme at Entrance

Typical grounding scheme at entrance switch of residental installation. only the grounded neutral wires are shown The detail used varies in different localities

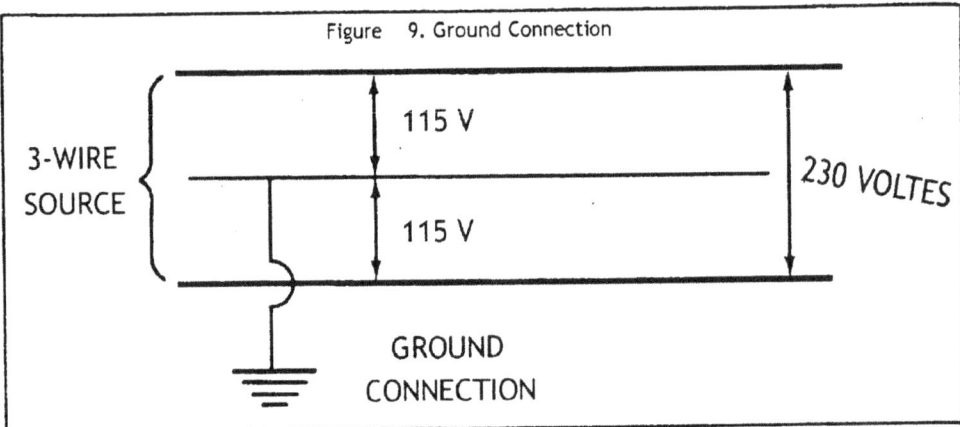

Figure 9. Ground Connection

volts. Thus, where we have a two-wire installation (one hot and one neutral) only 115-volt power is available (see Figure 9).

When three wires are installed (two hot and one neutral) either 115- or 230-volt power is available. In a three-wire system the voltage between the neutral and either of the hot wires is 115; between the two hot wires it is 230 volts.

The major advantage of a three-wire system is that it permits the operation of heavy electrical equipment such as laundry dryers, cooking ranges, and air conditioners, the majority of which require 230-volt circuits. In addition, the three-wire system is split at the service panel into two 115-volt systems to supply power for small appliances and electric lights. The result is a doubling of the number of circuits, and possibly a corresponding increase in the number of branch circuits, with a reduction of the probability of fire caused by overloading electrical circuits.

VI. Residential Wiring Adequacy

The use of electricity in the home has risen sharply since the 1930's. Many home owners have failed to repair or improve their wiring to keep it safe and up to date. The National Electrical Code recommends that individual residences be provided with a minimum of 100-ampere three-wire service. This type service is sufficient in a one-family house or dwelling unit to provide safe and adequate electric supply for the lighting, refrigerator, iron, and an 8,000-watt cooking range, plus other appliances requiring a total of up to 10,000 watts altogether.

Some homes have a 60-ampere, three-wire service. It is recommended that these homes be rewired for at least the minimum of 100 amperes recommended in the National Code since they are safely capable of supplying current only for lighting and portable appliances such as a cooking range and regular dryer (4,500 watts), or an electric hot-water heater (2,500 watts) and cannot handle additional major appliances.

Other homes today have only a 30-ampere, 115-volt, two-wire service. This system can safely handle only a limited amount of lighting, a few minor appliances, and no major appliances. Therefore, this size service is substandard in terms of modern household needs for electricity. Furthermore, it constitutes a fire hazard and a threat to the safety of the home and the occupants.

VII. Wire Size and Types

A   Wire Size

Electric power flows over wire. It flows with relative ease (little resistance) in some materials such as copper and with a substantial amount of resistance in iron. If iron wire were used it would have to be 10 times as large as copper wire.

Copper wire sizes are indicated by a number. No. 14 is most commonly used in residential branch circuits. No. 14 is the smallest permitted by the Code for use in a branch circuit with a 15-ampere capacity. No. 16, 18, and 20 are progressively smaller than No. 14 and are usually used for extension wires. As the number of the wire becomes smaller the size and current capacity of the wire increases. No. 1 is the heaviest wire usually used in ordinary household wiring.

Wire of correct size must be used for two reasons: current capacity and voltage drop.

1. When current flows through a wire it creates heat. The greater the amount of flow, the greater the amount of heat generated. (Doubling the amperes without changing the wire size increases the amount of heat by four times.) The heat is electric energy that has been converted into heat energy by the resistance of the wire; the heat created by the coils in a toaster is an example. This heat developed in an electrical conductor is wasted, and thus the electric energy used to generate it is wasted. If the amount of heat generated by the flow of current through the wire becomes excessive, a fire may result. Therefore, the code sets the maximum permissible current that may flow through a certain type and size wire.
The following are examples of current capacities for copper wire of various sizes.

Size wire (AWG)	#14	#12	#10	#8
Max. capacity, amperes	15	20	30	40

2. In addition to heat generation there will be a reduction in voltage as a result of attempting to force more current through a wire than it is capable of carrying. Certain appliances, such as induction-type electric motors, may be damaged if operated at too low a voltage.

B Wire Types

1. **Wire markings** - All wires must be marked to indicate the maximum working voltage, the proper type letter or letters for the type wire specified in the code, the manufacturer's name or trademark, and the AWG size or circular-mil area.

2. **Insulations used** There are a variety of wire types which can be used for a wide range of temperature and moisture conditions. The 1975 National Electrical Code should be consulted to determine the proper wire for specific conditions.

C Types of Cable

1. **Nonmetallic Sheathed Cable** - This type of cable consists of wires wrapped in a paper layer, followed by another spiral layer of paper, and enclosed in a fabric braid, which is treated with moisture-resistant and fire-resistant compounds. Figure 10 shows this type of cable, which often is marketed under the "Romex" name. This type of cable can be used only indoors and in permanently dry locations.

2. **Armored Cable** - This type of cable is commonly known by the BX or Flex-steel trade names. Wires are wrapped in a tough paper and covered with a strong spiral flexible steel armor. This type of cable is shown in Figure 11 and may be used only in permanently dry indoor locations. Armored cable must be supported by a strap or staple every 6 feet and within 24 inches of every switch or junction box, except for concealed runs in old work where it is impossible to mount straps.

3. **Other Cable** Cables are also available with other outer coatings of metals such as copper, bronze, and aluminum for use in a variety of conditions.

D Flexible Cords

Flexible cords are used to connect lamps, appliances, and other devices to outlets. Each wire consists of many strands of fine wire for flexibility. Extension cords in AWG sizes 16 to 18 are usually fine for lamps and smaller appliances, if the cord is not too long. A commonly accepted standard limits their length to 8 feet of unspliced cord. This keeps the cords short enough to prevent the excessive voltage drops, minimizes the possibility of fire caused by overheating of the wire due to overload, and also minimizes the danger of someone's tripping over them.

E Open Wiring

Open wiring is a wiring method using knobs, nonmetallic tubes, cleats, and flexible tubing for the protection and support of insulated conductors in or on buildings and not concealed by the structure. The term "open wiring" does not mean exposed, bare wiring. In dry locations when not exposed to severe

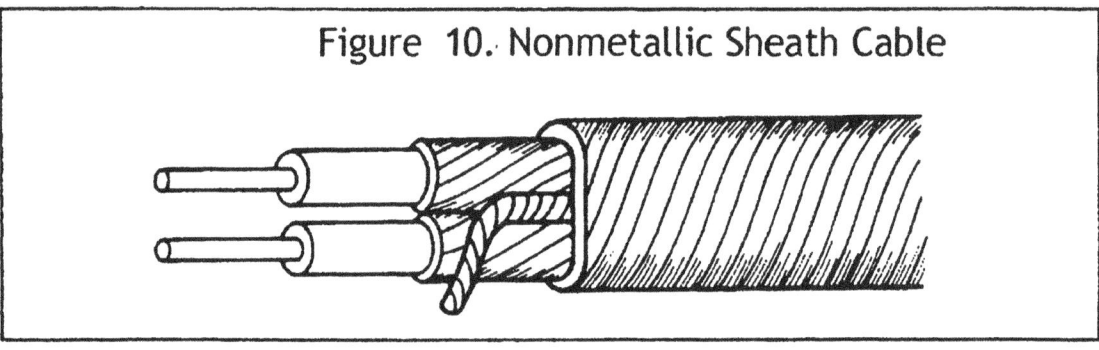

Figure 10. Nonmetallic Sheath Cable

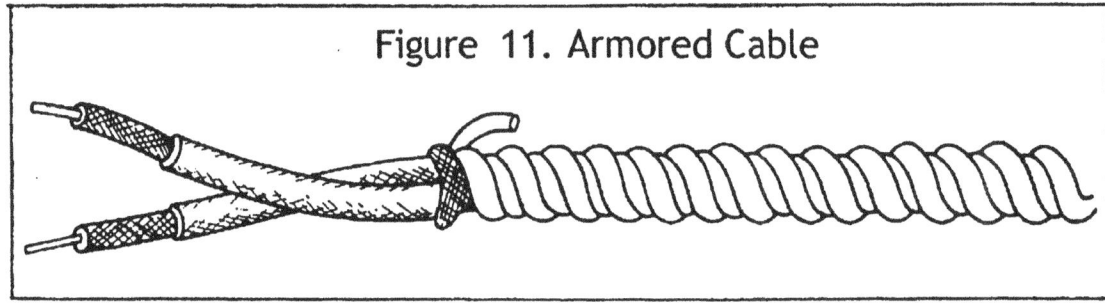

Figure 11. Armored Cable

physical damage, conductors may be separately encased in flexible tubing. Tubing should be in continuous lengths not exceeding 15 feet and secured to the surface by straps not more than 4 1/2 feet apart. They should be separated from other conductors by at least 2 1/2 inches and should have a permanently maintained airspace between them and any and all pipes they cross.

F Concealed Knob and Tube Wiring

Concealed knob and tube wiring is a wiring method using knobs, tubes, and flexible nonmetallic tubing for the protection and support of insulated wires concealed in hollow spaces of walls and ceilings of buildings. This wiring method is similar to open wiring, and like open wiring, is usually found only in older buildings.

VIII. Electric Service Panel

Service Switch
This is a main switch that will disconnect the entire electrical system at one

time. The main fuses or circuit breakers are usually located within the "Service Switch" box. The branch circuit fuse or circuit breaker may also be located within this box.

According to the code, the switch must be "externally operable." This condition is fulfilled if the switch can be operated without the operator's being exposed to electrically active parts. Older switches use external handles as shown in Figure 12.

Most of today's service switches do not have hinged switch blades. Instead, the main fuse is mounted on a small insulated block that can be pulled out of the switch. When this block is removed, the circuit is broken just as if the blades had been operated with a handle.

The neutral terminal or wire of a grounded circuit must never be interrupted by a fuse or circuit breaker. In some installations the service switch is a "solid neutral" switch. This means that the neutral wire in the switch is not broken by the switch or a fuse.

When circuit breakers instead of fuses are used in homes, the use of main circuit breakers may or may not be required. If it takes not more than six movements of the hand to open all the branch-circuit breakers, no main breaker or switch or fuse will be required ahead of the branch-circuit breakers. Thus, a house with seven or more branch circuits requires a separate disconnect means or a main circuit breaker ahead of the branch-circuit breakers (see Figure 13).

IX. Overcurrent Devices

The amperage (current flow) in any wire is limited to the maximum permitted by using an overcurrent device of a

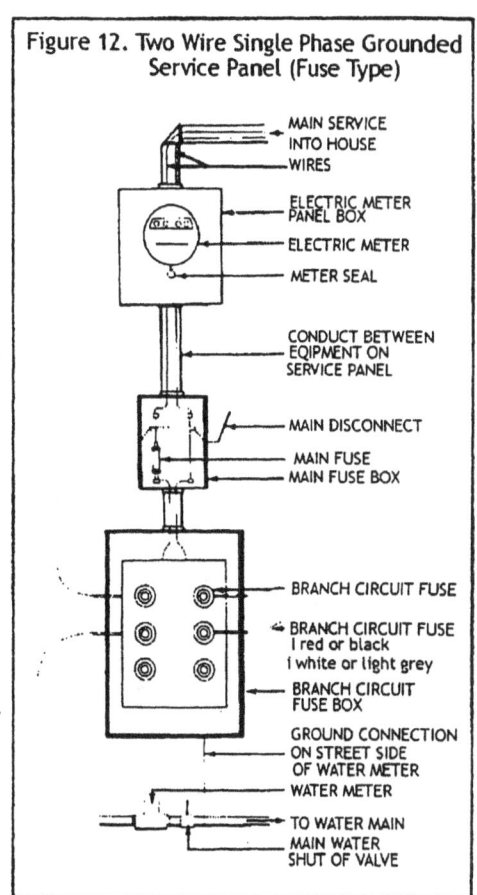

Figure 12. Two Wire Single Phase Grounded Service Panel (Fuse Type)

specific size as specified by the code. Two types of overcurrent devices are in common use: circuit breakers and fuses; both are rated in amperes. The overcurrent device must be rated at equal or lower capacity than the wire of the circuit it protects.

A   Circuit Breakers (Fuseless) Service Panels

A circuit breaker (see Figure 14) looks something like an ordinary electric light switch. There is a handle that may be used to turn power on or off. Inside is a simple mechanism that, in case of a circuit overload, trips the switch and breaks the circuit. The circuit breaker may be reset by simply flipping the switch. A circuit breaker is capable of taking harmless short-period overloads (such as the heavy initial current required in the starting of a washing machine or air conditioner) without tripping but protects against prolonged overloads. After the cause of trouble

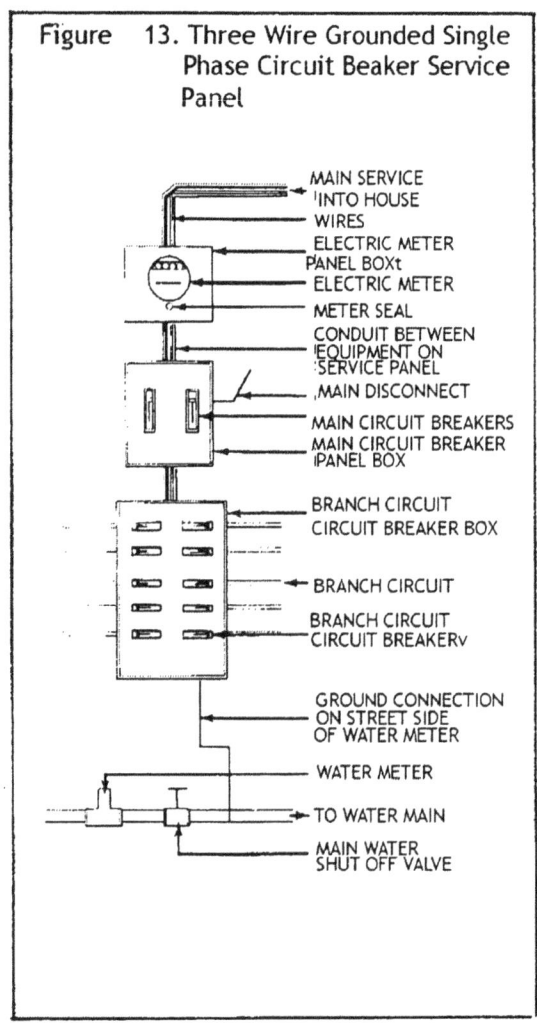

Figure 13. Three Wire Grounded Single Phase Circuit Beaker Service Panel

has been located and corrected, the power is easily restored by flipping the circuit breaker switch (circuit breakers are modern substitutes for fuses). Fuseless service panels are usually broken up into the following circuits.

1. A 100-ampere or larger main circuit breaker that shuts off all power.
2. A 40-ampere circuit for an appliance such as an electric cooking range. against the dangers of overloading
3. A 30-ampere circuit for clothes dryer, hot water heater, or central air conditioning.
4. A 20-ampere circuit for kitchen, small appliances, and power tools.
5. A 15-ampere circuit for general purpose lighting, TV, and vacuum cleaner.
6. Space for circuits to be added if needed for future use.

B Fused Ampere Service Panel or Fuse Box

Fuse-type panel boxes are generally found in older homes. They are equally as safe and adequate as a circuit breaker of equivalent capacity, provided fuses of the proper size are used.

A fuse (see Figure 15), like a circuit breaker, is designed to protect a circuit and short circuits and does this in two manners.

a. When a fuse is blown by a short circuit the metal strip is instantly heated to an extremely high temperature, and this heat causes it to vaporize. A fuse blown by a short circuit may be easily recognized because the window of the fuse usually becomes discolored.

b. In a fuse blown by overload the metal strip is melted at its weakest point, and this breaks the flow of current to the load. In this case the window of the fuse remains clear; therefore, a blown fuse caused by an overload may also be easily recognized.

Sometimes, although a fuse has not been blown, the bottom of the fuse may be severely discolored and pitted. This indicates a loose connection due to the fuse's not being screwed in properly.

Generally, all fused panel boxes are wired similarly for two- and three-wire systems. In a two-wire-circuit panel box the black or red hot wire is connected to a terminal of the main disconnect, and the white or light gray neutral wire is connected to the neutral strip, which is then grounded to the pipe on the street side of the water meter.

In a three-wire system the black and red hot wires are connected to separate terminals of the main disconnect, and the neutral wire is grounded the same as for a two-wire system (see Figure 12). Below each fuse is a terminal to which a black or red wire is connected. The white or light gray neutral wires are then connected to the neutral strip. Each fuse indicates a separate circuit.

1. **Non-tamperable Fuses** - All ordinary plug fuses, shown in Figure 15, have the same diameter and physical appearance regardless of their current capacity. Thus, if a circuit designed for a 15-ampere fuse is overloaded so that the 15-ampere fuse blows out, nothing will prevent a person from replacing the 15-ampere fuse with a 20- or 30-ampere fuse, which may not blow out. If a circuit wired with No. 14 wire (current capacity 15 amperes) is fused with a 20- or 30-ampere fuse and an overload develops, more current than the No. 14 wire is safely capable of carrying could pass through the circuit. The result would be a heating of the wire and a potential fire.

Type S fuses, shown in Figure 15, have different lengths and diameter threads for each different amperage capacity. An adapter is first inserted into the ordinary fuse holder, which adapts the fuse holder for only one capacity fuse. Once the adapter is inserted, it cannot be removed.

2. **Cartridge Fuses**

Figure 15 shows two different types of cartridge fuses. A cartridge fuse protects an electric circuit in the same manner as an ordinary plug fuse already described protects it. Cartridge fuses are often used as main fuses.

X. Electric Circuits

An electric circuit in good repair carries electricity through two or three wires from the source of supply to an outlet and back to the source.

A Branch Circuit

A branch circuit is an electric circuit that supplies electric current to a limited number of electric outlets and fixtures. A residence generally has many branch circuits. Each is protected against short circuits and overloads by a 15- or 20-ampere fuse or circuit breaker.

The number of outlets per branch circuit varies from building to building. The code requires enough light circuits so that 3 watts of power will be available for each square foot of floor area

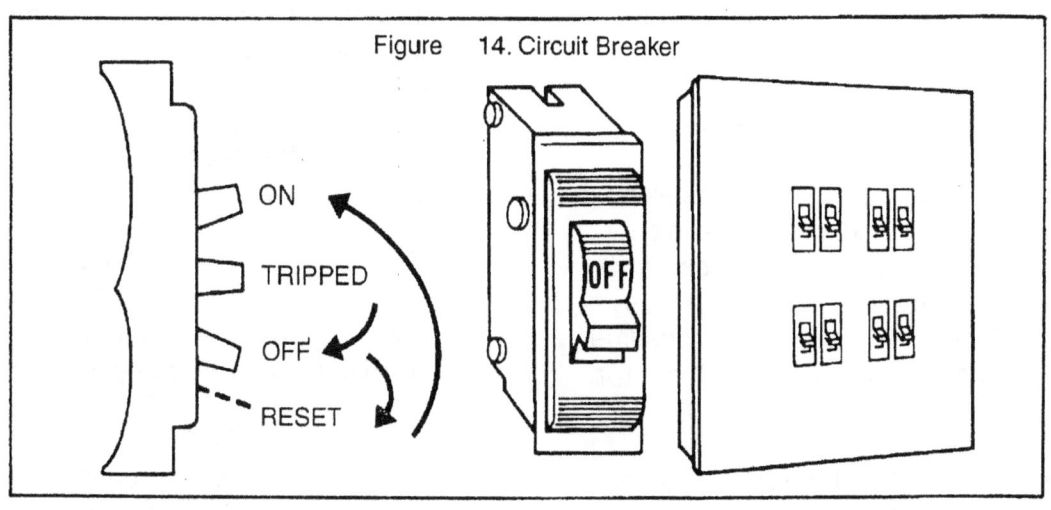

Figure 14. Circuit Breaker

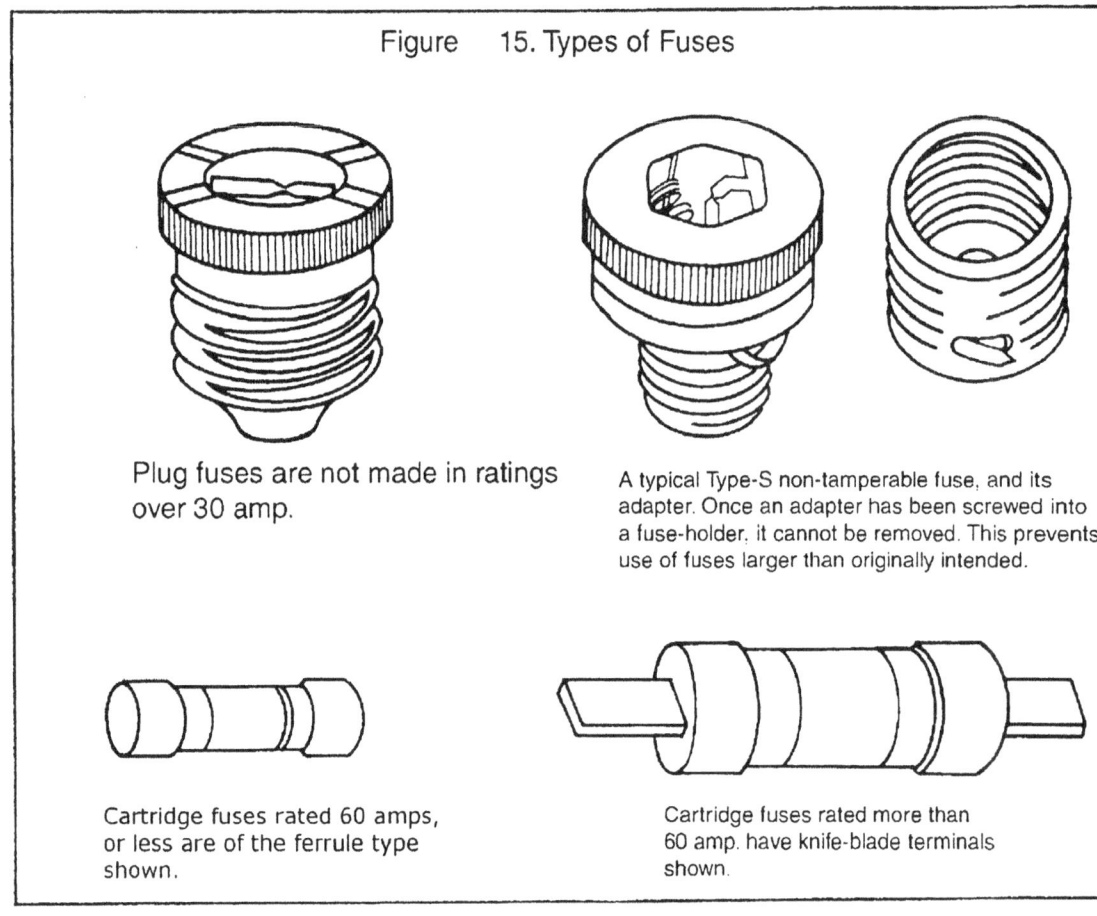

Figure 15. Types of Fuses

Plug fuses are not made in ratings over 30 amp.

A typical Type-S non-tamperable fuse, and its adapter. Once an adapter has been screwed into a fuse-holder, it cannot be removed. This prevents use of fuses larger than originally intended.

Cartridge fuses rated 60 amps, or less are of the ferrule type shown.

Cartridge fuses rated more than 60 amp. have knife-blade terminals shown.

in a house. A circuit wired with No. 14 wire and protected by a 15-ampere overcurrent protection device provides 15 X 115 or 1,725 watts; each circuit is obviously enough for 1,725/3 or 575 square feet.

Note that 575 is a minimum figure; if future use is considered, 500 or even 400 square feet per branch circuit should be used.

B **Special Appliance Circuits**

The branch circuit will provide electric power for lighting, radio, television, and small portable appliances. However, the larger electric appliances usually found in the kitchen consume more power and must have their own special circuit.

Section 220-3b of the code requires two special circuits to serve only appliance outlets in kitchen, laundry, pantry, family-room, dining room, and breakfast room. Both circuits must be extended to the kitchen; the other rooms may be served by either one or both of these circuits. No lighting outlets may be connected to these circuits, and they must be wired with No. 12 wire and protected by a 20-ampere overcurrent device. Each circuit will have a capacity of 20 X 115 or 2,300 watts, which is not too much when one considers that toasters often require over 1,600 watts.

C **Individual Appliance Circuits**

It is customary to provide a circuit for each of the following appliances:

1. Range
2. Water heater
3. Automatic laundry
4. Clothes dryer

5	Garbage disposer	
6	Dishwasher	
7	Furnace	
8	Water pump	

Note that these circuits may be either 115 volts or 230 volts, depending on the particular appliance or motor installed.

D Outlet Switch and Junction Boxes

The code requires that every switch, outlet, and joint in wire or cable be housed in a box. Every fixture must be mounted on a box. Most boxes are made of metal with a galvanized finish. Figure 16 shows a typical outlet box.

When a cable of any style is used for wiring, the code requires that it be securely anchored with a connector to each box it enters.

E Grounding Outlets

An electrical appliance may appear to be in good repair, and yet it might be a danger to the user. Consider a portable electric drill. It consists of an electric motor inside a metal casing. When the switch is depressed, the current flows to the motor, and the drill rotates. As a result of wear, however, the insulation on the wire inside the drill may deteriorate and allow the hot side of the power cord to come in contact with the metal casing. This will not affect the operation of the drill.

A person fully clothed using the drill in the living room, which has a dry floor, will not receive a shock, even though he is in contact with the electrified drill case. His body is not grounded, because of the dry floor. If, however, the operator should be standing on a wet basement floor, his body might be grounded, and when he touches the electrified drill case, current will pass through his body.

In order to protect man, the drill case is usually connected to the system ground by means of a wire called an "appliance ground." In this instance, as the drill is plugged in, current will flow between the shorted hot wire and the drill case and cause the overcurrent device to break the circuit. Thus the appliance ground has protected man. The appliance ground is the third wire found on many appliances.

The appliance ground on the appliance will be of no use unless the outlet into which the appliance is plugged is grounded. The outlet is grounded by being in physical contact with a ground outlet box. The outlet box is grounded by having a third ground wire, or a grounded conduit, as part of the circuit wiring.

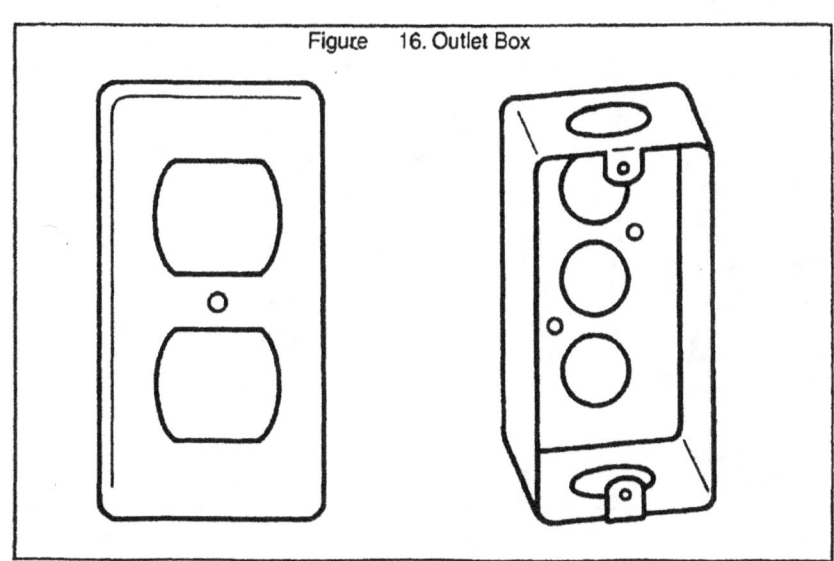

Figure 16. Outlet Box

All new buildings are required to have grounded outlets (as shown in Figure 17). The outlet may be tested by using a circuit tester. The circuit tester should light when both of its leads are plugged into the two elongated parallel openings of the outlet. In addition, the tester should light when one lead is plugged into the round third opening and the other is plugged into the hot side of the outlet.

If the conventional two-opening outlet is used, it still may be grounded. In this instance the screw that holds the outlet cover plate is the third-wire ground. The tester should light when one lead is in contact with a clean paint-free metal outlet cover plate screw and the hot side of the outlet. If the tester fails to light then the outlet is not grounded. If the outlet is not grounded then the tester will not function.

If a two-opening outlet is grounded, it may be adapted for use by a three-wire appliance by using an adapter. The loose-wire portion of the adapter should be secured behind the metal screw of the outlet plate cover.

Many appliances such as electric shavers and some new hand tools are double insulated and are safe without having a third ground wire.

XI. Common Electrical Violations

A   The most apparent requirements that a housing inspector must check are the existence of the power supply; the types, locations, and conditions of the wiring in use; and the existence of the number of wall outlets or ceiling fixtures required by his local code and their condition. In making his investigations, these considerations will serve as useful guides:

1   **Power Supply** - Where is it located, is it grounded properly, and is it at least of minimum capacity required to supply current safely for lighting and the major and minor appliances in the dwelling?

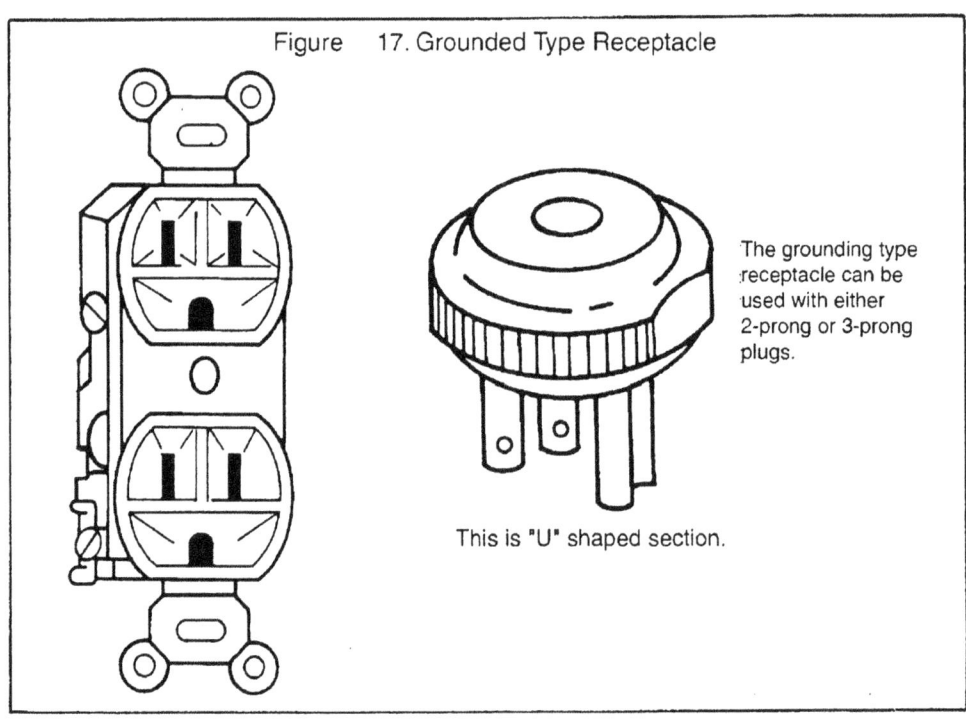

Figure 17. Grounded Type Receptacle

The grounding type receptacle can be used with either 2-prong or 3-prong plugs.

This is "U" shaped section.

2. **Panel Box Covers or Doors** - These should be accessible only from the front and should be sealed in such a way that they can be operated safely without the danger of contact with live or exposed parts of the wiring system.

3. **Switch, Outlets, and Junction Boxes** - These also must be covered to protect against danger of electric shock.

4. **Frayed or Bare Wires** - These are usually the result of long use and a drying out and cracking of the insulation, which leave the wires exposed, or else a result of constant friction and rough handling of the wire, which cause it to fray or become bare. Wiring in this condition constitutes a safety hazard, and correction of such defects should be ordered immediately.

5. **Electric Cords Under Rugs or Other Floor Coverings** - Putting electric cords in locations such as these is prohibited because of the potential fire hazard caused by continuing contact over a period of time between these heat-bearing cords and the flammable floor coverings. Direct the occupant to shift the cords to a safe location, explain why, and make sure it is done before you leave.

6. **Bathroom Lighting** - It should include at least one permanently installed ceiling or wall light fixture with a wall switch and plate so located and maintained that there is no danger of short circuiting from use of other bathroom facilities or splashing of water. Fixture or cover plates should be insulated or grounded.

7. **Lighting of Public Hallways, Stairways, Landings, and Foyers** A common standard here is sufficient lighting to provide illumination of 10 foot-candles on every part of these areas at all times. Sufficient lighting means that a person can clearly see his feet on all parts of the stairways and halls. Every public hall and stairway in a structure containing *less than three* dwelling units may be supplied with conveniently located light switches controlling an adequate lighting system that may be turned on when needed, instead of full-time lighting.

8. **Habitable Room Lighting** - The standard here may be two floor convenience outlets although floor outlets are dangerous unless protected by proper dust and water covers or one convenience outlet and one wall or ceiling electric light fixture. This number constitutes an absolute and often inadequate minimum given the contemporary widespread use of electricity in the home. The minimum should be that number required to provide adequate lighting and power to accommodate lighting and appliances normally used in each room.

9. **Octopus Outlets or Wiring** - This term is applied to outlets into which plugs have been inserted and are being used to permit more than two lights or portable appliances, such as a TV, lamp, or radio, to be connected to the electrical system. The condition occurs where the number of outlets is insufficient to accommodate the normal use of the room. This practice overloads the circuit and is a potential source of fire, which may be caused by overloading the circuit.

10. **Outlet Covers** - Every outlet and receptacle must be covered by a protective plate to prevent contact of its wiring or terminals with the body, combustible object or splashing water.

The following items are conditions that cause needless dangers and must also be corrected:

a. **Excessive or faulty fusing** - The wire's capacity must not be exceeded by the fuse or circuit breaker capacity or be left unprotected by faulty fusing or circuit breakers. Fuses and circuit breakers are safety devices designed to "blow" as a means of protection against overloadings of the electrical system or one or more of its circuits. Pennies under fuses are put there to bypass the fuse. These are illegal and must be removed. Overfusing is done for the same reason. The latter can be prevented by the installation of modern fuse stats, which prevent use of any fuse of a higher amperage than can be handled by the circuit it serves.

b **Cords run through walls or doorways and hanging cords or wires** - This is a makeshift-type installation and most often is installed by an unqualified handyman or do-it-yourself occupant. The inspector should check with his local electrical section to determine the policy regarding this type of insulation and govern his action in accordance with the electrical section's policies.

c **Temporary wiring** - This type of installation should not be allowed, with the exception of extension cords that go directly from portable lights and electric fixtures to convenience outlets.

d **Excessively long extension cords** - This requirement does not apply to specially designed extension cords for operating portable tools and trouble lights. Cities operating under modern code standards limit the length of loose cords or extension lines to a maximum of 8 feet. This is necessary because those that are too long will overheat if overloaded or if a short circuit develops and thus create a fire hazard. Even shorter lengths are feasible in housing with new or updated wiring systems that include one convenience outlet every 12 feet around the perimeter of the room.

e **Dead or dummy outlets** - These are sometimes installed to deceive the inspection agency. This is why all outlets must be tested or the occupants questioned to see if these are alive and functioning properly. A dead outlet cannot be counted to determine compliance with the code.

XII. Steps Involved in Actual Inspection

A **Testing Tools**

The basic tools required by an inspector of housing for making an electrical inspection are a fuse and circuit tester and a flashlight.

B **Danger of Techniques**

The first thing is to remember you are in a strange house and the layout is unfamiliar to you. The second thing to remember is that you are dealing with electricity *take no chances*. Go to the water meter and check the ground. It should connect to the water line on the street side of the water meter or else be equipped with a jumper wire. Do not touch any box or wire until you are sure of the ground. Go to the main fuse box and check all fuses in all boxes. Note the condition of the wiring and of the box itself and check whether it is overfused or not. Examine all wiring in the cellar. Make sure you are standing in a dry spot before touching any electrical device. Do not disassemble the fuse box or other devices. Decisions must be made on what you see. If in doubt, consult your supervisor.

Make note whether any fuse boxes or junction boxes are uncovered. Examine all wiring for frayed or bare spots, improper splicing, or rotted, worn, or inadequate insulation. Avoid all careless touching. When in doubt DON'T! If you see bare wire, have the owner call an electrician. Look for wires or cords in use in the cellar. Many work benches are lighted by an old lamp that was once in the parlor and now has a spliced or badly frayed cord or both. Be certain all switch boxes and outlets are in a tight, sound condition.

Make sure that the emergency switch for the oil burner is at the top of the cellar stairs, not on top of the unit.

If you find an electric clothes washer-clothes dryer combination in a dwelling, it should have a 240-volt circuit 30-ampere service connected to a separate fuse or circuit breaker. Washer-dryer combinations and other portable appliances in the entire house should be served by sufficiently heavy service. If either of these special lines is not available under the above-stated conditions, consult your supervisor.

An electric range needs a 50-ampere circuit, 240 volts. A dishwasher needs a 20-ampere, 120-volt circuit. A separate three-wire circuit must be installed for an electric water heater. Continue your inspection this way through the house. In the bathroom look for the usual items, but also check for dangerous items such as radios or plug-in portable electric heaters. Have them removed immediately. Such items have killed thousands of people either has a spliced or badly frayed cord or both. Be certain all switch boxes and outlets are in a tight, sound condition. Make sure that the emergency switch for the oil burner is at the top of the cellar stairs, not on top of the unit.

If you find an electric clothes washer-clothes dryer combination in a dwell-

ing, it should have a 240-volt circuit 30-ampere service connected to a separate fuse or circuit breaker. Washer-dryer combinations and other portable appliances in the entire house should be served by sufficiently heavy service. If either of these special lines is not available under the above-stated conditions, consult your supervisor.

An electric range needs a 50-ampere circuit, 240 volts. A dishwasher needs a 20-ampere, 120-volt circuit. A separate three-wire circuit must be installed for an electric water heater. Continue your inspection this way through the because they touched them after getting out of the bathtub or shower while still wet or because the appliance fell into the water. Look for brass pull chains in bathroom lighting fixtures. If one exists, have owner attach a string to the end of it as a temporary precaution, then order it replaced with a wall switch as required by the electrical code.

To sum up, in broad terms, the housing inspector's investigation of specified electrical elements in a house is made to detect any obvious evidence of an insufficient power supply, to ensure the availability of adequate and safe lighting and electrical facilities, and to discover and correct any obvious hazard. Because electricity is a technical, complicated field, the housing inspector, when in doubt, should consult his supervisor. He cannot, however, close the case until appropriate corrective action has been taken on all such referrals.

XIII. Wattage Consumption of Electrical Appliances

(100 watts = approximately 1 ampere)

Appliance	Watts
Air conditioner (central)	5,000
Air conditioner (window)	see name plate
Blanket	150
Blender	250
Chaffing Dish	600
Clock	3
Coffee Maker	600
Deep fryer	1,320
Dishwasher	1,800
Egg boiler	250
Electric shaver	10
Fan	75
Food mixer	200
Furnace (fuel fixed)	800
Frying pan	600
Garbage disposer	900
Griddle	1,300
Grill	600
Heater (radiant)	1,600
Heating pad	50
Hot-plate (2 burners)	1,650
Humidifier	500
Immersion heater	300
Iron	1,000
Ironer	1,650
Lighting	
Bed lamp	40
Ceiling light	100
Decorative lights	80
Dining light	150
Dresser lamps	60
Drop light	60
Floor lamp	400
Fluorescent	80
Sun lamp	275
Table lamp	100

Appliance	Watts
Radio	100
Range	8,000 to 16,000
Refrigerator	250
Roaster (large)	1,380
Rotisserie	1,400
Sewing machine	75
Soldering iron	200
Stereo hi-fi	300
Sump pump	300
Television	300
Toaster	1,100
Vacuum cleaner	400
Waffle iron	660
Washing machine	5,200
Water heater	2,500-4,500
Water pump	300

XIV. Motor Currents

Horsepower	Full load amperes			
	115 v	230 1-phase	230 2-phase	230 3-phase
1/4	5.8	2.9		
1/2	9.8	4.9	2.0	2.0
3/4	13.8	6.9	2.4	2.8
1	16.0	8.0	3.2	3.6

HUMAN RELATIONS ASPECTS OF A HOUSING INSPECTION

I. General Considerations

The term "housing inspection" is generally understood to mean a close-up observation of actual conditions that exist in a dwelling and on its premises. It is conducted by a trained, qualified, and competent appointed official to determine whether the observed conditions meet the minimum requirements specified by the local housing ordinance. In cases where the minimum requirements are not met, the inspection procedure offers an opportunity to begin the necessary action to bring the existing conditions up to a level that will be acceptable under provisions of the ordinance.

A. **Purposes of the Housing Inspection**

   For the occupant of the dwelling unit, the inspection should be an opportunity to compare the conditions in which he lives with those considered to be minimal to protect his health and safety. In addition it provides a check on the quality of maintenance given to the facilities of his dwelling unit since the last inspection.

   For the code enforcement or housing improvement agency, the inspection procedure provides a means for:

   1. Gathering data that can be combined with other, similar data to develop a comprehensive picture of housing conditions in the community as an aid to measure improvement progress.

   2. Executing its responsibility for protecting the health and safety of individual citizens as well as the public generally.

   The main focus of the housing agency's activities should be primarily related to the improvement of the housing quality of the community rather than to the mere enforcement of a housing ordinance.

B. **The Housing Inspection as a Technique for Improving Housing Quality**

   The inspection procedure should be considered a technique, which used in concert with other techniques, is intended to improve continually the housing quality throughout the community. The inspection procedure, if properly used, is an effective tool in achieving code compliance.

   1. It provides a reasonably accurate measurement of actual dwelling and premises conditions to indicate improvement or slippage in housing quality when compared with previously collected data.

   2. It provides a convenient opportunity for consultation to take place between the occupant and the inspector regarding conditions that do not meet code requirements.

   3. It provides a means of measuring the effectiveness of techniques, such as use of press, radio, TV, and neighborhood improvement projects, which may also be employed to help improve community housing quality.

   4. It provides information that can be later used if some form of legal action becomes necessary to bring about code compliance.

Legal action, as a form of persuasiveness, is often considered to be the least desirable. It can cause adverse publicity for the agency that can hinder its future work. It is costly. Legal action can cause a false impression to be formed by the public regarding the purposes of the agency and the functions of its personnel. It is a last-resort effort that is in a sense an admission of failure at being able to teach housing hygiene principles and persuade their acceptance.

C. The Community Housing Improvement Program

The success of a community housing improvement program generally depends upon several basic factors.

1. Adoption, by municipal officials, of a housing ordinance with realistic code provisions that will help maintain the quality of "good" housing and substantially improve the quality of "poor" housing conditions.
2. The code administration compliance program must be well planned and conducted in a systematic fashion.
3. The program must have sufficient financial support for an adequate number of personnel and other administrative needs.
4. Legal counsel and direct legal aid must be readily available to the program staff when needed.
5. Housing inspectors must be adequately trained and supervised so that they can conduct their work competently.
6. The general acceptance, support, and participation of the public in the housing improvement efforts of the program must be secured.

In the end, this last item will largely determine the measure of success or failure of the program.

The housing agency, as all other governmental units, is a tax-supported public agency that belongs to the people it serves. In the final analysis its future existence to continue serving the needs of the people will depend upon the people's wish to maintain it. This in turn depends upon their understanding of and satisfaction with the services of the agency and the performance of its personnel. Modern thinking is along the line of doing "with" people rather than "for or to" them. When applied to a housing agency and the public it serves, the word "with" implies everything that contributes to good human relations.

II. Human Relations and Attainment of Housing Goals

The term "human relations" as used here actually refers to two types of relationships between people: The personal one-to-one or person-to-person relationship and the relationship that exists between the agency and the general public.

They are interrelated. The public is composed of individuals with attitudes and feelings that when taken jointly make up the public sentiment. This sentiment forms the basis for the relationship that develops between the housing agency and the general public.

A The Housing Inspector and Public Relations

The housing inspector is more concerned with the one-to-one or person-to-person relationships than with the relationship between the agency and the public. The latter is more a responsibility of the supervisory or executive levels of the agency; the housing inspector, however, meets individual members of the public personally on a daily basis. What he does and how he does it, even what he does not do but should do, help to shape the individual's attitudes about the inspector as well as about the agency he represents. Individual attitudes added together form the basis of the public's opinion of the agency and are important in determining whether the public will or will not cooperate with the housing improvement efforts.

The effects of the housing inspector's contacts with the public can have even deeper implications. Since the only contact many members of the public may have with the municipal government is through the housing inspector, he may, to them, represent the municipal administration. This is especially true for the inner-city poverty area resident to whom the housing inspector may well be the municipal government. The housing inspector has more personal contact with members of the public than any other municipal employee, even the mayor. To a large degree, the success of his relationships may well determine the success or failure of many municipal programs other than the housing improvement program.

B **Anatomy of the Person -To - Person Communication Interaction**

Since the person-to-person relationships of the housing inspector have such far-reaching effects, it is important for him to have some idea of what takes place when two persons confront each other in an attempt to communicate.

When two persons meet and attempt to communicate with each other, their reactions to what is said by the other are dependent upon many factors. The behavior of an individual (John) in the presence of another person (Frank) is, at the same time, both a response and a stimulus to the actions of Frank. Because John knows that Frank will react to the manner in which John conducts himself, he (John) is likely to temper his behavior. John may, knowingly or unknowingly to himself, behave in such a way as to bring about certain responses from Frank. John's subsequent behavior thence depends upon whether or not he brings about the desired responses from Frank.

Of course this is an oversimplified explanation of a very complex matter explained in terms of stimulus and response, action and reaction. Under ordinary circumstances, the behavior of persons in interaction flows quite smoothly. This occurs if each party to the interaction has learned to anticipate the response that an action on his part will elicit, as well as to anticipate the responses he will make toward the actions of the other party. *Such interactions flow smoothly, however, only when both parties share the same definitions of their own and each other's acts, as well as an understanding of their relation with each other.*

On the assumption that the housing inspector understands his job to be that of teacher and motivator in addition to that of code enforcement officer, it is to his advantage to have a workable knowledge of the person-to-person communications technique. Armed with this advantage, his job of making people interested in the things they may not want to be interested in becomes easier.

C **How To Interest People In Things They Don't Want To Know**

Every normal human being is interested in many things. Certainly he is interested in himself, his family, and conditions that affect his daily life. To establish an effective communications link the housing inspector must fmd a way to relate what he wants to say with what the other person is already interested in. If he can do this, the inspector can reach him and teach him what he needs to know to improve his housing conditions. This is a two-step process; the inspector must:

- ☑ get the attention or interest of the subject;
- ☑ then do the teaching.

Everyone the inspector tries to reach will have some interest, some need, some desire, to which he can relate himself and his message. At the start, it must be something in which the subject is interested, not something in which the inspector is interested. He must find this need or desire and use it to anchor an emotional or intellectual bridge between himself and his subject. Then he can send his messages across tltis bridge to his subject.

I **How To Get The Interest Of The Subject**

Obviously, until the inspector has figured out what need or desire he can serve in the subject - and until he states convincingly to the subject - he cannot begin to interest the subject in anything. In fact, the person may not even know that he should have a particular need or desire. This may be especially true with dwellers of inner-city poverty areas who have lived in poor housing conditions so long that their sensibilities to react to these conditions have been dulled. In this instance the best starting place might be to reawaken these sensibilities.

To recognize the needs and desires of the subject, one must know as much about the subject as the subject knows himself - perhaps even more. To do this effectively, the inspector must first recognize and accept certain basic facts:

a. That there is no such thing as "one" or "the" public. All communities - and neighborhoods - have population subgroups based on religion, economic or social status, race, education, nationality, age, sex, and occupation.

b. Childhood rearing patterns vary in each of these subgroups so that the experiences, attitudes, and behavior of individuals belonging to each of these subgroups will be different. These differences may be evident in their attitude and behavior toward the municipal government, its representatives, and even members of other subgroups. Municipal officials the~selves constitute a subgroup that is further broken down by smaller sub groupings formed on the basis of rank, status, or the type of duties performed.

c. Inner-city dwellers in particular may confuse the housing inspector if he is unfamiliar with their problems.

Many of these residents have migrated from remote rural areas that kept them isolated from the mainstream of technological change that has occurred so rapidly in this country. They may have received little or no education or job training. Many came to the city with the sincere hope of improving their condition and becoming a member of the American society. Being unfamiliar with city ways, however, they soon found themselves in difficulty with the law, without a job, and in living conditions that were worse than those they had left in the rural hinterlands.

Often many do not recognize an illness, much less know where to get treatment, even though a health clinic may be just down the street. Some have never been trained to perform simple technical functions such as how to use a washing machine. To survive, many fathers have had temporarily to leave their families in search of work in other cities. Some never return, leaving the women to raise the family. Boys and young men grow up with deeprooted feelings of insecurity, never having had the model of their father to guide their development into manhood. Often any municipal employee represents the real or imagined oppression of the government and is a likely target on which to vent pent-up anxieties.

d. The housing inspector must realize that he also belongs to one or more population subgroups with attitudes and behavior patterns that are different from those found in other groups. As a housing inspector, he must neutralize the attitudes or behavior patterns that may evoke an undesired response from the subject. He must further make it· clear to the person with whom he is trying to establish a communications link that, although there are differences between them, he is unbiased and nonjudgmental in their relationship, and that he expects the same from the subject. These are generally expected characteristics of persons belonging to the subgroupings of municipal officials.

e. By using whatever background knowledge he can learn about the people with whom he must work, the inspector, with some tactful probing, should be able to determine their needs and desires and build a communications bridge to them by establishing a genuine interest in *them*.

2 How To Get Your Message Across

Once the communications bridge has been built, the housing inspector can begin sending messages across. The message he has to tell must be important to the subject, related to some basic need or desire of his, and related in his terms, not the inspector's.

Then he can hope to move the subject in the direction he wants him to go, that is, toward improving his housing conditions.

Every communication has three elements, each of which determines the value of the other two. There is the content of the message, what it is the inspector wants to say. There is the form of the message, how the content is expressed and transmitted, and this includes both the medium and words used. And there is the subject of the communications, the person to whom it is directed.

Obviously until all three of these content, form, and subject are carefully and successfully related to each other, the communication is not likely to have the desired result. The content must be properly and precisely related to the subject. How the message is stated must be properly and precisely related to the content and the subject of the communication. If these three are not effectively related, the intended message will fall short of communicating.

Finally, the communicator, that is, the inspector, must not be message oriented. Although his message may be important to the subject, it may also be new and different, and the importance of the message may have no impact on the subject. The inspector must be always conscious of whom he is trying to reach, of how that person thinks and feels; as he directs his efforts, he shapes his message and form of delivery, as best he can, to fit the subject. To do this, he must start with his subject in mind; that is where persuasive person-to-person communication starts.

D Interagency Relations

The housing inspector should realize that the housing improvement program is only one of manyprograms of municipal administration. During a normal work day, the housing inspector is likely to meet other municipal employees in the same neighborhoods working with the same people.

With the multiplicity of community and personal improvement programs in effect today, especially in inner-city poverty areas, the traffic of public employees can become bewildering, if not irritating, to the neighborhood residents. Naturally, all employees feel their work is important, and in their striving to achieve their goals, compete with other employees for the time, interest, and support of community residents. If competition for the attention of neighborhood residents becomes too intense, the result might well be the polarization of indi viduals around one or a few program activities — those that interest or benefit them mosL Or worse, the result might be sheer apathy and loss of support or interest in any program's efforts. Several things can be done to avert this very undesirable situation and make the efforts of all public employees mutually beneficial. They include the following:

1. The housing inspector should try to determine which employees have duties related to his or perform similar activities. These will usually be health, building, electrical, fire, and various public works employees. He should then try to learn as much as possible about the other employee's work that relates to his own. Then, if he discovers conditions that should be brought to the attention of other departments, he will know enough to determine whether the condition really does constitute a hazard or a violation of another ordinance. Unnecessary inspections can become costly to the municipal administration, time consuming and bothersome for the other employees as well as for the resident.

    A possible result of this type of needless activity can easily result in alienation of both the other city employees and the resident. Eventually the housing inspector will find himself without the participation and support of others in his program efforts.

2. The housing inspector should try to develop lines of liaison or channels of communications with employees of other units. Then, through these channels he should attempt either formally or informally to coordinate the planning and execution of his activities. For example, an occupant of a dwelling would rather have the housing and other necessary inspections done at the same time or on the same day rather than arrange separate appointments on different days.

3. Exchange information and views about the neighborhood and its residents. Keep it general and related only to topics that will directly help improve communications with the residents or otherwise help achieve the desired objectives. All persons regardless of their station in life have the right of freedom from invasion of privacy. The details of a person's life or living circumstances that the inspector may learn during his work should not be idly discussed.

    Perhaps the most important fact the inspector should keep in mind, regarding good interagency relations, is that, although his interest is primarily focused on one program area, he is part of a larger team working together to improve the conditions of the total community.

GLOSSARY OF HOUSING TERMS

TABLE OF CONTENTS

	Page
Airway ... Beam	1
Bearing Partition ... Butt Joint	2
Cabinet ... Coped Joint	3
Corner Bead ... Doorjamb, Interior	4
Dormer ... Flat Paint	5
Flue ... Gable	6
Gloss (Paint or Enamel) ... Insulation Board, Rigid	7
Insulation, Thermal ... Lintel	8
Lookout ... Millwork	9
Miter Joint ... Preservative	10
Primer ... Riser	11
Roll Roofing ... Shingles	12
Shingles, Siding ... Square	13
Stain, Shingle ... Termites	14
Termite Shield ... Varnish	15
Vent ... Weatherstrip	16

Glossary of Housing Terms

A

AIRWAY
A space between roof insulation and roof boards for movement of air.

APRON
The flat member of the inside trim of a window placed against the wall immediately beneath the stool.

ASPHALT
Most native asphalt is a residue from evaporated petroleum. It is insoluble in water but soluble in gasoline and melts when heated. Used widely in building for such items as waterproof roof coverings of many types, exterior wall coverings, and flooring tile.

ATTIC VENTILATORS
In houses, screened openings provided to ventilate an attic space. They are located in the soffit area as inlet ventilators and in the gable end or along the ridge as outlet ventilators. They can also consist of powerdriven fans used as an exhaust system. (See also LOUVER.)

B

BACK-FILL
The replacement of excavated earth into a trench or pier excavation around and against a basement foundation.

BALUSTERS
Usually small vertical members in a railing used between a top rail and the stair treads or a bottom rail.

BASE OR BASEBOARD
A board placed around a room against the wall next to the floor to finish properly between floor and plaster or dry wall.

BASE MOLDING
Molding used to trim the upper edge of interior baseboard.

BASE SHOE
Molding used next to the floor on interior baseboard. Sometimes called a carpet strip.

BATTEN
Narrow strips of wood used to cover joints or as decorative vertical members over plywood or wide boards.

BEAM
A structural member transversely supporting a load.

BEARING PARTITION
A partition that supports any vertical load in addition to its own weight.

BEARING WALL
A wall that supports any vertical load in addition to its own weight.

BED MOLDING
A molding in an angle, as between the overhanging cornice, or eaves, of a building and the sidewalks.

BLIND-NAILING
Nailing in such a way that the nailheads are not visible on the face of the work. Usually at the tongue of matched boards.

BLIND STOP
A rectangular molding, usually 3/4 by 1 3/8 inches or more in width used in the assembly of a window frame. Serves as a stop for storm and screen or combination windows and to resist air infiltration.

BOILED LINSEED OIL
Linseed oil in which enough lead, manganese, or cobalt salts have been incorporated to make the oil harden more rapidly when spread in thin coatings.

BOLTS, ANCHOR
Bolts to secure a wooden sill plate to concrete or masonry floor or wall or pier.

BOSTON RIDGE
A method of applying asphalt to wood shingles at the ridge or at the hips of a roof as a finish.

BRACE
An inclined piece of framing lumber applied to wall or floor to stiffen the structure. Often used on walls as temporary bracing until framing has been completed.

BUCK
Often used in reference to rough frame opening members. Door bucks used in reference to metal door frame.

BUILT-UP ROOF
A roofing composed of three to five layers of asphalt felt laminated with coal tar, pitch, or asphalt. The top is finished with crushed slag or gravel. Generally used on flat or low-pitched roofs.

BUTT JOINT
The junction where the ends of two timbers or other members meet in a square-cut joint.

C

CABINET
A shop- or job-built unit for kitchens or other rooms. Often includes combinations of drawers, doors, and the like.

CASING
Molding of various widths and thicknesses used to trim door and window openings at the jambs.

CASEMENT FRAMES AND SASH
Frames of wood or metal enclosing part or all of the sash, which may be opened by means of hinges affixed to the vertical edges.

COLLAR BEAM
Nominal 1- or 2-inch-thick members connecting opposite roof rafters. They serve to stiffen the roof structure.

COMBINATION DOORS OR WINDOWS
Combination doors or windows used over regular openings. They provide winter insulation and summer protection. They often have self-storing or removable glass and screen inserts. This eliminates the need for handling a different unit each season.

CONCRETE, PLAIN
Concrete without reinforcement, or reinforced only for shrinkage or temperature changes.

CONDENSATION
Beads or drops of water, and frequently frost in extremely cold weather, that accumulates on the inside of the exterior covering of a building when warm, moisture-laden air from the interior reaches a point where the temperature no longer permits the air to sustain the moisture it holds. Use of louvers or attic ventilators will reduce moisture condensation in attics. A vapor barrier under the gypsum lath or dry wall on exposed walls will reduce condensation in walls.

CONDUIT, ELECTRICAL
A pipe, usually metal, in which wire is installed.

CONSTRUCTION, DRY-WALL
A type of construction in which the interior wall finish is applied in a dry condition, generally in the form of sheet materials or wood paneling, as contrasted to plaster.

CONSTRUCTION, FRAME
A type of construction in which the structural parts are of wood or depend upon a wood frame for support. In building codes, if masonry veneer is applied to the exterior walls, the classification of this type of construction is usually unchanged.

COPED JOINT
Fitting woodwork to an irregular surface. In moldings, cutting the end of one piece to fit the molded face of the other at an interior angle to replace a miter joint.

CORNER BEAD
A strip of formed sheet metal, sometimes combined with a strip of metal lath, placed on corners before plastering to reinforce them. Also, a strip of wood finish three-quarters round or angular placed over a plastered corner for protection.

CORNER BOARDS
Used as trim for the external corners of a house or other frame structures against which the ends of the siding are finished.

CORNER BRACES
Diagonal braces at the corners of frame structure to stiffen and strengthen the wall.

CORNICE
Overhang of a pitched roof at the eave line, usually consisting of a facia board, a soffit for a closed cornice, and appropriate moldings.

COUNTERFLASHING
A flashing usually used on chimneys at the roofline to cover shingle flashing and to prevent moisture entry.

COVE MOLDING
A molding with a concave face used as trim or to finish interior corners.

CRAWL SPACE
A shallow space below the living quarters of a basementless house sometimes enclosed.

D

d
See PENNY.

DADO
A rectangular groove across the width of a board or plank. In interior decoration, a special type of wall treament.

DECK PAINT
An enamel with a high degree of resistance to mechanical wear, designed for use on such surfaces as porch floors.

DENSITY
The mass of substance in a unit volume. When expressed in the metric system (in g. per cc.), it is numerically equal to the specific gravity of the same substance.

DIMENSION
See LUMBER, DIMENSION.

DOORJAMB, INTERIOR
The surrounding case into and out of which a door closes and opens. It consists of two upright pieces, called side jambs, and a horizontal head jamb.

DORMER
A projection in a sloping roof, the framing of which forms a vertical wall suitable for windows or other openings.

DOWNSPOUT
A pipe, usually metal, for carrying rainwater from roof gutters

DRESSED AND MATCHED (TONGUED AND GROOVED)
Boards or plans machined in such a manner that there is a groove on one edge and a corresponding tongue on the other.

DRIER, PAINT
Usually oil-soluble soaps of such metals as lead, manganese, or cobalt, which, in small proportions, hasten the oxidation and hardening (drying) of the drying oils in paints.

DRIP CAP
A molding placed on the exterior top side of a door or window frame to cause water to drip beyond the outside of the frame.

DRY-WALL
See CONSTRUCTION, DRY WALL.

DUCTS
In a house, usually round or rectangular metal pipes for distributing warm air from the heating plant to rooms, or air from a conditioning device, or as cold air returns. Ducts are also made of asbestos and composition materials.

E

EAVES
The overhang of a roof projecting over the walls.

F

FACE NAILING
To nail perpendicular to the initial surface or to the junction of the pieces joined.

FACIA OR FASCIA
A flat board, band, or face, used sometimes by itself but usually in combination with moldings, often located at the outer face of the cornice.

FLASHING
Sheet metal or other material used in roof and wall construction to protect a building from seepage of water.

FLAT PAINT
An interior paint that contains a high proportion of pigment, and dries to a flat or lusterless finish.

FLUE
The space or passage in a chimney through which smoke, gas, or fumes ascend. Each passage is called a flue, which, together with any others and the surrounding masonry, make up the chimney.

FLUE LINING
Fire clay or terracotta pipe, round or square, usually made in all of the ordinary flue sizes and in 2-foot lengths, used for the inner lining of chimneys with a brick or masonry work around the outside. Flue lining in chimneys runs from about a foot below the flue connection to the top of the chimney.

FLY RAFTER
End rafters of the gable overhang supported by roof sheathing and lookouts.

FOOTING
A masonry section, usually concrete in a rectangular form wider than the bottom of the foundation wall or pier it supports.

FOUNDATION
The supporting portion of a structure below the first floor construction, or below grade, including the footings.

FRAMING, BALLOON
A system of framing a building in which all vertical structural elements of the bearing walls and partitions consist of single pieces extending from the top of the foundation sill plate to the roofplate and to which all floor joists are fastened.

FRAMING, PLATFORM
A system of framing a building in which floor joists of each story rest on the top plates of the story below or on the foundation sill for the first story, and the bearing walls and partitions rest on the subfloor of each story.

FRIEZE
In house construction, a horizontal member connecting the top of the siding with the soffit of the cornice or roof sheathing.

FROSTLINE
The depth of frost penetration in soil. This depth varies in different parts of the country. Footings should be placed below this depth to prevent movement.

FURRING
Strips of wood or metal applied to a wall or other surface to even it and usually to serve as a fastening base for finish material.

G

GABLE
The triangular vertical end of a building formed by the eaves and ridge of a sloped roof.

GLOSS (PAINT OR ENAMEL)
A paint or enamel that contains a relatively low proportion of pigment and dries to a sheen or luster.

GIRDER
A large or principal beam of wood or steel used to support concentrated loads at isolated points along its length.

GRAIN
The direction, size, arrangement, appearance, or quality of the fibers in wood.

GRAIN, EDGE (VERTICAL)
Edge-grain lumber has been sawed parallel to the pith of the log and approximately at right angles to the growth rings, i.e., the rings form an angle of 45 or more with the surface of the piece.

GUSSET
A flat wood, plywood, or similar type member used to provide a connection at the intersection of wood members. Most commonly used at joints of wood trusses. They are fastened by nails, screws, bolts, or adhesives.

GUTTER OR EAVE TROUGH
A shallow channel or conduit of metal or wood set below and along the eaves of a house to catch and carry off rainwater from the roof.

H

HEADER
(a) A beam place perpendicular to joists and to which joists are nailed in framing for chimney, stairway, or other opening.
(b) A wood lintel.

HEARTWOOD
The wood extending from the pith to the sapwood, the cells of which no longer participate in the life processes of the tree.

HIP
The external angle formed by the meeting of two sloping sides of a roof.

HIP ROOF
A roof that rises by inclined planes from all four sides of a building.

I

INSULATION BOARD, RIGID
A structural building board made of wood or cane fiber in and 25/32" thicknesses. It can be obtained in various size sheets, in various densities, and with several treatments.

INSULATION, THERMAL
Any material high in resistance to heat transmission that, when place in the walls, ceiling, or floors of a structure, will reduce the rate of heat flow.

J

JACK RAFTER
A rafter that spans the distance from the wallplate to a hip, or from a valley to a ridge.

JAMB
The side and head lining of a doorway, window, or other opening.

JOINT
The space between the adjacent surfaces of two members or components joined and held together by nails, glue, cement, mortar, or other means.

JOINT CEMENT
A powder that is usually mixed with water and used for joint treatment in gypsum-wallboard finish. Often called "spackle."

JOIST
One of a series of parallel beams, usually 2 inches thick, used to support floor and ceiling loads, and supported in turn by larger beams, girders, or bearing walls.

K

KNOT
In lumber, the portion of a branch or limb of a tree that appears on the edge or face of the piece.

L

LANDING
A platform between flights of stairs or at the termination of a flight of stairs.

LATH
A building material of wood, metal, gypsum, or insulating board that is fastened to the frame of a building to act as a plaster base.

LEDGER STRIP
A strip of lumber nailed along the bottom of the side of a girder on which joists rest.

LIGHT
Space in a window sash for a single pane of glass. Also, a pane of glass.

LINTEL
A horizontal structural member that supports the load over an opening such as a door or window.

LOOKOUT
A short wood bracket or cantilever to support an overhanging portion of a roof or the like, usually concealed from view.

LOUVER
An opening with a series of horizontal slats so arranged as to permit ventilation but to exclude rain, sunlight, or vision. See also ATTIC VENTILATORS.

LUMBER
Lumber is the product of the sawmill and planning mill not further manufactured other than by sawing, resawing, and passing lengthwise through a standard planing machine, cross cutting to length, and matching.

LUMBER, BOARDS
Yard lumber less than 2 inches thick and 2 or more inches wide.

LUMBER, DIMENSION
Yard lumber from 2 inches to, but including, 5 inches thick, and 2 or more inches wide. Includes joists, rafters, studs, plank and small timbers. The actual size dimension of such lumber after shrinking from green dimension and after machining to size or pattern is called the dress size.

LUMBER, MATCHED
Lumber that is dressed and shaped on one edge in a grooved pattern and on the other in a tongued pattern.

LUMBER, SHIPLAP
Lumber that is edge-dressed to make a close rabbeted or lapped joint.

LUMBER, YARD
Lumber of those grades, sizes, and patterns which are generally intended for ordinary construction, such as framework and rough coverage of houses.

M

MASONRY
Stone, brick, concrete, hollow-tile, concrete-block, gypsum-block, or other similar building units or materials or a combination of the same, bonded together with mortar to form a wall, pier, buttress, or similar mass.

MEETING RAILS
Rails sufficiently thicker than a window to fill the opening between the top and bottom sash made by the parting stop in the frame of double-hung windows. They are usually beveled.

MILLWORK
Generally all building materials made of finished wood and manufactured in millwork plants and planing mills are included under the term "millwork." It includes such items as inside and outside doors, window and doorframes, blinds, porchwork, mantels, panelwork, stairways, moldings, and interior trim. It normally does not include flooring, ceiling, or siding.

MITER JOINT
The joint of two pieces at an angle that bisects the joining angle. For example, the miter joint at the side and head casing at a door opening is made at a 45 angle.

MOISTURE CONTENT OF WOOD
Weight of the water contained in the wood, usually expressed as a percentage of the weight of the ovendry wood.

MOLDING
A wood strip having a curved or projecting surface used for decorative purposes.

MORTISE
A slot cut into a board, plank, or timber, usually edgewise, to receive tenon of another board, plank, or timber to form a joint.

N

NATURAL FINISH
A transparent finish which does not seriously alter the original color or grain of the natural wood. Natural finishes are usually provided by sealers, oils, varnishes, water-repellent, preservatives, and other similar materials.

NONLOADBEARING WALL
A wall supporting no load other than its own weight.

NOTCH
A crosswise rabbet at the end of a board.

O

O.C. ON CENTER
The measurement of spacing for studs, rafters, joists, and the like in a building from center of one member to the center of the next.

P

PLYWOOD
A piece of wood made of three or more layers of veneer joined with glue and usually laid with the grain of adjoining plies at right angles. Almost always an odd number of plies are used to provide balanced construction.

PLUMB
Exactly perpendiular; vertical.

PORCH
A roofed area extending beyond the main house. May be open or enclosed and with concrete or wood frame floor system.

PRESERVATIVE
Any substance that, for a reasonable length of time, will prevent the action of wood-destroying fungi, borers of various kinds, and similar destructive life when the wood has been properly coated or impregnated with it.

PRIMER
The first coat of paint in a paint job that consists of two or more coats; also the paint used for such a first coat.

PUTTY
A type of cement usually made of whiting and boiled linseed oil, beaten or kneaded to the consistency of dough, and used in sealing glass in sash, filling small holes and crevices in wood, and for similar purposes.

Q

QUARTER ROUND
A small molding that has the cross-section of a quarter circle.

R

RAFTER
One of a series of structural members of a roof designed to support roof loads. The rafters of a flat roof are sometimes called roof joists.

RAFTER, HIP
A rafter that forms the intersection of an external roof angle.

RAFTER, VALLEY
A rafter that forms the intersection of an internal roof angle. The valley rafter is normally made of doubled 2-inch-thick members.

RAIL
Cross members of panel doors or of a sash. Also the upper and lower members of a balustrade or staircase extending from one vertical support, such as a post, to another.

RAKE
The inclined edge of a gable roof (the trim member is a rake molding).

RIDGE
The horizontal line at the junction of the top edges of two sloping roof surfaces.

RIDGE BOARD
The board placed on edge at the ridge of the roof into which the upper ends of the rafters are fastened.

RISE
In stairs, the vertical height of a step or flight of stairs.

RISER
Each of the vertical boards closing the spaces between the treads of stairways.

ROLL ROOFING

Roofing material, composed of fiber and saturated with asphalt, that is supplied in rolls containing 108 square feet in 36-inch widths. It is generally furnished in weights of 45 to 90 pounds per roll.

ROOF SHEATHING

The boards or sheet material fastened to the roof rafters on which the shingle or other roof covering is laid.

ROUTED

See MORTISED.

RUN

In stairs, the net width of a step or the horizontal distance covered by a flight of stairs.

S

SASH

A single light frame containing one or more lights of glass.

SATURATED FELT

A felt which is impregnated with tar or asphalt.

SCAB

A short piece of wood or plywood fastened to two abutting timbers to splice them together.

SEALER

A finishing material, either clear or pigmented, that is usually applied directly over uncoated wood for the purpose of sealing the surface.

SEMIGLOSS PAINT OR ENAMEL

A paint or enamel made with a slight insufficiency of nonvolatile vehicle so that its coating when dry, has some luster but is not very glossy.

SHAKE

A thick handsplit shingle, resawed to form two shakes; usually edge grained.

SHEATHING

The structural covering, usually wood boards or plywood, used over studs or rafters of a structure. Structural building board is normally used only as wall sheathing.

SHEATHING PAPER

See PAPER, SHEATHING

SHINGLES

Roof covering of asphalt, asbestos, wood, tile, slate, or other material cut to stock lengths, widths, and thicknesses.

SHINGLES, SIDING
Various kinds of shingles, such as wood shingles or shakes and nonwood shingles, that are used over sheathing for exterior sidewall covering of a structure.

SHIPLAP
See LUMBER, SHIPLAP.

SIDING
The finish covering of the outside wall of a frame building, whether made of horizontal weatherboards, vertical boards with battens, shingles, or other material.

SIDING, BEVEL (LAP SIDING)
Wedge-shaped boards used as horizontal siding in a lapped pattern. This siding varies in butt thickness from 1/2 to 3/4" and in widths up to 12 inches. Normally used over some type of sheathing.

SIDING, DROP
Usually 3/4" thick and 6 and 8" in width with tongued-and-grooved or shiplap edges. Often used as siding without sheathing in secondary buildings.

SIDING, PANEL
Large sheets of plywood or hardboard which serve as both sheathing and siding.

SILL
The lowest member of the frame of a structure, resting on the foundation and supporting the floor joists or the uprights of the wall. The member forming the lower side of an opening, as a door sill, window sill, etc.

SOFFIT
Usually the underside covering of an overhanging cornice.

SOIL COVER (GROUND COVER)
A light covering of plastic film, roll roofing, or similar material used over the soil in crawl spaces of buildings to minimize moisture permeation of the area.

SOIL STACK
A general term for the vertical main of a system of soil, waste, or vent piping.

SOLE OR SOLE PLATE
See PLATE.

SPAN
The distance between structural supports such as walls, columns, piers, beams, girders, and trusses.

SQUARE
A unit of measure - 100 square feet - usually applied to roofing material. Sidewall coverings are sometimes packed to cover 100 square feet and are sold on that basis.

STAIN, SHINGLE
A form of oil paint, very thin in consistency, intended for coloring wood with rough surfaces, like shingles, without forming a coating of significant thickness or gloss.

STAIR CARRIAGE
Supporting member for stair treads. Usually a 2-inch plank notched to receive the treads; sometimes termed a "rough horse."

STOOL
A flat molding fitted over the window will between jambs and contacting the bottom rail of the lower sash.

STORM SASH OR STORM WINDOW
An extra window usually placed on the outside of an existing window as additional protection against cold weather.

STORY
That part of a building between any floor and the floor or roof next above.

STRING, STRINGER
A timber or other support for cross members in floors or ceilings. In stairs, the support on which the stair treads rest, also stringboard.

STUD
One of a series of slender wood or metal vertical structural members placed as supporting elements in walls and partitions. (Plural: studs or studding.)

SUBFLOOR
Boards or plywood laid on joists over which a finish floor is to be laid.

T

TAIL BEAM
A relatively short beam or joist supported in a wall on one end and by a header at the other.

TERMITES
Insects that superficially resemble ants in size, general appearance, and habit of living in colonies, hence, frequently called "white ants." Subterranean termites do not establish themselves in buildings by being carried in with lumber, but by entering from ground nests after the building has been constructed. If unmolested they eat out the woodwork, leaving a shell of sound wood to conceal their activities, and damage may proceed so far so to cause collapse of parts of a structure before discovery. There are about 56 species of termites known in the United States; but the two main species, classified from the manner in which they attack wood, subterranean (ground-inhabiting) termites, the most common, and drywood termites, found almost exclusively along the extreme southern border and the Gulf of Mexico in the United States.

TERMITE SHIELD
A shield, usually of noncorrodible metal, placed in or on a foundation wall or other mass of masonry or around pipes to prevent passage of termites.

THRESHOLD
A strip of wood or metal with beveled edges used over the finished floor and the sill of exterior doors.

TOENAILING
To drive a nail at a slant with the initial surface in order to permit it to penetrate into a second member.

TREAD
The horizontal board in a stairway on which the foot is placed.

TRIM
The finish materials in a building, such as moldings, applied around openings (window trims, door trim) or at the floor and ceiling of rooms (baseboard, cornice, picture molding).

TRIMMER
A beam or joist to which a header is nailed in framing for a chimney, stairway, or other opening.

TRUSS
A frame or jointed structure designed to act as a beam of long span, while each member is usually subjected to longitudinal stress only, either tension or compression.

TURPENTINE
A volatile oil used as a thinner in paints, and as a solvent in varnishes. Chemically, it is a mixture of terpenes.

U

UNDERCOAT
A coating applied prior to the finishing or top coats of a paint job. It may be the first of two or the second of three coats. In some usage of the word, it may become synonymous with priming coat.

V

VAPOR BARRIER
Material used to retard the movement of water vapor into walls and prevent condensation in them. Usually considered as having a perm value of less than 1.0. Applied separately over the warm side of exposed walls or as a part of batt or blanket insulation.

VARNISH
A thickened preparation of drying oil or drying oil and resin suitable for spreading on surfaces to form continuous, transparent coatings, or for mixing with pigments to make enamels.

VENT
A pipe or duct which allows flow of air as an inlet or outlet.

VERMICULITE
A mineral closely related to mica, with the faculty of expanding on heating to form lightweight material with insulation quality. Used as bulk insulation and as aggregate in insulating and acoustical plaster and in insulating concrete floors.

W

WATER-REPELLENT PRESERVATIVE
A liquid designed to penetrate into wood and impart water repellency and a moderate preservative protection. It is used for millwork, such as sash and frames, and is usually applied by dipping.

WEATHERSTRIP
Narrow or jamb-width sections of thin metal or other material to prevent infiltration of air and moisture around windows and doors.

www.ingramcontent.com/pod-product-compliance
Lightning Source LLC
Chambersburg PA
CBHW081814300426
44116CB00014B/2358